PIPE FITTINGS

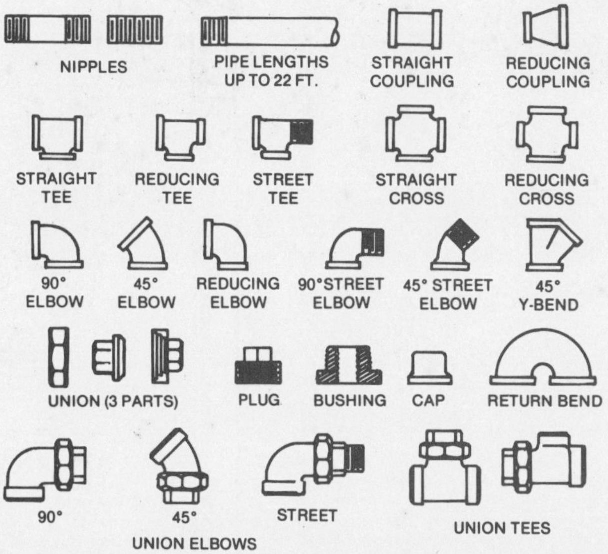

Here are the common steel pipe fittings. Nipples are simply short lengths of pipe threaded on both ends. Reducing fittings join two different sizes of pipe.

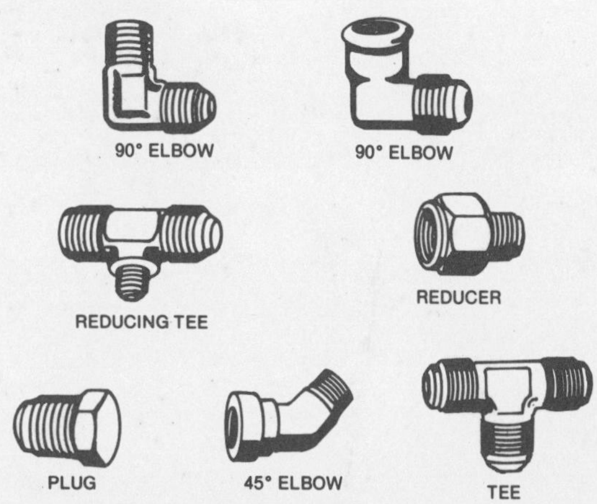

Compression fittings of the flared-tube type are the easiest for the novice to handle when working with copper tubing.

STANDARD STEEL PIPE (All Dimensions in Inches)					
Nominal Size	Outside Diameter	Inside Diameter	Nominal Size	Outside Diameter	Inside Diameter
1/8	0.405	0.269	1	1.315	1.049
1/4	0.540	0.364	1 1/4	1.660	1.380
3/8	0.675	0.493	1 1/2	1.900	1.610
1/2	0.840	0.622	2	2.375	2.067
3/4	1.050	0.824	2 1/2	2.875	2.469

SQUARE MEASURE

144 sq in = 1 sq ft
9 sq ft = 1 sq yd
272.25 sq ft = 1 sq rod
160 sq rods = 1 acre

VOLUME MEASURE

1728 cu in = 1 cu ft
27 cu ft = 1 cu yd

MEASURES OF CAPACITY

1 cup = 8 fl oz
2 cups = 1 pint
2 pints = 1 quart
4 quarts = 1 gallon
2 gallons = 1 peck
4 pecks = 1 bushel

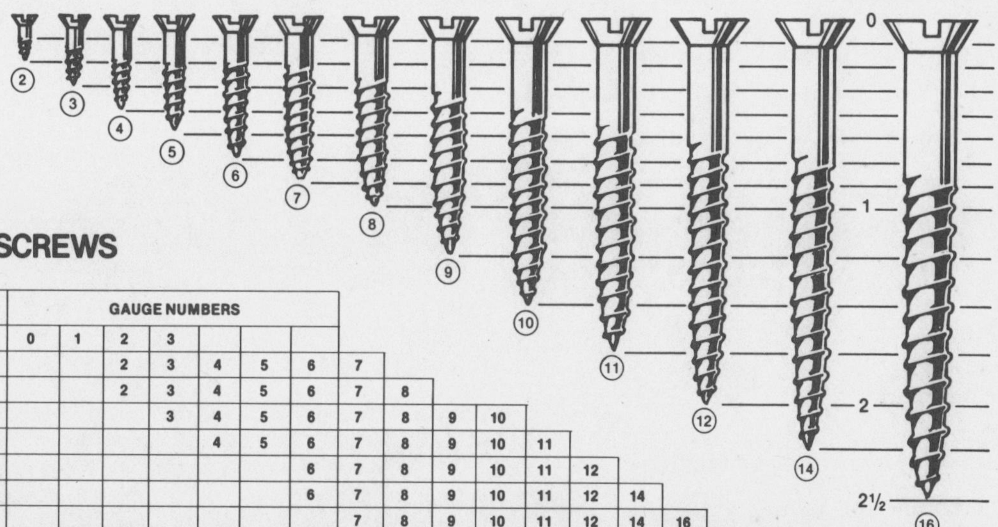

WOOD SCREWS

LENGTH	GAUGE NUMBERS																	
1/4 INCH	0	1	2	3														
3/8 INCH			2	3	4	5	6	7										
1/2 INCH			2	3	4	5	6	7	8									
5/8 INCH				3	4	5	6	7	8	9	10							
3/4 INCH					4	5	6	7	8	9	10	11						
7/8 INCH							6	7	8	9	10	11	12					
1 INCH							6	7	8	9	10	11	12	14				
1 1/4 INCH								7	8	9	10	11	12	14	16			
1 1/2 INCH							6	7	8	9	10	11	12	14	16	18		
1 3/4 INCH									8	9	10	11	12	14	16	18	20	
2 INCH									8	9	10	11	12	14	16	18	20	
2 1/4 INCH										9	10	11	12	14	16	18	20	
2 1/2 INCH													12	14	16	18	20	
2 3/4 INCH														14	16	18	20	
3 INCH															16	18	20	
3 1/2 INCH																18	20	24
4 INCH																18	20	24

WHEN YOU BUY SCREWS, SPECIFY (1) LENGTH, (2) GAUGE NUMBER, (3) TYPE OF HEAD—FLAT, ROUND, OR OVAL, (4) MATERIAL—STEEL, BRASS, BRONZE, ETC., (5) FINISH—BRIGHT, STEEL BLUED, CADMIUM, NICKEL, OR CHROMIUM PLATED.

In this volume . . .

LEARN TO TAKE great pictures of your sailboat or runabout. See page 356.

YOU CAN EVEN get good pictures of a houseboat. See tips on lighting, posing.

MAKE ANY WALL a beautiful brick wall easily and quickly, and without any foundation problems. This wall is covered with lightweight plastic moldings that need no extra support. Choose your color and pattern. For details, see page 450.

YOU CAN BUILD THIS ATTRACTIVE POOLHOUSE for much less than you think. It offers a screened ar for barbecues, a lavatory and dressing room, a sundeck and a playhouse for the youngsters. Instructions start on page 558.

HERE'S A BEAUTY—a coffee table with a lift-off top that becomes a spacious serving tray. It's a handsome project to make for your own home, or a fine gift for someone else. See the article on page 472.

Look what you'll find in other volumes!

MAKE THE CEILING fit the decor. The ceiling of your living room or dining room can be something more than just a flat expanse of plaster. Use ceiling tile, and it's one of the easiest do-it-yourself projects. See the article on page 616 of Vol. 4.

HERE'S A BEAUTIFUL AND FUNCTIONAL entertainment wall, with plenty of storage space—all made with standard ready-to-use kitchen cabinets. Simply stack the cabinets like building blocks. Supplement them with simple plywood boxes. See Vol. 4, page 484.

NOW YOU CAN SEW YOUR OWN CAMP GEAR. It's fun, it can cut costs, and in many cases it will improve quality. Several manufacturers now produce kits for everything from booties to sleeping bags, from jackets to tents. The man is trying on some of the results. For details, see the article on page 538 of Vol. 4.

HERE'S A NEAT AND SIMPLE IDEA—a footboard table that fits right over a twin bed. It's shown here between two beds along one wall, but it works nicely with a single bed, too. Find this, and another bright idea for the kids' room, in Vol. 5, page 672.

WHAT CAMPER can resist these views of the wilderness? Little-known, unspoiled wilderness areas have adventure-away-from-it-all appeal. The article in Vol. 4 on page 545 tells you not only where to go, but what you can expect when you get there.

THEY'VE JUST ARRIVED by plane, and are about to shove off to explore the wilderness in canoes. They're in for the time of their lives—if they're properly equipped. See outfitting tips from an expert in Vol. 4, page 581.

MAKE INSTANT FURNITURE from kitchen cabinets. See Vol. 4, page 484.

THIS KID studies under his bed, an ingenious space-saving idea. See Vol. 5, page 668.

NOVELTY CANDLES make fine gifts for children. See Vol. 4, page 554.

Popular Mechanics

do-it-yourself encyclopedia

in 20 volumes

a complete how-to guide for the homeowner, the hobbyist—
and anyone who enjoys working with mind and hands!

All about:

home maintenance
home-improvement projects
wall paneling
burglary and fire protection
furniture projects
finishing and refinishing furniture
outdoor living
home remodeling
solutions to home problems
challenging woodworking projects
hobbies and handicrafts
model making
weekend projects
workshop shortcuts and techniques
hand-tool skills
power-tool know-how
shop-made tools
car repairs
car maintenance
appliance repair
boating
hunting
fishing
camping
photography projects
radio, TV and electronics know-how
clever hints and tips
projects just for fun

volume 3

ISBN 0-87851-068-0
Library of Congress Catalog Number 77 84920

MANUFACTURED IN THE UNITED STATES OF AMERICA

contents

VOLUME 3

LEITZ 6x24 TRINOVID

BAUSCH & LOMB 9x35
PORRO PRISM TYPE

How to choose and use binoculars

By ROBERT BRIGHTMAN

Whether you use them for nature study, car rallies, indoor sports or girl-watching, there's a lot to know about binoculars if you want the latest features at the best price

MIIDA 7x28 STRAIGHT THROUGH

SEE ALSO

Backpacking . . . Boat camping . . .
Boating, safety . . . Boating, white-water . . .
Camping . . . Canoes . . . Hunting . . .
Map reading . . . Sailboats

WHAT IS a binocular? Are field glasses and opera glasses binoculars? No. A binocular always uses a set of prisms in its optical system. Without prisms, binoculars would be about three times as long and their fields of view would be very narrow—like looking through a 10-in.-long pipe. Field glasses are limited in power (magnification), seldom more than five times (5X); opera glasses are usually 2X to 3X.

How far can you see with binoculars? The same as with the naked eye! All binoculars do is bring the object closer. You can see the moon with the naked eye, and it is 240,000 miles away. But with 10X glasses the moon will seem to appear 24,000 miles away—or 10 times closer.

The first time you shop for a binocular, the salesman will invariably ask what power glass you want. If you're indecisive, he may recommend an 8X glass—generally, a good all-around choice for most outdoor work.

ZEISS 8x50 CENTRAL FOCUSING

SWIFT 7x50
AMERICAN STYLE

BUSHNELL 7x50
INSTA-FOCUS

If you examine an eight-power glass closely, you will see numbers near the eyepiece end reading 8x30, 8x40 or 8x50. The first number refers to the power; the second to diameter in millimeters of the objective lenses (large lenses opposite the eyepieces.) The larger the objective lens—in the same power—the brighter the image. Thus, if you want a glass for stargazing, select one with a large objective lens: 40 or 50-mm. But, as the objective gets bigger, so does the binocular—heavier, too.

Another term you may come across is "relative brightness," a method of comparing image brightness of glasses with different powers and objectives—sort of a common denominator. To obtain it, divide the objective lens diameter (40-mm, for example) by the power (10X, let's say); this gives 4. Square this number (4x4) and you get 16—the relative brightness of a 10x40 binocular. The lower the magnification—with the same objective—the higher the relative brightness. Also, the larger the objective—with the same power—the higher the relative brightness.

BINOCULAR APPLICATIONS

USE	6x30	7x35	7x50	8x30	9x35	10x50	16x50
General	E	G		E			N
Indoor Sports	E			G		N	N
Outdoor Sports		E	G	E			N
Boating		E		E	G		G
Hunting		E		G	E	N	N
Nature Study	G	E			E		G
Travel	E			G		N	N
Plane Spotting	N				G	E	E
Night Use		G	E				N

E—Excellent G—Good N—Not recommended

Note: When shopping for a binocular, you may see intermediate sizes such as 6x20, 6x24, 8x32, 8x40. Use the recommendations nearest to the glass you are examining.

Another important buying criterion is the field of view. Obviously, the wider the field of view, the easier it is to keep a moving object or animal in view. If a wide field of view is important (for game spotting or horse racing) select a glass with a low or medium power: 6X or 7X is best.

The field of view can be measured by the angle formed by two lines drawn from the observing position to the two opposite edges of the visible field seen through the glass. It is commonly indicated by the number of yards (or feet) visible between the lines 1000 yards from the binocular. For example, a glass with a field of view of 128 yards at 1000 yards has a 7.3° angle of view.

However, an extra-wide field of view may not be an advantage, if gained at the expense of clarity. A true wide-angle binocular should show a sharp field of view in the center of the field. If you have to refocus to get sharp edges, try another glass.

Chromatic aberration, an annoying fault found in some cheap binoculars, shows up as a color fringe when you look at a post or tree against a bright sky. It tends to make a halo around the image, thus affecting the definition.

How about antireflection coatings? Very important. All binoculars now have them in *some* form, but a good one should have *all* reflecting optical surfaces coated to prevent internal glare. A cheap glass will have such a coating only on visible glass surfaces—outside the eyepieces and objective lenses.

How can you tell if internal optical parts have been coated? Quite easily. Hold the binocular at arm's length at your waist so that an overhead lamp is reflected from the objective lens. Shift the glass slightly until you can see a series of reflections of the lamp in the lens—one for each optical surface of the prisms and lenses. If the reflections you see have a decided purple or blue cast, then you can be reasonably sure that all of the internal surfaces are coated.

What about independent or central focusing (IF or CF)? Each eyepiece of an IF system must be adjusted separately. However, this system permits the manufacturer to make a more nearly dustproof and waterproof binocular. The CF system allows you to change the focus for both eyes at once as you follow rapidly moving action such as a horse race or hockey game where the action ranges from one end of a field to another.

To focus an IF glass, close one eye and move the eyepiece back and forth in front of the opened eye until the image is as sharp as possible. Do the same for the other eye. Adjust for interpupillary distance by moving the two sides of the binocular until they match the distance between the eyes. To focus a CF glass, close the right eye (or cover the right objective lens) and move the center wheel back and forth until you get a sharp image with your left eye. Next, close the left eye and rotate the right *eyepiece* until the image for the right eye is as sharp as possible. The glass should now be accurately focused.

These adjustments will compensate for eyeglasses. However, if you persist in wearing them when using a binoclar, you can get one with either flat or reversible eyecups for use with or without your eyeglasses.

What about binocular design? There are three basic styles: German and American Porro prismatic and straight through. German style—the original—is characterized by two parallel tubes, side by side, connected by cover plates at top and bottom. In an effort to increase rigidity and provide a firm optical alignment that wouldn't get out of whack under hard usage, Bausch & Lomb pioneered a one-piece barrel—the so-called American style.

This type of construction is also featured by Zeiss, Leitz and most Japanese makers. From an optical standpoint, American and German styles are identical. Both use Porro prisms to reflect light back and forth and to erect the image.

The straight-through binocular, made under the trade names of Trinovid (Leitz), Dialyt (Zeiss) and Miida (Japanese), uses three prisms in each half instead of two as found in a Porro prismatic binocular. It also has five reflecting surfaces instead of four. While this extra surface

MAINTENANCE TIPS

- Don't drop your binocular; you won't if you always use it with the strap around your neck.
- Keep lenses free of dust and fingerprints. Use lens tissue or camel's hair brush for cleaning.
- Your name and address should appear somewhere on carrying case.
- Salt spray should be wiped off immediately with a damp cloth.
- Store binocular in clean, dry place.
- If your binocular ever needs repair, write to manufacturer for instructions as to where it should be sent.

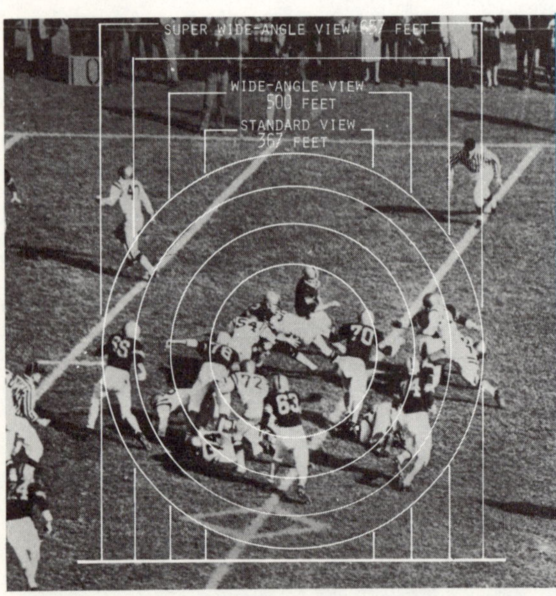

PARTIAL VISION is the result (above, left) when you try to use binoculars without removing your eyeglasses. The image at the right provides full vision. Wide-angle binoculars (comparable sizes shown at left) offers advantages over a standard binocular when used for watching football, horse racing and similar sports where action ranges over a wide field and is fast-moving. Wide-angle glasses are also recommended for hunting, plane-spotting.

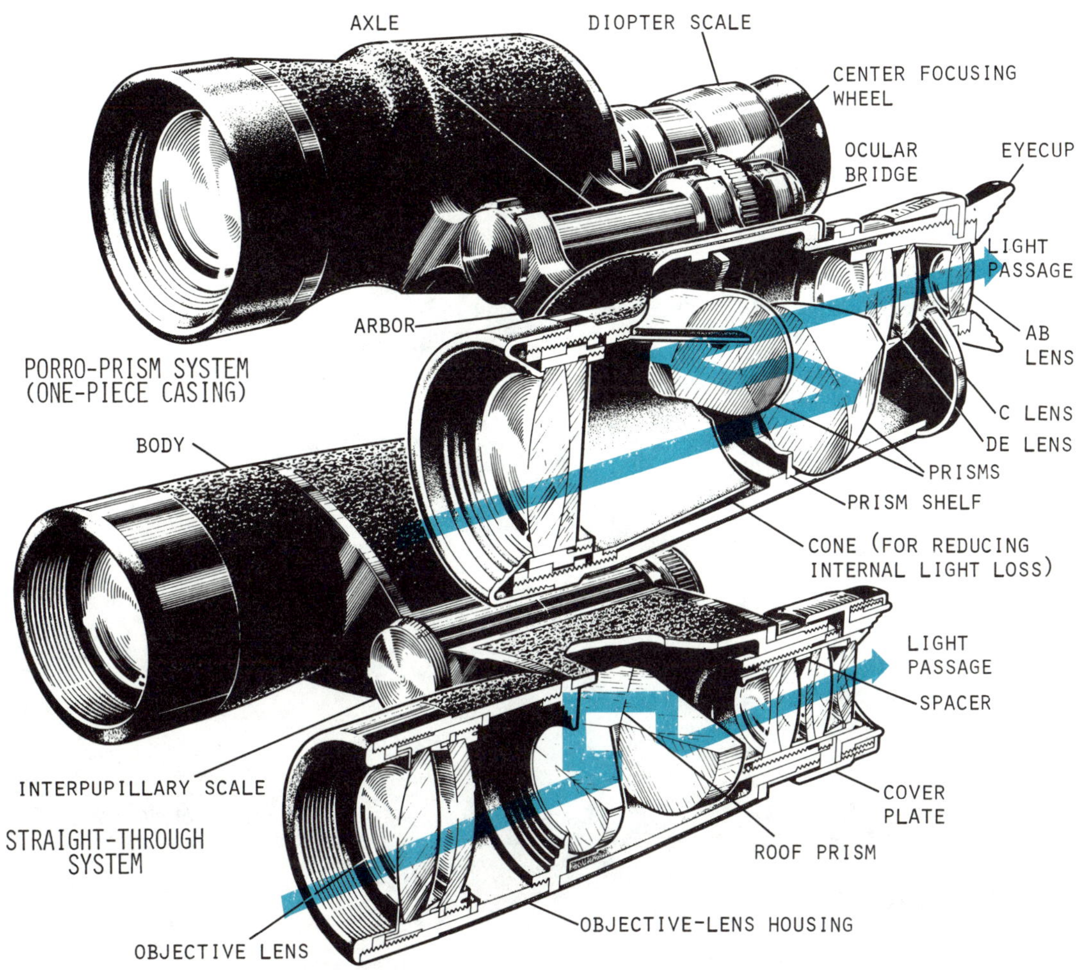

represents a four to six-percent loss in light transmission, it permits a lighter, more compact binocular. Where weight is a factor, such as on a hunting trip, the straight-through glass has much to recommend it.

Zoom glasses. Newest products in the field are binoculars with a zoom feature which allows you to come in very close at the turn of a control. You can zoom for 6X to 12X, or 7.5X to 15X manually or with a push-button electric control. The electric models are handy, but somewhat heavier.

How about price? You can pay from $18 to $500 or more for binoculars, depending on quality, type, and country of origin. Japanese models cost less than German or American-made units. The straight-through glasses are more expensive than the prismatic, and zoom models cost more than non-zooms.

Begin shopping by deciding which type and power you need, then check the different makes available in this model. Look for quality differences. If the price is low, check for chromatic aberrations and lack of coated lenses. But don't reject a glass on price alone, because some less expensive models *do* have all lenses coated and *have* eliminated chromatic aberrations.

SIX POINTS TO CHECK BEFORE BUYING

- Shake the binocular; nothing should rattle inside.
- After adjusting and focusing, you should see a single image, no overlaps.
- Lenses and prisms should be coated.
- Focusing should be smooth and easy. Be wary of glasses that bind or have a loose point when focusing.
- Image should be crisp and clear, no color fringes should appear.
- Check for distortion. A straight line (edge of building or flagpole) should remain reasonably straight when moved towards edge of binocular field.

Bend the light path and you shrink the optics. It's done with mirrors in Vivitar's new 600-mm "solid cat" lens (1); conventional telephoto of a mere 400-mm towers over it. Roof-prism design shrinks Honeywell Pentax monocular (3) which doubles as a 22X microscope (2), and Minolta Pocket binoculars (4) which fold compactly (5).

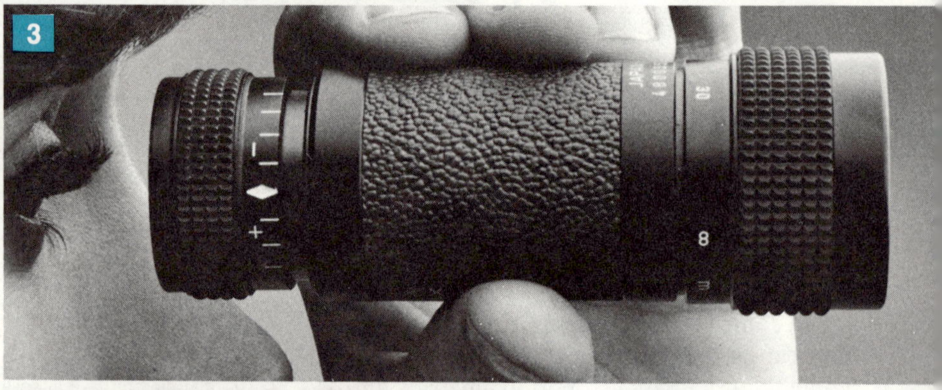

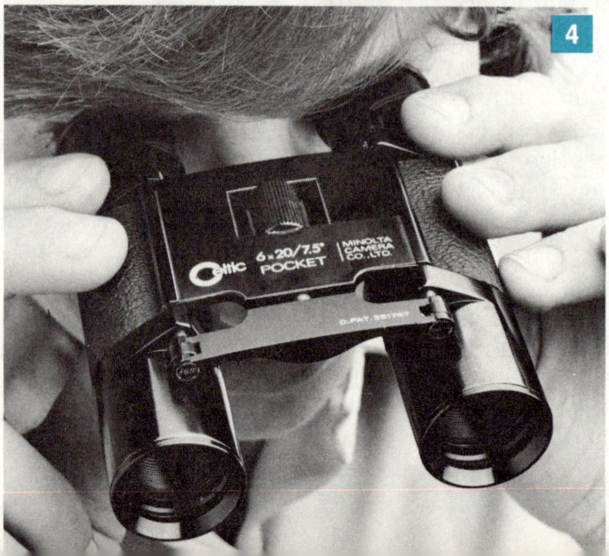

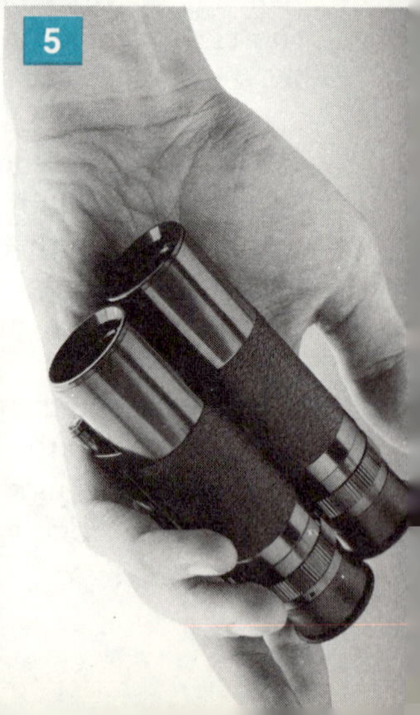

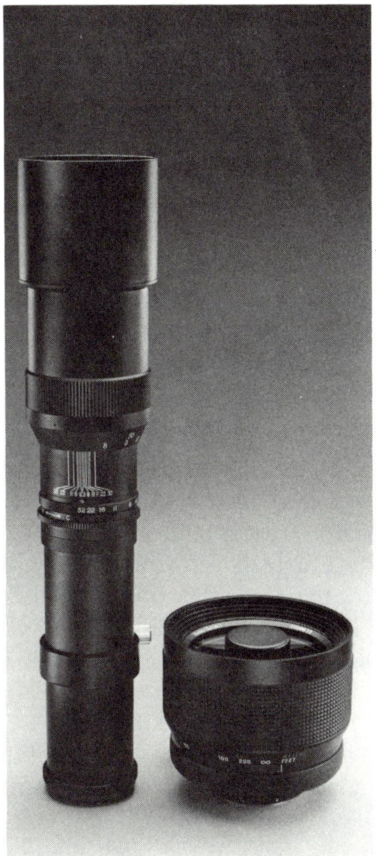

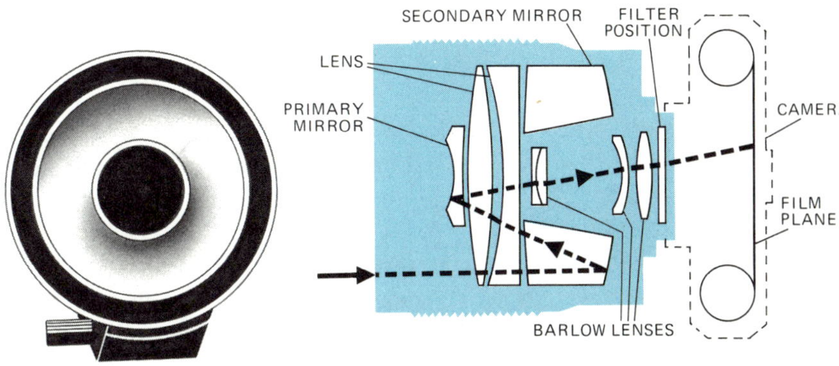

VIVITAR "solid cat" (above) reflects the light twice to lengthen the path while shortening the lens; light enters in a ring around the primary mirror at the lens's front. Barlow lenses at rear of the lens act as teleconverters to magnify the image and increase the power. To keep the filters small and economical, they fit at the rear of the lens. Camera mounts are interchangeable

Big performance from small optics

■ HOW DO YOU SHRINK a pair of binoculars? Or a camera lens? You fold it—not by bending the glass, but by using prisms and mirror surfaces to bend the light rays that pass through the optical system.

That's the secret behind a raft of new optical devices which have been made incredibly compact without serious losses in performance.

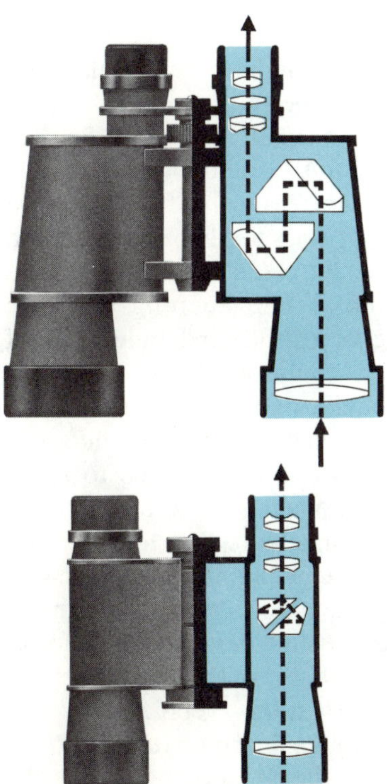

COMPACT BINOCULARS below are (clockwise from upper left corner); Bushnell, Minolta/Celtic Compact 6x20, Minolta Celtic Compact 8x20 and Minolta/Celtic Pocket 6x20. The binocular in the center is a full-size 7x35 Scope model shown for size comparison. Straight tubes of the Pocket model are due to roof-prism design (lower left diagram), that folds light back on itself. Compare this to the conventional design above it

MAGNIFICATION of 600-mm telephoto lens is 12 times that of a normal 50-mm lens. Compare the lower shot taken with 600-mm "solid cat" to upper shot taken with a normal lens. Note how bright spots in the out-of-focus foliage behind the child in the 600-mm shot register as circles. These blurry doughnuts are one of the drawbacks of using all catadioptric mirror lenses

Most dramatic of this new breed is Vivitar's "solid cat" 600-mm telephoto lens. Just 3¾ inches long, it has a focal length of 600-mm (23.6 inches). That's 12 times the focal length and magnification of a normal 50-mm lens, in a housing only about twice as long as a 50, though considerably wider.

Mirror lenses are not new. What distinguishes the Vivitar from other such "catadioptric" designs, however, is that it's practically solid, with little airspace between its elements—hence the nickname "solid cat."

Solid construction saves space. The Vivitar 600 is about half the length of many conventional, airspaced 500-mm mirror lenses and an inch shorter than the shortest 500. Solid construction also makes the lens more rugged and more stable in changing temperatures. And it concentrates the lens's weight close to the camera, making it easier, though still chancy, to take shots with the camera supported only by hand.

Mirror lenses have their drawbacks, though. They have only one f-stop, nearly always f/8. Neutral-density filters must be fitted if you want the exposure you'd get from smaller apertures. (To keep filters small and economical, they fit behind the lens.) Out-of-focus light spots register as blurry doughnuts instead of fuzzy dots. Contrast is often so low that focusing can be difficult. To these drawbacks add the disadvantages of weight (at 3 pounds, 5½ ounces, the "solid cat" is about a pound heavier than most mirror 500s) and high price (approximately $800).

Still to come are 800 and 1200-mm "solid cats" where compactness should really pay off in those super-telephoto focal lengths and help offset the disadvantages of using such unique telephoto lenses.

prisms for binoculars too

Binoculars also use light-folding techniques—the bulge in their shape and the offset that puts the objective lenses farther apart than the eyepieces are both due to the use of prism systems. What's new here is the extensive trend to "roof prism" designs that turn the light path around enough extra corners to equal the path length of a standard binocular while keeping the tube straight and free of offsets and bulges. Roof prisms have been around a while, too, but in recent years binocular makers such as Konica, Redfield and Asanuma have taken advantage of this design's compact, tubular shape to make folding models. Minolta has now taken this a step farther, with binoculars that fold but still have the convenience of center-wheel focusing. Still another approach to compact designs is taken by Minolta, Bushnell and others who reverse the binocular offset, so that the objectives are closer together than the eyepieces.

And for the ultimate in compactness, try a monocular. Again, they're not new, but the latest wrinkle in them is the use of closeup attachments, such as the one that makes the Pentax monocular a 22X microscope with stand.

"DECLAWED" MOUSE TRAPS make good holders for birds' food, such as the pieces of bread shown here.

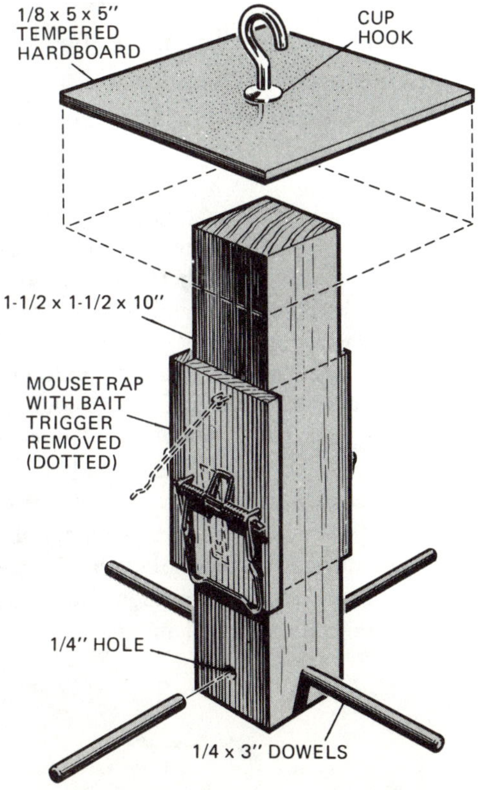

By H. D. BUTTS

Four-station bird feeder

USING FOUR common mouse traps to hold suet, bread and other tidbits for your feathered friends, this hanging bird feeder can be quickly mass-produced in your home workshop and sold for a handsome profit. As you see, after the bait trigger and wire are removed from it, each trap is fastened to a side of a length of 1½-in.-sq. wood. Holes are drilled at the lower end for ¼-in. dowel perches, and a 5-in.-sq. roof of ⅛-in. hardboard is attached to the top with a brass cup hook. Paint the feeder a rustic brown.

SEE ALSO
Bird photography . . . Birdhouses . . . Outdoor photography

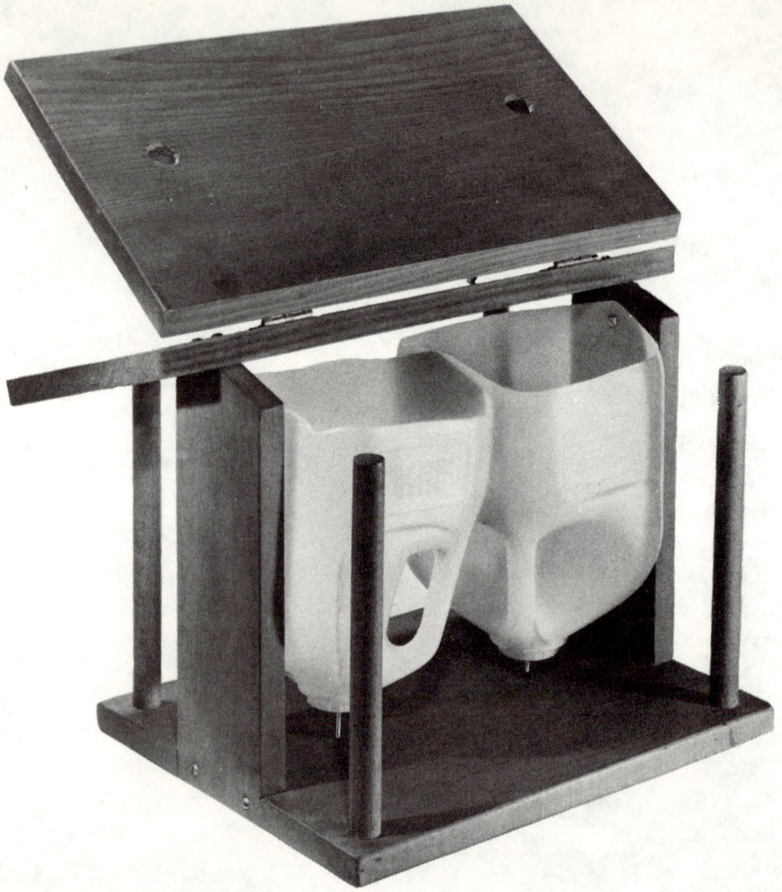

UNFASTENED half of hinged roof allows access to the feed containers; they are two bottomless plastic gallon jugs.

By LAURENCE J. RASMUSSEN

Automatic bird feeder

Here's a way to recycle a couple of plastic gallon jugs and at the same time make an attractive bird feeder. Made from weatherproof redwood, it automatically dispenses food and has a tilting disc to discourage squirrels

■ TO DELIGHT the bird-watchers in your home, build this year-round, self-dispensing feeder that will attract birds in any season.

The bird feeder, of weatherproof redwood, consists of a notched floor, four dowel posts, two peaked sides and a hinged slanting roof. It gives ample room at front and back to view birds as they eat.

The post is a length of ½-in. x 8½-ft. galvanized iron pipe set into the ground 3 ft. The top end of the pipe is threaded to receive the pipe flange that is screwed to the floor of the feeder. A 12-in. dia. aluminum disc with a 1-in. dia. center hole is loosely held to the pipe with a machine washer and ½-in. electrician's tape wound around the pipe beneath the washer. This loose, tilting object can sometimes help prevent squirrels from reaching the feeder. (If desired, more than one disc can be attached.)

The receptacles are two inverted, bottomless plastic gallon jugs, each screwed to a feeder side with a ½-in. sheet-metal screw. The necks of these jugs are cut off below the threads of the cap and each straddles a nail in the floor of the feeder to give them stability when empty in a strong wind. A discarded leather belt can be used as the roof hinge; simply nail it along each edge with ½-in. wire brads spaced 1 in. apart.

SEE ALSO
Bird photography . . . Birdhouses . . . Outdoor photography

LIGHTLY secured disc that will tip easily is meant to discourage squirrels from reaching the feeder.

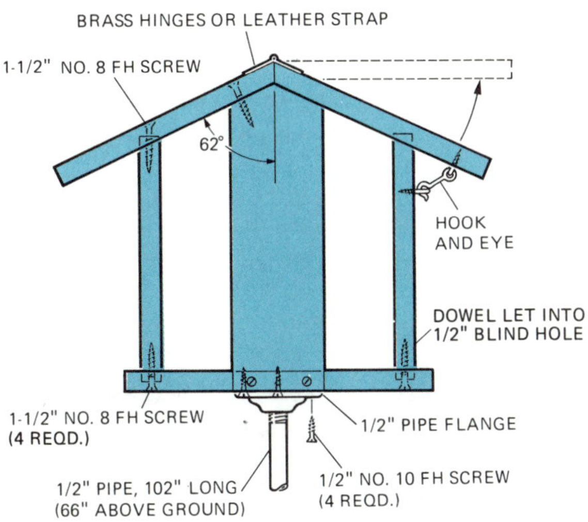

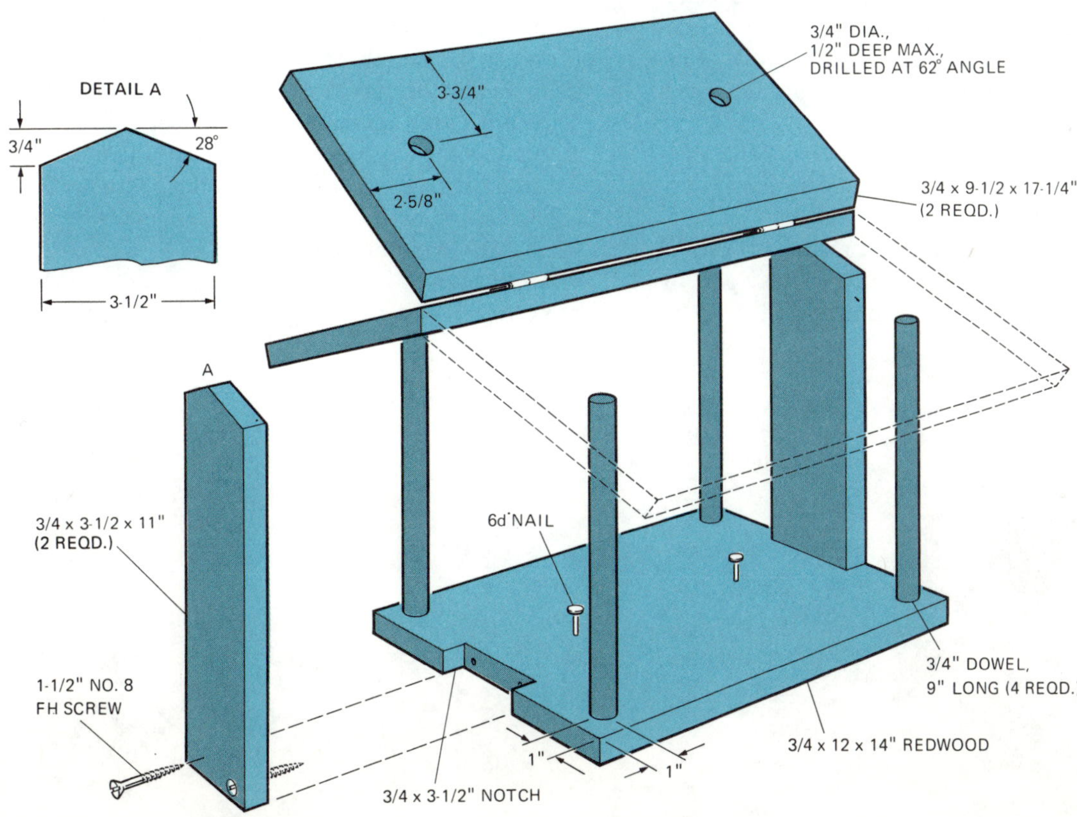

Birdhouses galore

By ROSARIO CAPOTOSTO

Provide suitable shelter and nesting facilities, and birds will return to your yard year after year

BUILD A BIRDHOUSE just like your own home! Obviously yours will differ from this, but you can use the same construction techniques.

■ THESE UNIQUE houses not only will attract birds to your yard, but they'll also add a touch of beauty to your property.

The 16-apartment purple martin cupola is designed for mounting on a garage roof. However, it can be made without the sub-base and simply mounted on a pole. The rustic red barn is a duplex for tree swallows. And the third birdhouse is most unique; you build it as a replica of your own house. The one shown, with four rooms, was made for Carolina wrens.

The houses were designed for the habits of the specific birds named above, but with minor changes they can be adapted to other species. Space limitations prohibit listing the specifications for the 50-odd species that will live in man-made houses, but you can obtain such information in your library.

A well-built birdhouse should be durable, waterproof and constructed of wood at least ½-in. thick to provide insulation.

Most important, it should be made so it can be opened for cleaning. The cupola comes apart by withdrawing screws. The barn is hinged to lift up when a screw is withdrawn from a screweye. The replica house can be lifted off its base when four screws are withdrawn.

All plywood must be exterior grade, and all joints are assembled with galvanized or aluminum 1½-in. finishing nails and water-resistant plastic resin glue.

replica house

The easiest way to make working drawings of your home is to work from enlarged photographs of each side taken head-on.

Assuming that the photos are smaller than the model you want to build, here's what to do: Determine the length you want the model to be. Measure the length of the house in the photo, then divide the larger number by the smaller. The sum is the factor you use to scale all elements. A simple example: If you want the model to be 16 in. long and the house in the photo measures 8 in., then multiply all measurements by 2 when drawing your plans.

An easier way if you have a 35mm camera and projector: Focus the image of the house to the

HOT-MELT GLUE makes it easy to assemble the precut doors, windows and other pieces of trim.

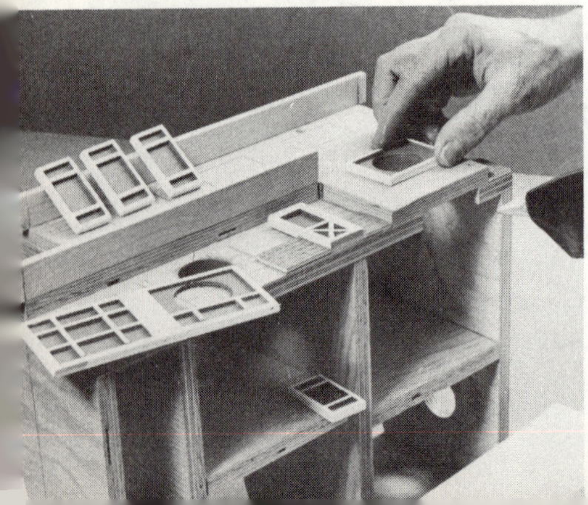

CLAPBOARD SIDING is available in preformed strips at hobby shops. House will soon be off-limits, kitty!

REALISTIC dollhouse cedar shingles are applied with hot glue. Start at bottom and work up.

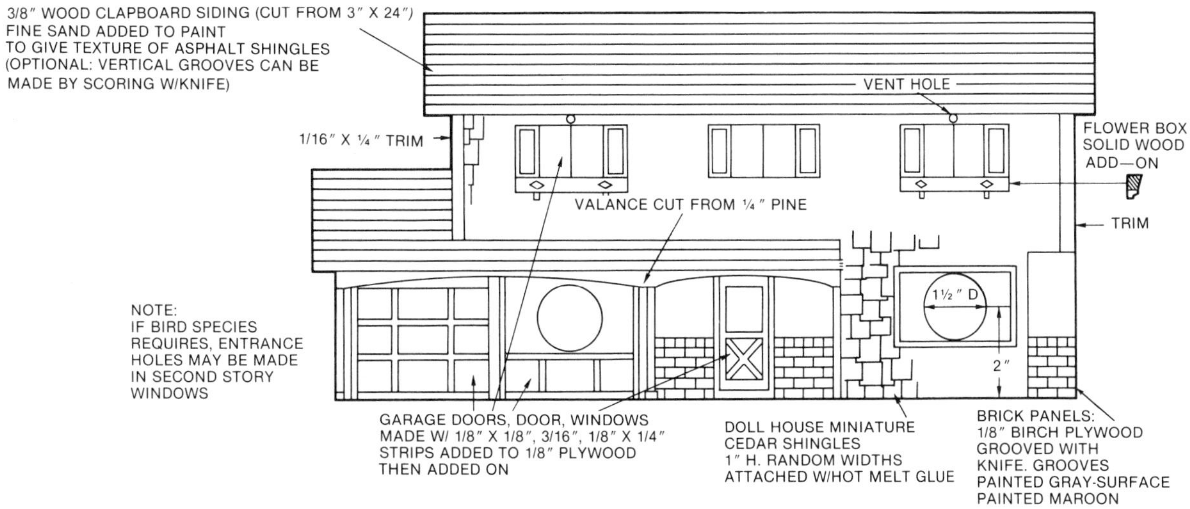
3/8" WOOD CLAPBOARD SIDING (CUT FROM 3" X 24")
FINE SAND ADDED TO PAINT
TO GIVE TEXTURE OF ASPHALT SHINGLES
(OPTIONAL: VERTICAL GROOVES CAN BE
MADE BY SCORING W/KNIFE)
VENT HOLE
1/16" X ¼" TRIM
FLOWER BOX
SOLID WOOD
ADD—ON
VALANCE CUT FROM ¼" PINE
TRIM
1½" D
2"
NOTE:
IF BIRD SPECIES
REQUIRES, ENTRANCE
HOLES MAY BE MADE
IN SECOND STORY
WINDOWS
GARAGE DOORS, DOOR, WINDOWS
MADE W/ 1/8" X 1/8", 3/16", 1/8" X 1/4"
STRIPS ADDED TO 1/8" PLYWOOD
THEN ADDED ON
DOLL HOUSE MINIATURE
CEDAR SHINGLES
1" H. RANDOM WIDTHS
ATTACHED W/HOT MELT GLUE
BRICK PANELS:
1/8" BIRCH PLYWOOD
GROOVED WITH
KNIFE. GROOVES
PAINTED GRAY-SURFACE
PAINTED MAROON

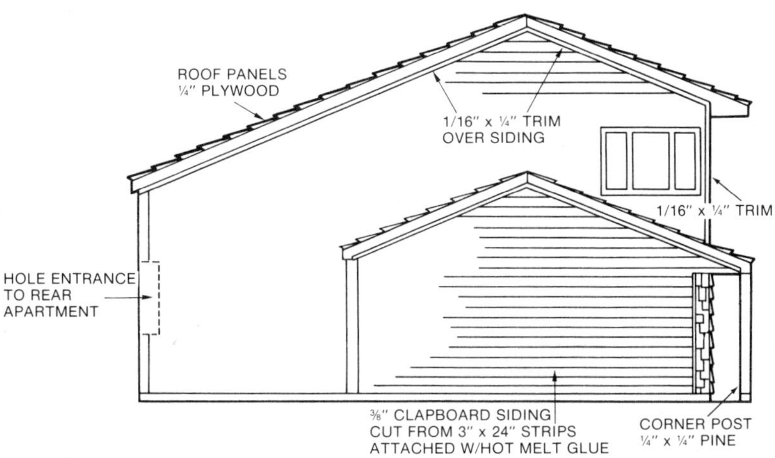
ROOF PANELS
¼" PLYWOOD
1/16" x ¼" TRIM
OVER SIDING
1/16" x ¼" TRIM
HOLE ENTRANCE
TO REAR
APARTMENT
⅜" CLAPBOARD SIDING
CUT FROM 3" x 24" STRIPS
ATTACHED W/HOT MELT GLUE
CORNER POST
¼" x ¼" PINE

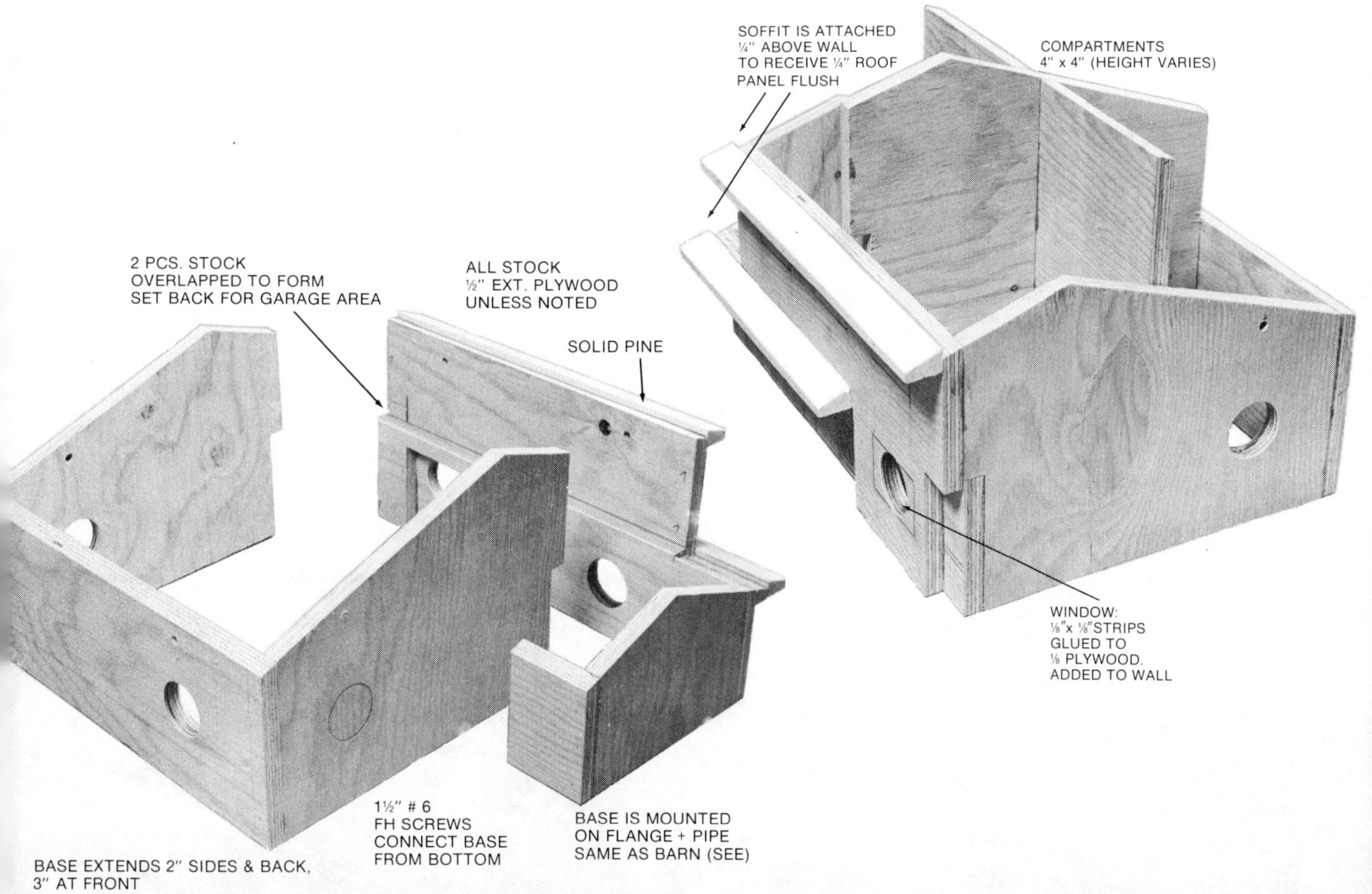
SOFFIT IS ATTACHED
¼" ABOVE WALL
TO RECEIVE ¼" ROOF
PANEL FLUSH
COMPARTMENTS
4" x 4" (HEIGHT VARIES)
2 PCS. STOCK
OVERLAPPED TO FORM
SET BACK FOR GARAGE AREA
ALL STOCK
½" EXT. PLYWOOD
UNLESS NOTED
SOLID PINE
WINDOW:
⅛"x ⅛"STRIPS
GLUED TO
⅛ PLYWOOD.
ADDED TO WALL
1½" # 6
FH SCREWS
CONNECT BASE
FROM BOTTOM
BASE IS MOUNTED
ON FLANGE + PIPE
SAME AS BARN (SEE)
BASE EXTENDS 2" SIDES & BACK,
3" AT FRONT

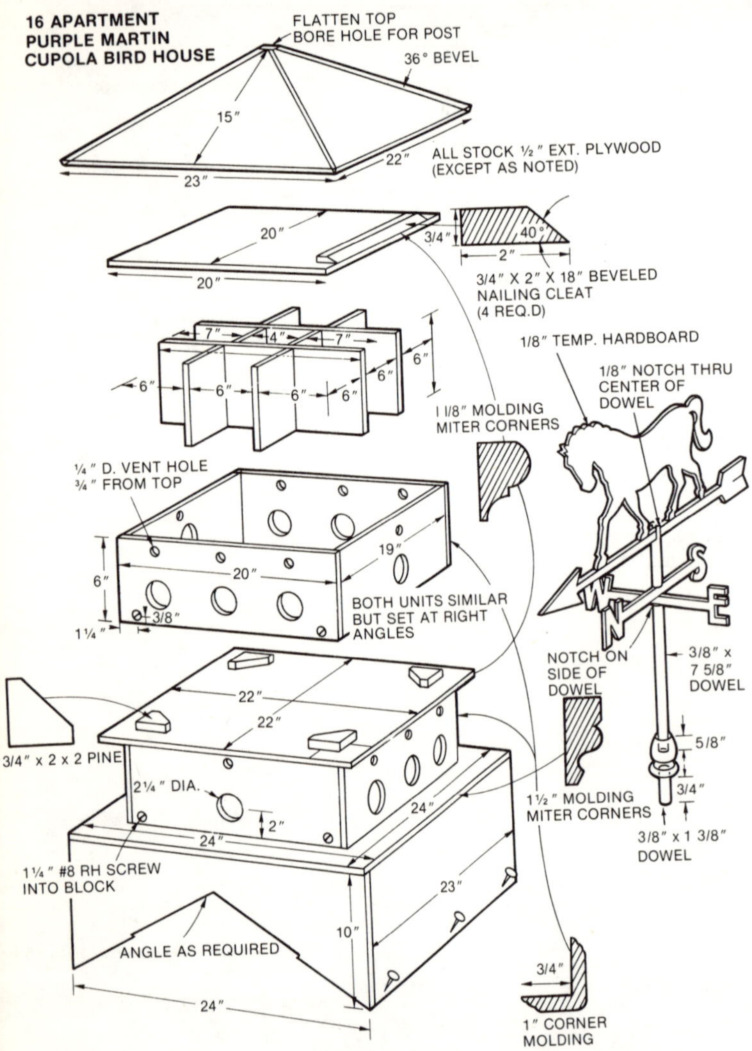

desired size, then trace it on paper.

Your house obviously will be different from mine, but you probably can use similar materials. Some supplies are available at hobby shops where dollhouse materials are sold. That's where I obtained the lap siding and cedar shingles, as well as thin strips for windows and doors. However, be sure any materials are weather resistant; some are made of paperlike materials.

I made the brick facing by cutting shallow grooves in ⅛-in. birch plywood. To simulate textured shingles I used the same lap siding as on the sides and mixed fine sand into the paint. The soffits are beveled strips of solid wood. Roof panels, cut from ¼-in. plywood, are butted to the strips.

Windows and doors are made by gluing thin strips to ⅛-in. plywood. All such parts are prepainted, then assembled with hot-melt glue. This glue is excellent for assemblies of this kind because it sets in about 15 seconds and makes a strong, waterproof bond.

The windows, flower boxes and doors are attached before adding the cedar shingles and siding. Both these materials are secured with hot-melt glue. Be sure to leave the small vent holes clear when surfacing. Paint the house, then add the prepainted trim strips.

1" SQUARES

PURPLE MARTIN apartment is designed as a cupola for a garage, but can be mounted on a pole if desired.

MARTIN HOUSE has 16 apartments, can be taken apart floor by floor for cleaning.

PAINT HOUSE and trim separately before assembling. Do not paint the inside of any birdhouse.

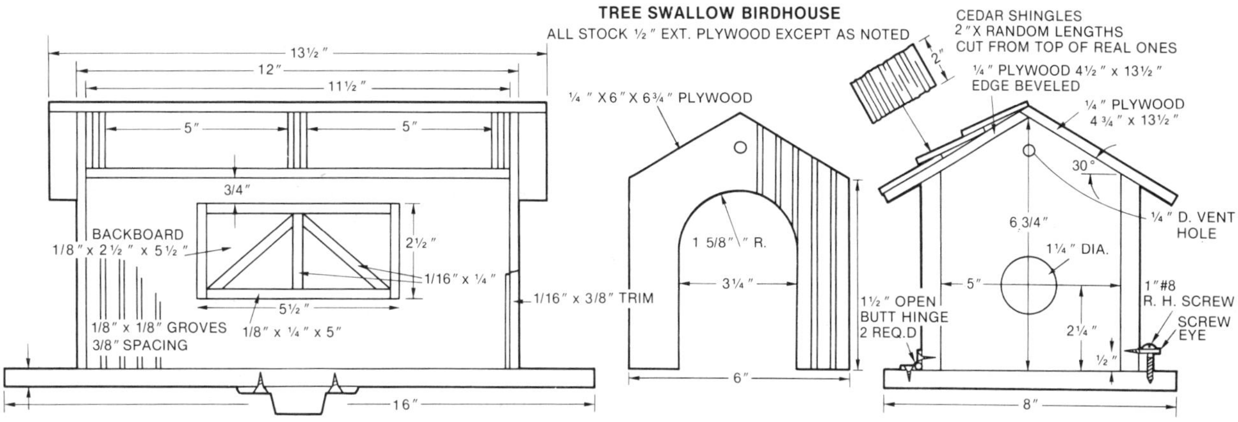

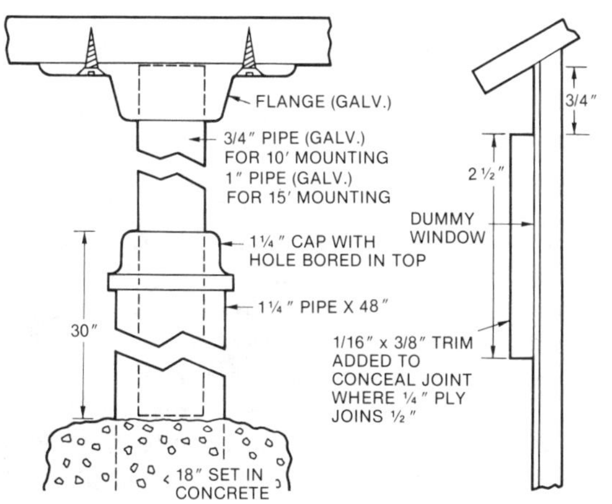

Attach the base to the house walls with four screws. Do not use glue, so you can lift the house off the base for cleaning.

cupola

Trace your roof pitch angle onto a piece of cardboard held against the edge of the roof. Cut and test for fit, then cut the ends of the sub-base with a sabre saw. Cut all parts to size, and cut entrance holes with a hole saw. Attach the room dividers, starting with the center pieces. Add sides, then tops. Locate corner blocks so sections will fit over them without forcing.

The roof panels require compound cuts. Tilt the saw blade 36° and set the miter gauge at 52½° to make these cuts. Hold roof pieces with masking tape during assembly.

Various moldings are used to ornament edges and corners. Paint the house and trim separately. Cut the weathervane from ⅛-in. hardboard and assemble with hot-melt glue.

barn

Side walls and "doorway" pieces are grooved by making shallow cuts with a table saw. Assemble the box and add end panels before attaching the roof.

Surface the roof with real cedar shingles, using only the thin upper few inches. Cut them to random widths and overlap previous course with each succeeding course.

RUSTIC RED BARN, mounted on a pole, is a duplex for tree swallows. Groove sidewalls with shallow saw cuts.

ASSEMBLE the box, then add the end siding panels. Use water-resistant glue and brads at all joints.

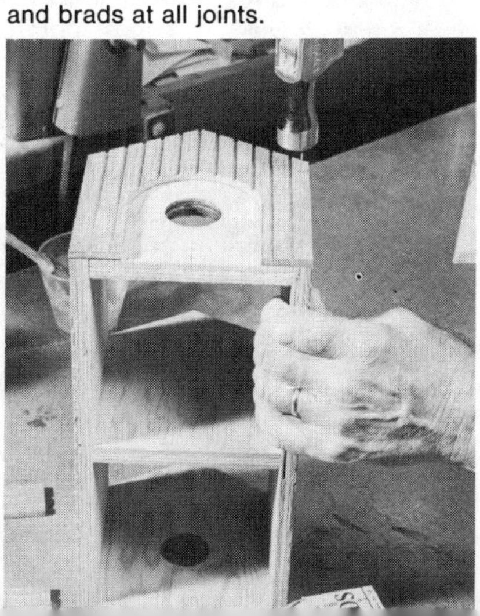

CEDAR SHINGLES are cut from the thin ends of real ones, fastened in place with a brad pusher.

Perspiring windows

Why do our windows sweat on the inside? We have storm sash and storm doors; the house is insulated and the clothes dryer is vented.—John Cvercko, Campbell, Ohio

Your storm sash are leaking cold air into the space between the storms and the inner sash. If you seal the storms with self-adhesive weatherstripping, you will likely solve this problem—certainly minimize it to the extent that it is no longer objectionable.

Fireplace cleaning

How can I clean the smoked-up interior of my fireplace? Although it has apparently been used for years, I've just moved to my present address and do not need it for heating.—Randall Wolff, Springfield, Ill.

You can look forward to a messy, tiresome job done in a most awkward working position—with the final issue in some doubt, if you're looking forward to spanking-clean firebrick. Of several procedures, the best I've tried is the use of a strong solution of trisodium phosphate—most household cleaners contain it—applied with a stiff-bristle scrubbing brush, or bristle brush and wire brush. If the coating is old and hardened, it may take several applications to get down to the bricks. Rinse after each scrubbing, wear rubber gloves and goggles to protect your eyes from spatters.

When the fireplace has been cleaned, you can then do as many interior decorators do and paint the inside black, using a special fire-resistant paint that is sold by most fireplace supply stores.

Clock origin

I acquired an old clock that caught my eye because of its unusual ornamentation. It has a long door veneered in a beautiful curly wood and a door panel consisting of nine pieces of beveled glass set in brass framing. It strikes on a long chime rod, has Arabic numerals, a brass and silvered dial and is driven by two brass weights. It's a hanging clock, about 35 in. tall and 12 in. wide. The question is, who made it and where? No one I've contacted seems to know.—George Hyde, Atlanta.

It's not possible to give you a positive answer without seeing it, but I'm guessing—and this is strictly a guess—that the clock was made in either Germany or Austria. The strike on a single chime rod and the multipaneled glass door in brass framing would seem to indicate this origin.

In-and-out home repairs

By necessity I must become a lady "handyman" and I need some elementary "how-tos," such as patching small cracks in walls and ceilings—what patcher to use and what kind of paint? Outside trim needs painting; what kind of paint do I use? Heating is a forced warm-air system; how often should filters be changed? There are small leaks in basement walls; how do I patch them? Screens have some whitish spots; how can these be removed? With kerosene?—A.V., Ind.

Small cracks in plastered walls and ceilings are usually filled with spackling compound, applied with a wide putty knife and sanded smooth after it dries.

Use a water-soluble interior paint on walls and ceilings; color, your choice. Apply it with a roller a narrow strip at a time and usually across the width—so that you can roll to a wet edge when rolling on the second strip.

On outdoor trim, brush or scrape off all loose material and "feather" the edges of blisters flush so that they will not show under new paint. Use a paint especially compounded for outside trim. If "trim" includes sash frames, be careful not to "paint them in." After painting loosen each sash to break the seal. Be sure to lower the upper sash and raise the lower one so you can paint the exposed outer edge of the upper rail of the latter. Do this work only during the warmer months.

Hold an unused furnace filter up to good light and note its clarity; when this "see-through" has been reduced 50 percent, or less, used filters should be replaced.

As a rule, small cracks in basement walls can be filled with a masonry waterproof paint. Apply paint to cracks first; then do the whole wall.

Whitish spots that usually appear on aluminum screening can be removed with a detergent. Don't use kerosene; it's a fire hazard.

Discolored rush chair seats

I have two chairs with artificial rush seats and after long use these seats have become soiled and discolored. After I washed them with detergent they turned grayish white. What happened? How do I restore the original color?—Earl Edwards, Dayton, Ohio.

It's likely that these seats were coated with shellac, the four-pound cut—which used to be a common treatment. Use a stiff-bristle brush on the seats to remove dust and any loose material; then try to stain them back to their original color. Apply an oil stain that matches the finish on the wood parts of the chairs; wipe it on the rush lightly and then let it dry thoroughly.

Armchair studio for wildlife photos

This windowsill birdfeeder has a one-way mirror to allow you to snap nature photos without going outdoors

By CHARLES SMITH

SETUP IS SIMPLE: Log with holes to hold seed acts as a feeder to attract birds, doubles as a natural background. One-way mirror hides camera from birds.

BLACK AND WHITE print of color photo shows how easy it is to get a "deep-woods" picture from easy chair.

MUCH AS I ADMIRE nature photographers who stalk birds through chilly woods for days, I prefer to get bird shots like this without leaving my armchair—and I do.

My secret is a windowsill bird feeder, with a piece of one-way mirror backing up the window's glass. Invisible to the birds, I just sit back and click my camera. It takes some patience—but not the field photographer's dedication—and no discomfort.

You can have the mirror cut to any size you wish, according to your budget. I started with a 5 by 7-inch mirror, but soon found so many friends and family members nosing the glass to watch the birds outside that I soon switched to a 12 by 30-inch size. For safety and convenience, frame the glass. I used a rabbeted wood frame, but you could tape the glass in a frame of fiberboard just as well.

The mirror cuts down the light reaching your camera, but you can still shoot, hand-held or on a tripod, with high-speed films. Using these films means you can use natural lighting, and that you'll get natural-action blurs when the birds move. But it can also result in cluttered backgrounds, and the faster film has more grain.

You can use slow black-and-white films or Kodachrome for wire-sharp, low-grain photos of unblurred action if you mount one or two electronic flash units on the windowsill as illustrated, and run extension sync cords to the camera. (Holes in the window sash or sill are optional.) Since this makes the birds much brighter than their background, there's no more background clutter.

My feeder is a log with holes drilled into it to hold seeds. It also makes a natural-looking setting. When I use flash, I attach my lights to a 2x4 base and adjust them before putting the light assembly outside, so as to disturb the birds as little as possible.

fine gift for a shut-in

Don't count on good shots your first day—it takes several days from the time you first start putting seed out till your birds find out where it is. Even when you're not taking photographs, the endless antics of the birds entertain family and guests. And if you're looking for a gift for someone who must spend a lot of time indoors, the bird logs and mirror, installed, make a fine one, whether they are used with camera or not.

SEE ALSO

Bird feeders . . . Birdhouses . . . Dryers, photo . . . Enlarging, photo . . . Film . . . Lenses, photo . . . Montages, photo . . . Outdoor photography . . . Photography . . . Telephotos

An expert's bird-carving secrets

By PENELOPE ANGELL

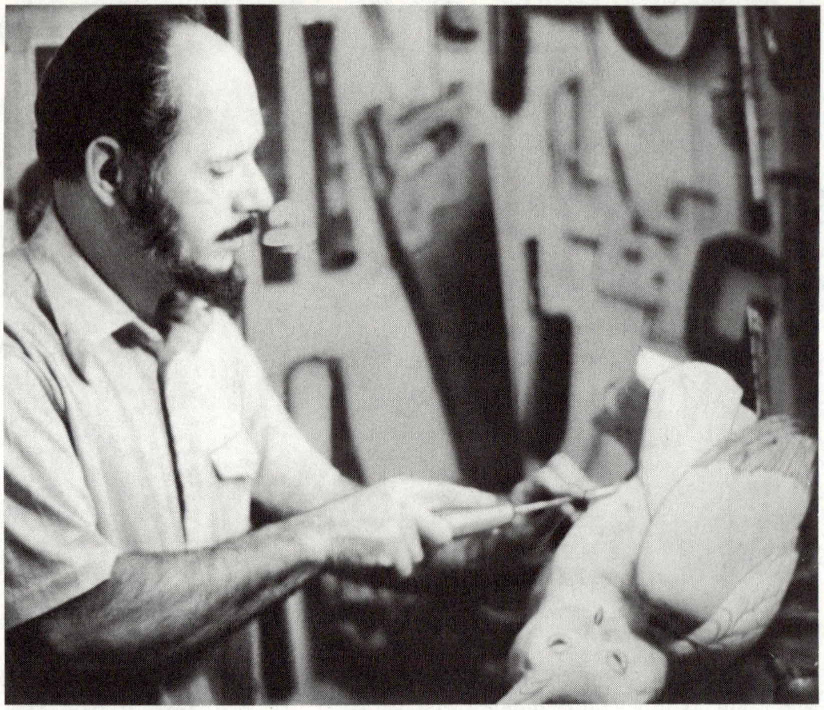

PHILLIP ZELLER carves a 22-in.-high great horned owl. Later this bird will be mounted on a section of hollow tree trunk.

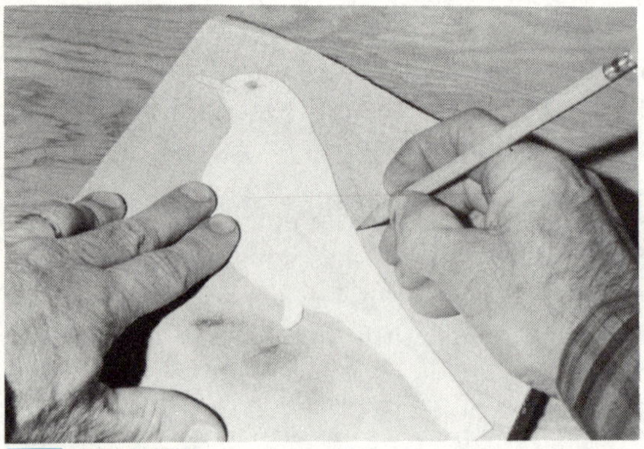

1 **ZELLER** begins by outlining a pattern on basswood; the beak runs with the grain.

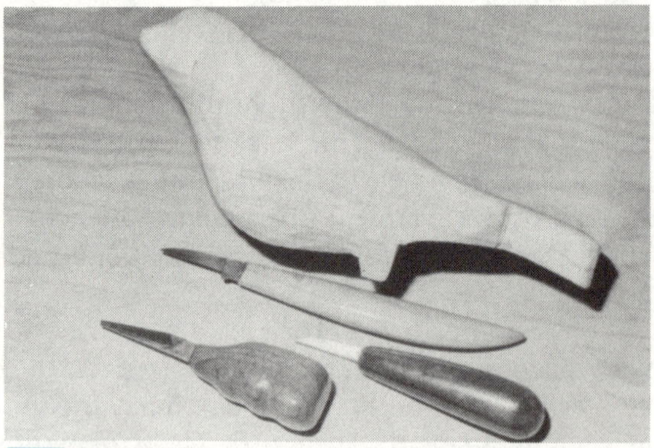

2 **CUT OUT** the rough shape with a bandsaw. Begin to round areas as needed.

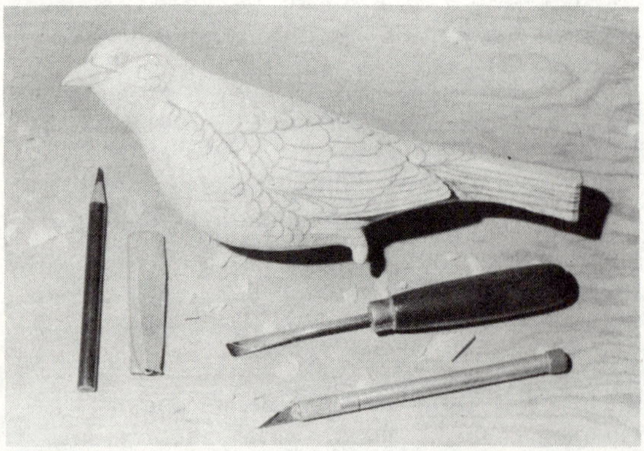

3 **CARVE OUT** areas to shape the bird and draw in each individual feather.

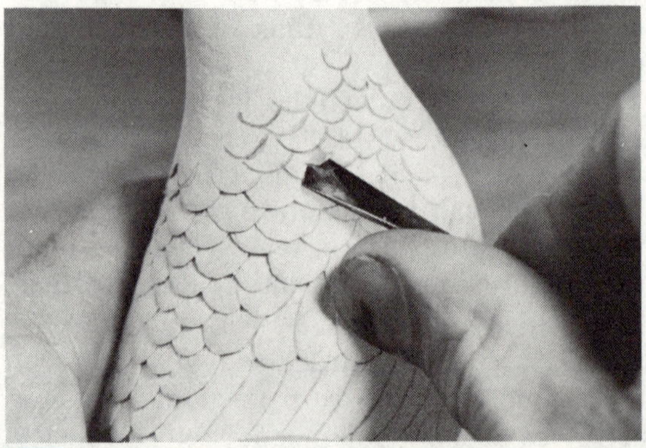

4 **OUTLINE FEATHERS** with a modeler's knife. Begin carving with skew chisel at tail.

DISPLAYED in their natural environment, Zeller's birds look even more realistic. Two bluebirds (upper left) make their home on the bough of a blossoming tree. Although most birds are life-size, these flying widgeons (bottom left) are one-third size. Water is made of plastic resin and grass that bends in the wind is wood. Wings of the colorful yellow-shafted flicker (above right) are separate wood pieces.

■ ONE WOMAN was positive the bird was stuffed. Another viewer thought real feathers had been glued to a wood body. Phillip Zeller's life-like bird carvings have been fooling people across the country.

Zeller devotes his time to carving the birds from basswood, a light wood that he sometimes hollows to make even lighter.

As Zeller explains it, there is more to creating a bird than carving. He spends much time in research, studying pictures and actual birds. A knowledge of metalwork is also needed as most carvings have metal feet and legs, and metal is used to make parts of the birds' environment. Assembling the bird—gluing individually carved feathers, attaching the feet and balancing the bird in its setting—is part of each project. Treat-

SEE ALSO

Bottle craft . . . Carving, wood . . . Gifts, Christmas . . . Hobby centers . . . Internal carving . . . Laminating wood . . . Marquetry . . . Tools, hand . . . Veneering . . . Wood sculpture

THERE ARE 450 individual feathers on this purple gallinule. He feeds in a plastic-resin pond with lilies carved of wood. His feet are metal.

ing the bird with oil paint in natural colors means careful mixing of paints to get the right hues.

Zeller's most popular birds are the familiar ones—cardinals, chickadees and wrens. Game birds appeal to male customers, and songbirds are often women's favorites.

The time it takes to make a bird ranges from a week (about 80 hours) for a robin, to two or three months (300 to 400 hours) for an owl, pheasant or other large bird. This includes painstaking attention to detail. Sometimes he chooses the bird's environment, perhaps a particular piece of driftwood, before he decides the bird's position. He finally sells the pieces for $500 to $10,000.

The advice Zeller considers most important for novice wood carvers is: Study birds as much as possible. Get pictures of birds, watch them and note how they move and hold themselves. Serious carvers would benefit by borrowing study skins—birds that are stuffed but not mounted—from schools or museums. He suggests carving a bird from a composite of pictures and information.

The mistake most often made by carvers, according to Zeller, is in shaping a bird's head and bill. Often the back part of the bill isn't narrowed enough. He suggests following photos closely and gradually tapering the bill from back to front. A common error is misshaping feet. Usually, Zeller uses metal feet.

To carve a lifelike bird, you must, like Zeller, really know the bird. As a friend said of him, "People can take a piece of wood and make a bird, but Phil takes the wood and it *is* a bird."

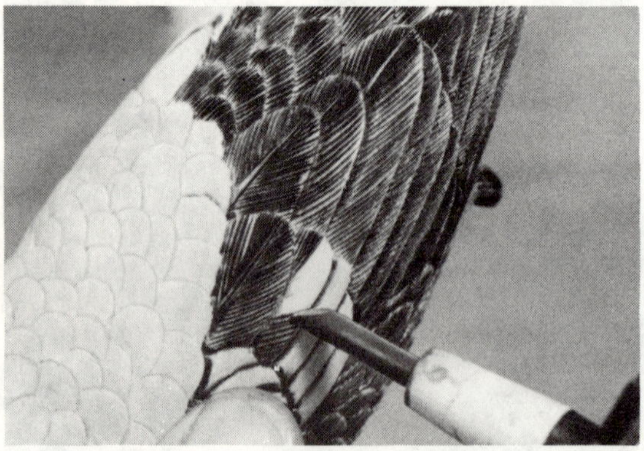

5 **BURN** central feather shaft and barbs on both sides with an electric pencil.

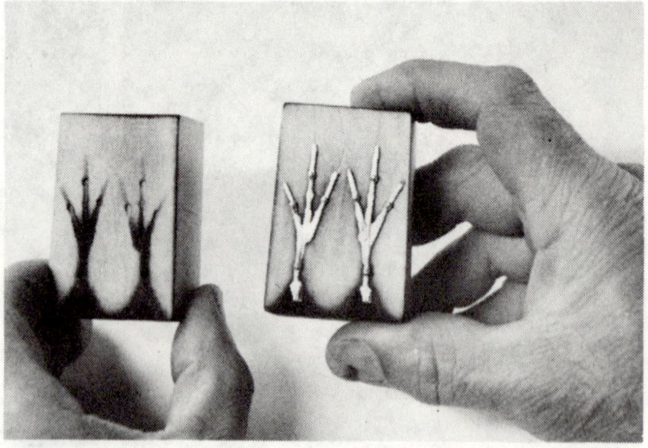

6 **TO MAKE FEET,** pour molten metal in a wood mold held in a vise. Legs are wire.

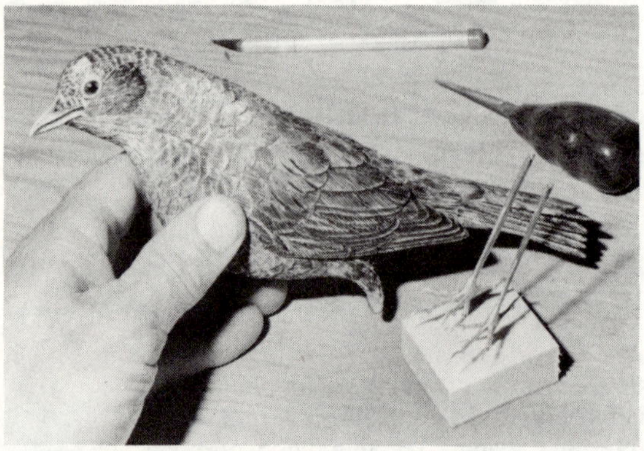

7 **BIRD** is completely burned and ready to paint. Front leg wires attach to base.

8 **REAL OR NOT?** It's hard to determine as this robin perches in tall grass.

By JAMES FINNERAN

Carve these sea gulls in flight

■ WITH A HAND-HELD power tool you don't have to be a master carver to make these handsome sea gulls.

1. Draw the pattern. Make a full-scale drawing of the sea gull. Transfer the outline to basswood or other soft wood. Use 1½ in.-thick wood for the bodies and ⅜-in.-thick wood for the wings.

2. Cut out the pieces. With a jigsaw cut out the pieces. Bevel-cut the wings at a 15° angle.

3. Glue the wings to the body. Apply Elmer's Glue-All to mating surfaces and wait until glue gets tacky. Then press parts together.

4. Shape the bird. Use the drum sander attachment in the power tool to shape the bird. Bore a hole the diameter of coathanger wire in the bottom of each bird.

5. Apply finish. First brush white alkyd primer on the birds and base. When dry apply an oil stain. Make highlights while stain is wet by rubbing with a turpentine-soaked rag.

Bore holes in the base for the attaching wires. Cut coathanger wire to 5-, 6- and 7-in. lengths; attach birds to the base.

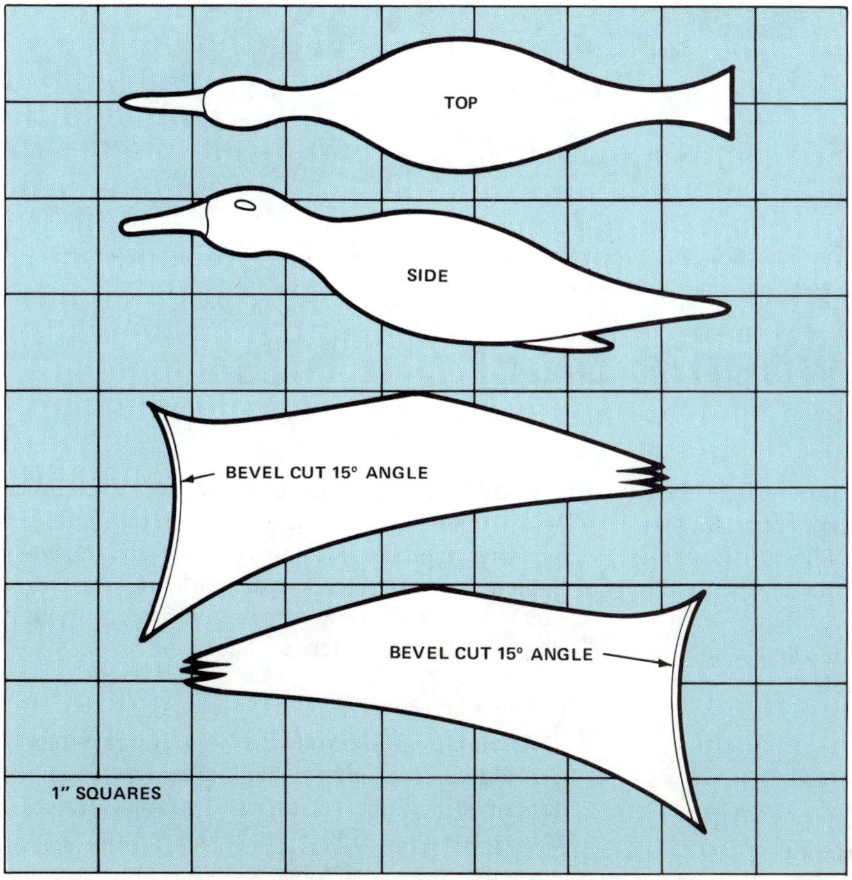

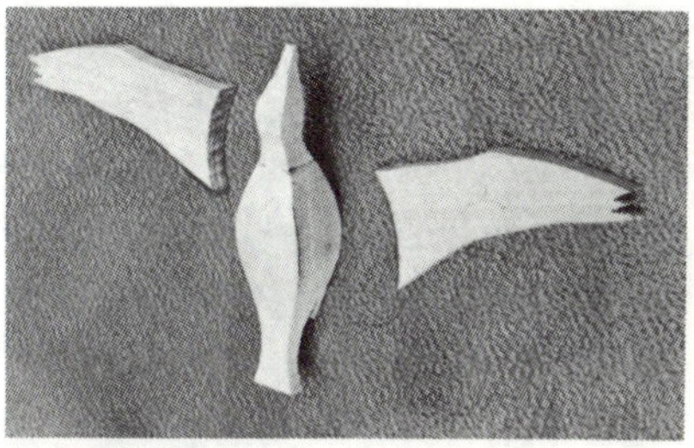

CUT OUT the three pieces.

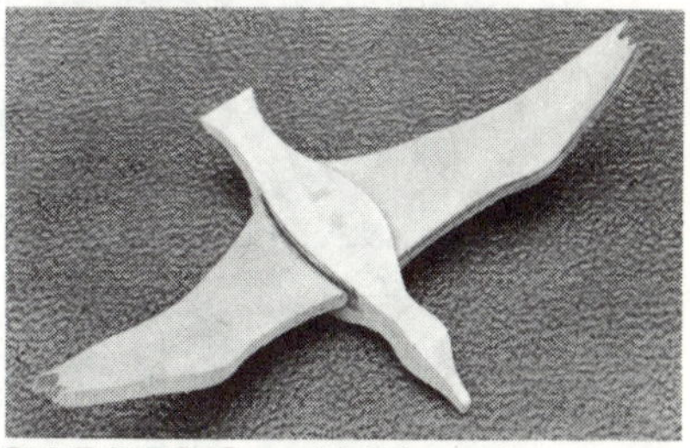

GLUE PIECES and let them dry.

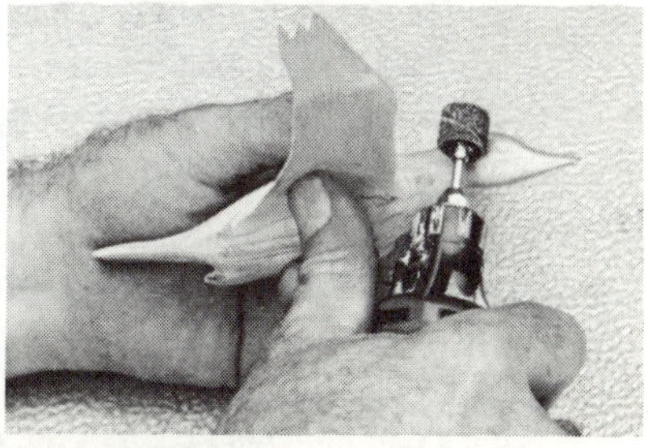

SHAPE BIRDS with a hand power tool.

COLEMAN'S TWO-BURNER stove and oven runs full blast for two hours on three and a half pints of fuel.

What to do when a blackout hits

By GURNEY WILLIAMS III

■ YOUR TELEVISION picture shrinks to a disappearing dot. Lights flicker out. Motors groan and die. The family huddles in the eerie quiet. It's a blackout. And despite all the myths about the simple joys of candlelit living, it's just about as romantic as a drought. There's nothing very enjoyable about a blackout.

SEE ALSO

Electrical wiring . . . Emergencies . . . Fire extinguishers . . . Wiring, electrical

Is there anything anyone can do? There is. Make plans while your lights are on. Join a growing number of homeowners who are enlightened about blackouts. Begin before the current goes off. Follow some simple precautions during the outage. Here's what to do:

before a blackout

Assemble a "Blackout Box"—a power-outage first-aid kit containing a small investment in self-contained lighting, cooking and heating devices costing less than $150. (For $1000, you can hook your house to a standby generator to see you through.) Recommended kit contents include camping equipment and canned food in a kitchen cabinet or closet—and make sure everything is in working order. Lanterns, stoves and catalytic heaters designed for camping can be used at home with proper precautions. If you haven't yet gone camping but want to try it, you might consider buying equipment that will double for both outings and outages. Whatever you buy, it's helpful to choose items that will let you use the same fuel in all your equipment. Here's what the Coleman Co. recommends for use in the home during blackouts:

A double-mantle lantern. This type of lamp has been used by campers for more than 75 years. The two mantles—the little sheaths of thread in the middle of the lamp—produce 220 candlepower, roughly equivalent to 100 and 75-watt bulbs burning next to each other at the same time. Most will hold about two pints of stove and lantern fuel, a distilled naphtha that won't clog wicks. The unit will burn eight hours on a single filling of one quart.

Stove. Some campers try to get by with Lilliputian pots and pans. The stove you buy for a blackout—assuming your range is electric—should be big enough to handle pots you normally use in the kitchen. Most deluxe two-burner stoves have space for 11-inch pans and will run about two hours, with both burners on full blast, on 3½ pints of fuel. You can add a stove-top oven—essentially a box with a temperature gauge—for baking.

Don't use charcoal grills indoors. Even a small grill will produce more carbon monoxide than a car's engine. In such concentrations, carbon monoxide—a colorless, odorless gas, heavier than air—can be hazardous. There's no need to cook inside.

Heater. A catalytic heater works by conducting fuel from a tank through a wick to a platinum burner. The platinum catalyst keeps the temperature down, leading to safe, efficient heating; clothing won't catch fire if it should come in contact with a "cat" heater. Most heaters will keep glowing in your kitchen or bedroom up to 37 hours on a tank (three quarts) of fuel. That's a lot of heat from very little fuel.

You'll need a small battery-powered *flashlight,* a supply of *fuel, matches, canned foods* and a *manual can opener,* a *cooler* and a *hot drink container.*

Total cost of this Blackout Box: less than $150. You should also have at least one battery-powered portable radio to keep you posted on the latest news during a power failure. Check the condition of the batteries once a month.

other items

Manufacturers offer other useful items for blackout use. L. L. Bean, Inc. (380 Alder St., Freeport, ME 04033) lists many products that would be handy. The Kangaroo Kitchen (Model No. 5297) can be used to boil, broil, bake, smoke, steam, toast and fry, and can pressure-cook an entire meal in 20 minutes. It's fueled by a 14-ounce propane cylinder.

Bean also offers kerosene lamps, an Aladdin Blue Flame Heater, and a handy coffeemaker. A kerosene table lamp and a hanging lamp operate

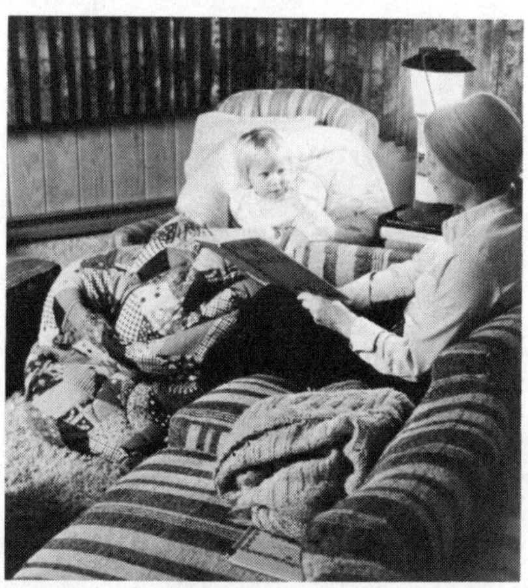

LIQUID-FUEL mantle lamps can provide light equal to a 175-watt bulb in this Coleman double-mantle model.

FAMILY MEALS are easily cooked indoors or out on campstoves like this Kangaroo Kitchen from L. L. Bean.

COFFEE KIT like L. L. Bean's Kar-'N-Home provides hot water for drinks without using public power.

for about 50 hours on a gallon of kerosene. They are nickel-plated and offer a light that varies in intensity from a single candle glow to a 100-watt bulb.

Bean's Aladdin Blue Flame Heater also operates on kerosene and burns without odor or smoke. It has a heat output of 9000 B.T.U. per hour, holds 1.3 gallons of fuel and will burn from 16 to 25 hours.

The firm's coffeemaker operates from a 12-volt automobile circuit or (when the current is on) from a standard household circuit. It comes complete with four cups and spoons and has a six-cup capacity.

The Swedish-made Optimus stove is made for small cooking chores; the top doubles as a cooking pan. It has a self-cleaning burner, runs on gas, and one-third of a pint will operate the stove for one hour and 15 minutes.

CAMPING EQUIPMENT lends itself to blackout situations. Coleman's two-burner stove takes 11-inch pans. Two-mantle lamp (rear) has 220 candlepower.

during the blackout

Oddly enough, one of the first things to do after the lights go out is to pull the plugs on your refrigerator and freezer and turn off your electric water heater, water pump and—if summer—airconditioner. Leave the pulled plugs in conspicuous positions—on the floor in front of the refrigerator, for instance, so you'll remember to reconnect appliances one by one when power returns.

There are a couple of reasons for turning off appliances. This helps the power company restore normal service. If circuits are overloaded when power returns, it may cut out again. And within the first few seconds after restoration, there's sometimes a surge of extra power. If your refrigerator or airconditioner is old, this surge can be enough to cause a breakdown. Don't take a chance on ruining your appliances.

Completely shut down, your house becomes a covered campground—except for one important difference: Cooking, heating and lighting equipment use up air. When you light them indoors, be sure to maintain ventilation by slightly opening windows on opposite sides of the room. If there's only one window in the room, open it several inches and leave it open as long as any fuel is burning.

Another point of safety: Catalytic heaters flare up for a few seconds when started. Flames may rise 2 or 3 feet above the heater head. So light heaters *outside* and carry the units into the house (in an upright position, held from beneath).

Hot meals and a space heater provide modest warmth; your refrigerator, meanwhile, will hold enough cold air to preserve food for two days or

HOME GENERATORS like these from Onan pump 1000 to 5500 watts into house circuits. Small units keep things going if switched from furnace to freezer to TV, lights and other appliances.

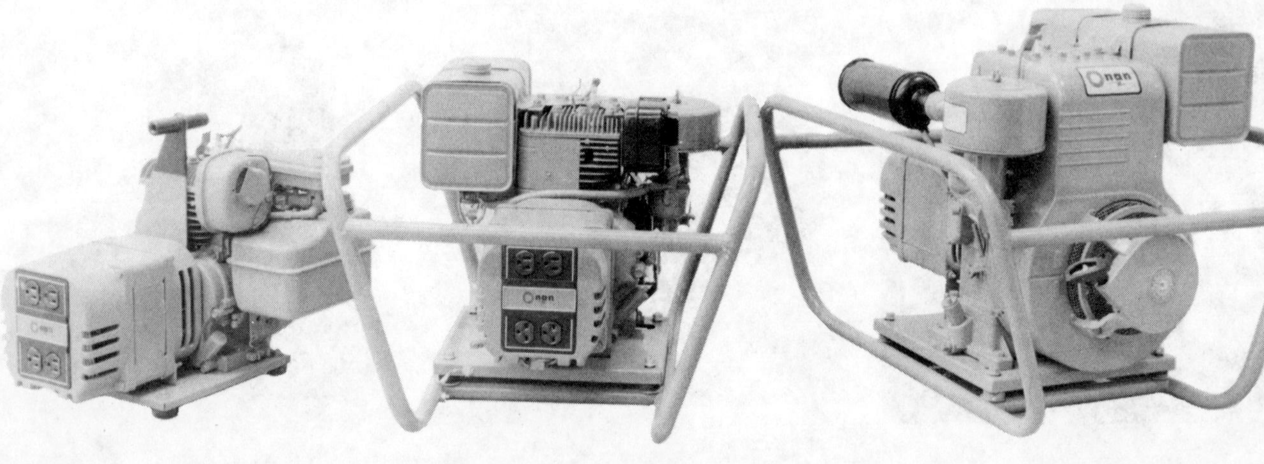

BLACKOUT CHECKLIST

If you know a blackout is coming, here's what you should do:

TURN UP the refrigerator and freezer controls to maximum. Treat the refrigerator and freezer just like Pandora's Box: Don't open door unless you have to. Food will generally stay solid for 48 hours in a fully loaded freezer if you keep door closed. (If the freezer is less than full, food will thaw faster; freezer full of meat generally stays cold longer.)

REVIEW ALL directions on how to use camping equipment safely.

FILL AND TEST all of your equipment *outside the house* to forestall any spills of fuel in kitchen.

IF LOCAL supplies and laws permit, fill your bathtub and/or other large containers with water in the event that your electric water pump or the local water system is affected by the blackout. Toilets can be flushed by pouring in a bucketful of water.

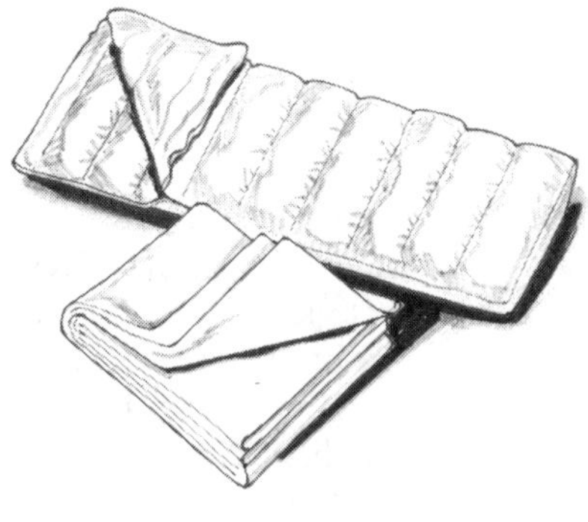

BRING OUT from storage all extra blankets and sleeping bags; you'll need them if your heat goes off.

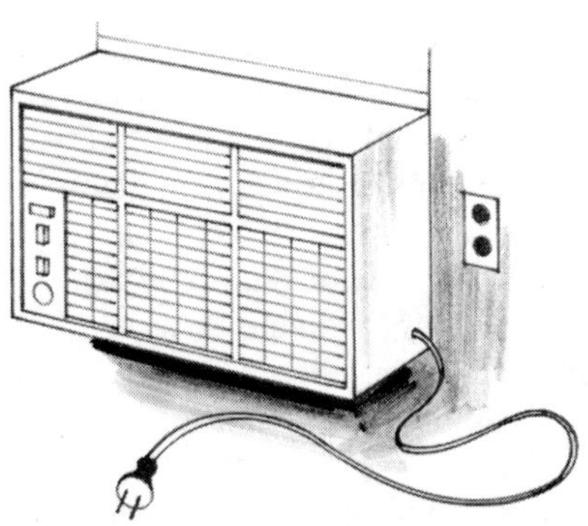

WHEN THE BLACKOUT begins, unplug your appliances such as the refrigerator, freezer, furnace and pumps; turn off all but a few lights. When power returns plug in appliances one at a time until all are safely on.

IF YOUR stove is electric, make coffee, soup or a hot drink on the campstove and store in a vacuum container. This will free both burners of your campstove for cooking the next meal.

so if you plan ahead before you open the door. Then pull out the food you need with the speed of a thief emptying a safe. Milk, juice, sandwich meats or other foods you know you'll consume in the course of a day can be removed and kept in a cooler (outside if it's cold) so you can leave the refrigerator alone. Whatever you do, resist the temptation to open the freezer door to see how frozen food is faring. Such testing drains cold air, particularly in vertical freezers, and hastens thawing.

What if your frozen foods *do* thaw? If they're later refrozen, their quality can deteriorate. You may notice a strange odor or color when you open them. But the danger of deterioration during a two-day blackout is minimal even if partial thawing occurs, particularly if foods are tightly sealed. You may want to remove ice cream containers before they leak. Otherwise, food experts advise, leave your freezer alone and don't worry about frozen foods for the first two days without power.

After two days, move food to a working freezer if possible, and check each food item for spoilage before you cook it. Heed the old saying: When in doubt, throw it out. If no working freezer is available after two days, follow directions on the side of many frozen-food packages and cook the products, if they haven't spoiled. Then keep them as cold as possible until you eat them.

after the blackout

Plug in the refrigerator, freezer and other appliances. Make sure all camping gear is turned off. Put the gear away according to directions (don't pack away cat heaters, for instance, until they've cooled for 20 or 30 minutes).

Camper-style living in your home is one way to ease through a blackout. The Cadillac way to go, by comparison, is to make your own electricity with a self-contained generator.

Several manufacturers produce complete standby power systems for the home that take up no more space than a lawnmower. Some models come with dollies so they can be trundled out of storage sheds when needed and hooked into your system at your electric meter.

There's a wide variety of models for home use. Onan, some of whose models are shown on page 346, makes 25 different generators between 1000 and 5500 watts. What wattage is right for you? One way to estimate is to add the approximate running wattage of all devices that might have to operate simultaneously at any point during the blackout. Then pick the generator that delivers the total you need. Here's the wattage some typical appliances require:

Lights (per bulb)	7½-300
Freezer	300-800
Refrigerator	250-750
Well or sump pump	300-600
Furnace blower	300-600
Electric range (per element)	650-1200
TV (color)	200-500
TV (black and white)	100-300
Washing machine	100-700
Clothes dryer	200-1200
Coffeemaker	600-1200

The heart of the generator is a gasoline-powered engine (diesels are available, too) driving an alternator. Most generators start with a pull cord and, in seconds, an alternator turns out full power. Current feeds through heavy cable to a feed-in plug at your meter. Some generator makers provide a special switch—usually optional (Onan calls its device Power Sentry)—that disconnects the house from outside utility lines. This switch, which should be UL-approved, provides an important safety feature: It locks the house circuits into the generator, so home-produced current can't feed back into power lines and endanger linemen.

In blackouts, simply throw the special switch, crank the generator and add appliances one by one. With lower-wattage units, rotate the use of the generator's limited output for efficiency. Turn on the freezer for a few hours at midday, for instance; then turn it off in the evening when you want lights or TV. If you exceed your unit's capacity, a circuit breaker on the generator will cut you off, and the engine will stop running. If that happens, turn off some of your appliances and reset the circuit breaker.

Generators make about as much noise as a late-model lawnmower. Since they must be operated outdoors (they produce carbon monoxide like any gas engine), noise isn't likely to bother *you.* Your neighbors may feel otherwise. Most units transmit interference to radios and TVs, too, but generator dealers can tell you how to install a simple interference suppressor at a cost of a few dollars.

special generator hookups

The overall cost depends on the generator capacity and extras. Onan has a 2000-watt generator and a 3000-watt unit, each in several models. The Power Sentry switch can be added and you can buy gadgetry to switch your house over to generator power automatically when the system senses a blackout.

The Power Sentry can be hooked up by experienced amateurs, but codes in some areas require that a licensed electrician do the work. Local dealers will be familiar with standards and inspection systems you'll have to follow. Part of the installation involves opening up your meter, so you'll have to call your power company, too.

hook up to RV

If you already own a recreational vehicle with a 120/240-volt generator, Onan makes other equipment to enable you to hook your house lines to your camper in an emergency. The basic kit includes the Power Sentry and heavy twist-lock power cord.

Your home-generated power will cost a lot more than electricity from a utility. The 3000-watt model, for instance, uses a gallon of gas per hour at full load to run its 8-hp engine. But during an outage, it'll seem a small price to pay to keep your furnace and freezer operating and some lights burning through the blackout.

Consider any standby generator an insurance policy; you hope you'll never use it, but it's there if needed.

Carbide blades—performance at a price

YOU MAY NOT need tungsten-carbide-tipped blades for your circular saw. If yours is a light-production workshop, if you rarely work with tough or exotic materials or if you sharpen your own blades regularly, the premium prices of carbide blades probably aren't justifiable.

But if your shop really hums with activity, if you want exceptionally smooth cuts in materials like expensive veneer plywood, or if you've figured the cost of having steel blades sharpened as often as they should be, carbide blades can start to look like a bargain.

They can hustle through materials that mean instant dullness for ordinary steel blades—hardboards, high-pressure laminates and laminated panels, asbestos and soft (nonferrous) metals such as brass and aluminum.

Best of all, they'll stay sharp 10 times longer, on the average, than steel blades will in the same applications. The reason is that tungsten carbide, a manmade substance, is extremely hard—three times harder than the hardened steel used for files.

Not every carbide-tipped blade is right for every use, of course, and they do suffer from two major disadvantages. The first is high initial cost: Carbide blades commonly cost four or more times as much as the nearest steel equivalents.

The second disadvantage is sharpening—it's costly, too; usually several times as much as commercial sharpening of a comparable steel blade. Don't think you can do it yourself, either—it requires a diamond wheel. If you take a green silicon-carbide wheel to a carbide blade, you're almost certain to wreck the geometry of the tips.

You'll have to work out the cost equation for your own situation. When this article was written a 10-inch steel blade was more economical to buy and sharpen than a 24-tip carbide blade after ten sharpenings (which would equal one carbide sharpening). But after that point, the carbide blade quickly becomes more economical.

After half a dozen or more sharpenings, a carbide blade may have lost its clearances (excess carbide that makes it possible to regrind a tip to the correct shape) and will be ready for replacement.

Retipping an entire blade is not economical. It's good to know that if you break one or two blade tips, they can be replaced, however.

In use, the tips of a carbide blade act as tiny chisels, each carrying a chip of material out of the work-piece. A blade's face-rake angle (also called hook angle) determines the angle at which each tip strikes the work. Most carbide blades for home-workshop use have positive rake angles, larger on rip blades and smaller on combination and crosscutting blades.

The way tips are ground also helps to determine a blade's characteristics. Square grind is usually for ripping; alternate top bevel (ATB) is for combination and crosscut blades. Grinds

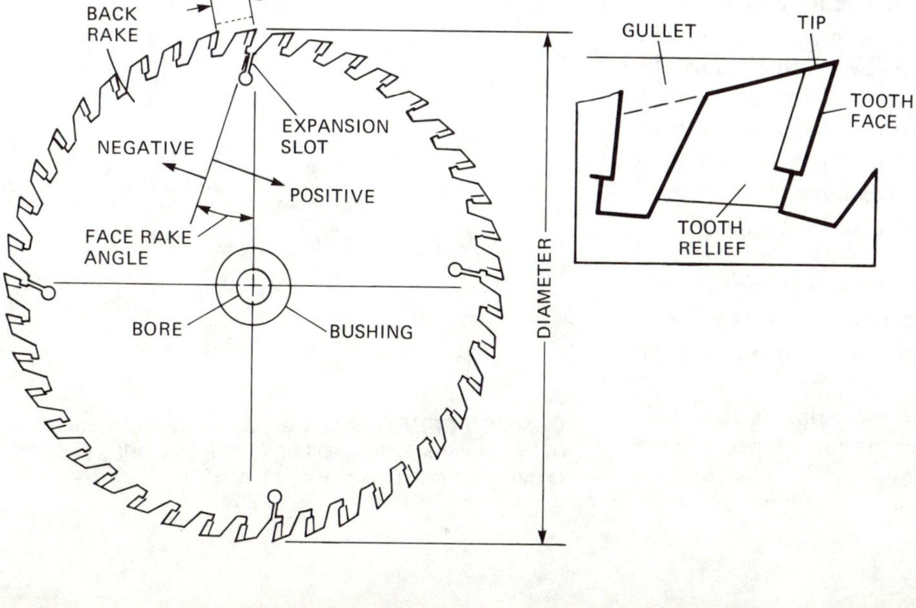

ANATOMY of a typical carbide-tipped blade is shown. Rotation is clockwise for blade in position shown. Expansion slots provided on many-toothed blades allow rim to expand without warping body of the blade.

SEE ALSO
Bench saws . . .
Circular saw accessories . . .
Circular saw blades . . .
Circular saws, portable . . .
Power-tool maintenance . . .
Power-tool stands . . .
Radial-arm saws . . .
Safety, workshop . . .
Saws, bench . . . Table saws

EIGHT-TIP blade for portable saws does rough carpentry.

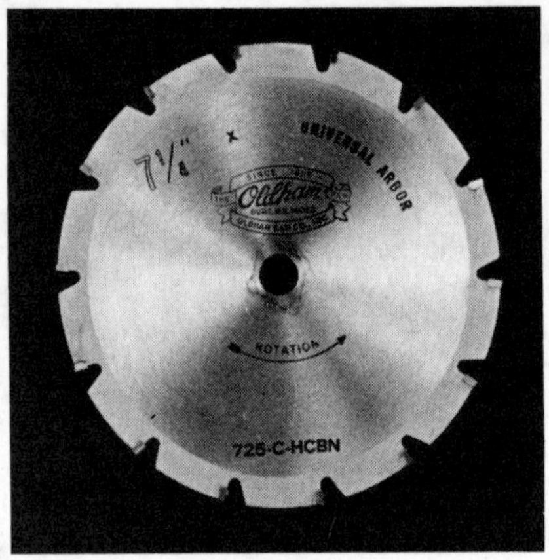

NAIL-CUTTING blade sold by Brookstone has a negative face rake angle.

COMBINATION blade with 20 alternately beveled tips both rips and cross cuts.

SQUARE-GRIND blade is for ripping and rough crosscutting.

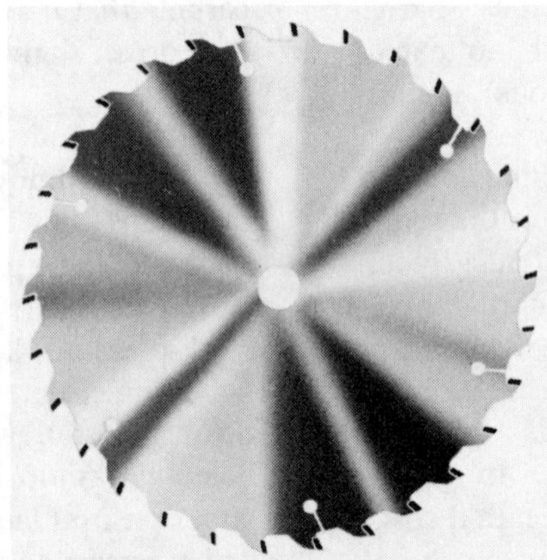

LUXITE blade is for radial-arm saws; 12-in., 30-tip model is shown.

FOR ADVANCED woodworking, 10-in.-dia., 60-tip blade cuts silky smooth.

using two ATB tips to one square tip (2-1 or raker grind) and four ATB tips to one square tip are also found on combination and smooth-crosscutting blades. Triple-chip grind (TCG) may also be used on high-grade blades for the do-it-yourselfer, but is not common.

Like most hard materials, tungsten carbide is also brittle. Carbide blades require gentle handling to prevent tip breakage. Keep them in their original packages if possible; if they must be stacked, put cardboard spacers between blades.

It's always important that your saw run true, without play. For true running with minimum wobble, blade makers recommend stabilizers, also called stiffeners. These are discs clamped on both sides of the blade.

Work should be held firmly, clamped when possible. Stop using a carbide blade at the first sign of dullness—tips are easier to break when dull.

As a general rule, the more tips on the blade you choose, the smoother the cut will be—but the sharpening will cost more.

CARBIDE TIP GRINDS (10 and 12-in.-dia. blades)

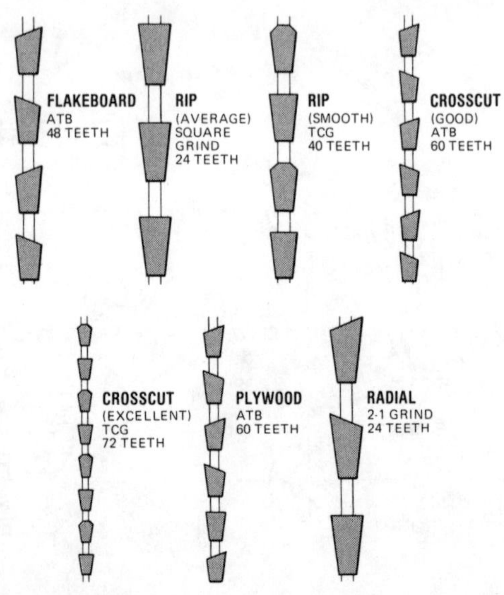

COMMON GRIND patterns are alternate top bevel (ATB), square, 2-1 (raker) and triple-chip grind (TCG) is found on the higher-priced blades.

How to survive a blizzard in your car

Every winter people lose their lives when they are trapped in their cars during sudden blizzards. Here's what you need to know to survive if you ever face this situation

By ROBERT LUND

TUESDAY, Nov. 10, 1940. A fine fall day in the Minneapolis-St. Paul area. Temperature 60°. Jacket and sweater weather, if you were going to be outside, but not cold by Minnesota standards. Most people stayed up beyond their normal bedtime. The following day was a holiday, Armistice Day (since changed to Veterans Day) and you could sleep late Wednesday morning.

Next day, Wednesday. The temperature dropped during the night and snow was falling by the time the late sleepers rolled out. But nothing unusual. The weather is always flip-flop in Minnesota in November.

But Armistice Day, 1940, was unlike any other Nov. 11 in the recorded history of Minnesota. Old-timers who survived the brutality nature visited on Minneapolis-St. Paul that day still recall the experience with a shiver.

In a 24-hour period, the temperature plunged 60°. The light wind, light snow of the early part of the day built into a snarling, howling blizzard. The wind was so powerful a man could not stand against it. Snow piled up layer by layer—5 inches, 10 inches, 15 inches. The official measurement was 16 to 20 inches. Farm animals were frozen alive in open fields.

The human bodies were found later. Forty-nine people died in the storm, some from exposure, some from over-exertion—trying to shovel out—some in their cars.

Winter is especially tough on people who have to use their cars. By listening to weather forecasts, you can plan some nonessential driving for times when conditions are likely to be favorable. But this isn't much of a solution for drivers who have to drive five or six days a week, good weather or bad. Snowstorms in the top tier of states are difficult to predict. Freak storms can come on without warning—with no mention of the storm in the weather forecast.

You can take a lot of the risk and worry out of winter driving by equipping your car with some basic gear and knowing what to do should you become snowbound to a point where you can't move your car.

what to carry

There are two different lists of take-alongs to consider. One is a list of on-car or in-car items. The second is an emergency pack.

Most drivers living in snowbelt states already have the on-car/in-car items. These include snow tires, traction devices—chains, mats, sandbags—a good spare tire (be sure it's inflated), jack and lug wrench, jumper cables, a spray deicer for windows, a graphite spray for door locks, shovel, tow cable or chain, extra fuses and a junior tool-kit—pliers, screwdriver and adjustable wrench. Spray-can chemicals are available for melting ice to give traction under the wheels. Or you can make your own. For a good "home brew," mix sand and salt or use granite poultry grit. These can be stored in milk cartons.

That's a fairly standard list of equipment for keeping a car moving under most nonemergency conditions. But what if you get caught in a blinding blizzard, snow as high as the headlights and no CB radio.

If you have a survival kit in your car, you don't do anything. You sit there until the storm stops and you can dig your way out. Or you wait for a rescue crew. If the idea of a survival kit reads like dramatic nonsense, check the newspapers this winter on the number of motorists who wind up in the hospital—or worse—as a result of being stranded.

The survival kit should contain certain basics, but beyond that you can get as elaborate as you wish. Here is the basic list suggested by the Minnesota Para-Rescue Team and the Minnesota State Automobile Assn. (AAA).

SEE ALSO
Autos, gas mileage . . . Chains, tire . . . Citizens band radio . . . Emergencies . . . Recreational vehicles

Face mask, first-aid kit, matches and candles, a small knife, safety pins, aspirin, 40 to 60 cents in dimes, compass, flashlight with spare batteries, paper towel, facial tissue or toilet paper and a supply of food. The Para-Rescue Team recommends storing the supplies in a three-pound coffee can with a plastic lid.

take high-energy food

The food should include honey, semisweet chocolate, instant coffee or a mocha mix, raisins or other dried fruit in small packets, candy bars (heavy on the chocolate) and gum. Experts don't include it on their lists, but I recommend carrying a jar of peanut butter. It will keep for months without spoiling and is a rich source of protein. Another item I've found handy is an icepick or awl. Or substitute one of those old-fashioned can openers with a point at one end and a fold-in corkscrew in the center.

Thick mittens or work gloves should be tied to the coffee can with strips of cloth—bright red or orange. If you get in trouble, you can use the strips to signal or tie them to the antenna to attract attention. You should also have a half-dozen emergency flares for signaling at night, and three or four reflectors.

Even though you are bundled up for winter driving, it's wise to pack extra clothing. Take along high boots or snowmobile boots, a stocking cap or winter hat with ear flaps and a padded jacket or heavy coat. The jacket or coat can be a castoff you happen to have around the house.

That's the basic list. If you want to go first class, add a thermal or space blanket, sleeping bag, thermal underwear, a hand-heating gadget, transistor radio (so you don't drain the battery playing the car radio), snowshoes and all the fancy stuff sold for snowmobilers and skiers.

first rule: don't panic

Now that you have all the gear, what do you do if you get zonked a hundred miles from nowhere?

The first rule, according to veterans of Minnesota winters, is don't panic. The storm will end eventually.

Stay in or near the car. You can leave it to find help if you know exactly where you are or you can see lights or human activity within walking distance. But if you don't know the territory, it's better to stay with the car. Even if you know where you are, don't try to walk for help until the storm lets up.

Don't attempt to push or shovel the car out of a heavy drift by yourself. You can try digging out if you have three or four people with you to share the shoveling.

If you shovel or exert yourself in any way that causes you to perspire, ventilate your clothes. Wet clothes lose insulation.

Keep front windows cracked an inch or so to let fresh air enter the car at all times. A freezing or wind-driven snow that drifts can seal a car so tight you can't get oxygen.

Don't sack out for any length of time. It's all right to doze, but it's important to exercise to keep warm. Move around in the car, climb from front seat to back, shake your arms and legs, clap your hands—anything to keep up your circulation. If there are others in the car, take turns sleeping. Someone should be on watch to signal for help if a rescue crew shows up.

keep a light on

Turn on the dome light of the car at night and leave it on. Road crews and snowmobile rescue units can see a small light from a long distance. You can turn on the engine to run the heater and play the radio at times, providing you are certain no exhaust is seeping into the car.

How long will you have to wait to be rescued? That depends on the intensity of the storm, how long it lasts and how many other motorists are in the same fix. Rescue crews in the Midwest usually get to snowbound cars on heavily traveled roads within 24 to 36 hours. If you are in the boondocks, you might have to wait three or four days.

Useful items to be carried at all times

First-aid kit, $2.50—$6
Flares (set of three), $1.75 set
Tire inflator, $1 each
Flashlight (magnetic), $2 each
Tire pressure gauge, $1.50—$5
Fire extinguisher (1 lb.), *$3.75 each
Jumper cables, *$7.95 pair
Blanket, $5—$8
Graphite aerosol spray, 75 cents each
Wiping cloth, 50 cents each
Chock blocks, $2 pr.
Warning triangle, *$7.49 each
Pencil and notebook, 50 cents each

*AAA price or est. retail price

Specific items to be carried in winter

Small snow shovel, *$2.35 each
Ice scraper—snow brush, $1.50 each
Reinforced tire chains, $20 set
Traction mats, *$1.95 pr.

*Items available through American Automobile Assn. (AAA).

Camp-cruising by kayak

By E.P. HADDON

■ THE BOAT may be small, but your trip can be a long one. So far I've paddled about 3000 miles in my present kayak, and today's touring models make it possible to copy safely the Eskimos' mode of travel. But for the long solo passages I enjoy, I've found you can do some customizing and improve on a good thing.

A little planning can make a kayak cockpit as shipshape as a submarine, with all essential safety and convenience gear stowed securely right at your fingertips. To plan placements aboard my 17-foot folding Klepper Aerius II kayak, I assembled the frame first without its Hypalon hull-covering. In the past, I had tested arrangements for storage of gear and supplies in a Folbot and other kayaks I have owned. Fitting out hard-shell fiberglass kayaks can be done in much the same way.

First, I installed a nylon pocket that holds a nylon storm suit ready for instant use. Next to it came a canteen and a quart-size plastic Gatorade bottle with sipper tube. These are attached to the inside gunwale next to a knee, and held in place with ½-inch nylon straps like those used on backpacks. On the opposite gunwale, four small tackle boxes are conveniently held in place with

SEE ALSO
Accident prevention, water . . .
Boating, white-water . . . Camping . . . Canoes . . .
Kayaks . . . Map reading

THIS 71-YEAR-OLD author-adventurer knows how to select and secure his gear carefully. He's looking forward to more long, solo, paddle-powered voyages.

SUPPLIES ARE PACKED for a month-long exploration of 850 miles of Texas and Mexico shoreline.

STOW CANTEENS, foul weather gear, anchor and fishing tackle where you can reach them easily.

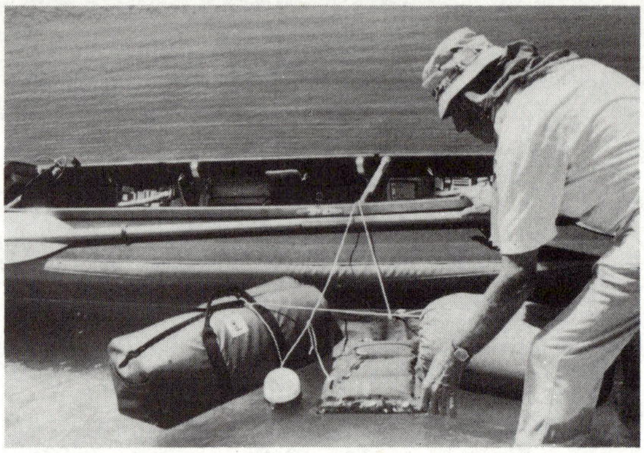

DUFFEL BAGS, sleeping bag, spotlight and all "waterproof" and "floatable" items should be tested first and then secured to the boat.

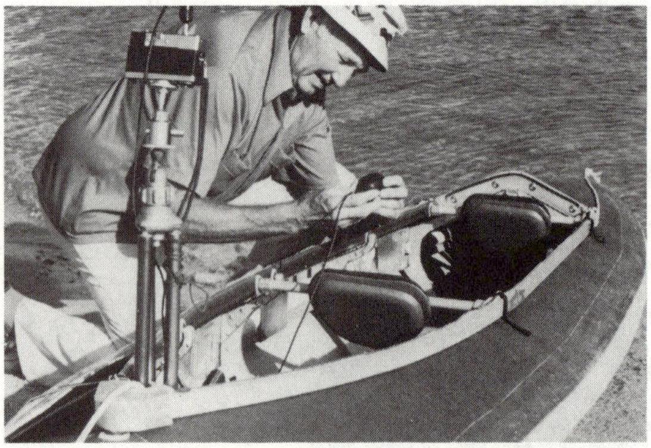

FOR PHOTOS en route, Haddon mounts a tripod with one leg through the mast socket and uses a rubber tube with bulb extended to paddler.

Velcro tabs. One drop of instant glue permanently attaches tabs on each box and matching tabs on the gunwale. No fisherman has ever had lures within such easy reach. A single Velcro tab secures a small, liquid-filled compass to the kayak floor or to the deck when traveling offshore or in foggy weather.

Because of a kayak's low center of gravity, particularly with air-filled side sponsons, there is little likelihood of capsizing it, but cargo bags, spotlights, sleeping bags and camera cases should be pretested for waterproof quality. Then attach them to the kayak with ⅛-inch nylon lines to prevent loss. During an emergency, they can also provide added buoyancy. As a precaution, cargo bags may be lined with three-mil plastic garbage bags tied off with rubber bands. Life preservers are required equipment.

For kayakers who travel along steep, rocky shores, a 20-ounce Mitey Brush anchor can be useful. Tossed into shoreline bushes or among rocks, its 50 feet of ⅛-inch nylon line holds the hull firmly against the shore for easy stepping out. Metal points on this anchor are flexible enough to permit yanking it free if necessary.

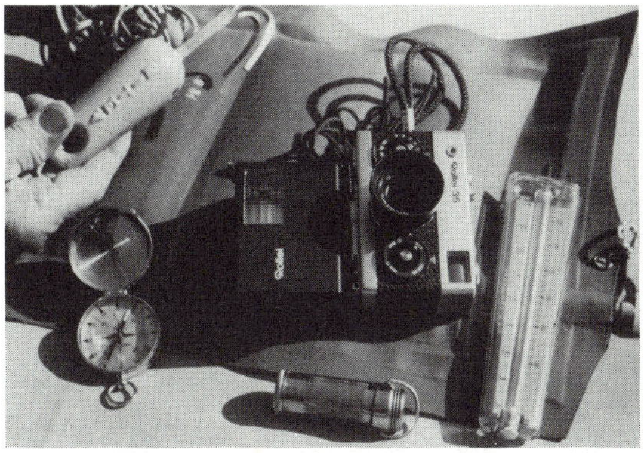

COMPASS, wind-speed indicator, waterproof match container and waterproof bag are some of the items you may want to Velcro-mount.

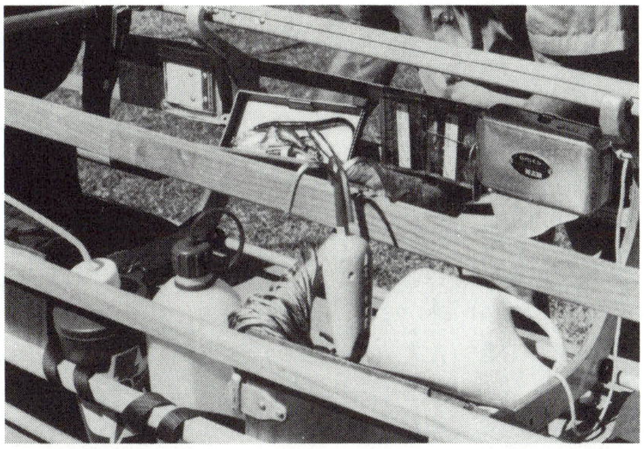

MITEY BRUSH anchor for tossing ashore hangs on gunwale; a tackle box and various kit bags are tied or held in place with Velcro.

I also use a Klepper inflatable camera bag for flotation and cushioning. A pocketable Dwyer wind-velocity meter is another useful accessory.

I simplify photography aboard by anchoring my tripod in the mast step with a bungee cord. The camera is snapped with an air tube and bulb taped to the floor where I can push it with one foot. By prefocusing, I can record anything from scenics to fish being landed.

Customizing means fitting out and installing aids and equipment that are selected and positioned just right for you. Velcro tabs, shock and bungee elastic cord, oversize rubber bands slit from discarded inner tubes and nylon line are good for securing accessories. Nylon cord, like the surplus type used for static lines of parachutes, will lash gear in place, but still untie easily, as a rule, when the knots get wet. Make good use of the line for lanyards on items like your bail scoop, searchlight and inflatable cushion, as well as cargo duffel. A pull on a color-coded line from your paddling position can bring your bailer quickly to hand without your leaving your seat. The tie-lines keep gear from floating away after an unlikely capsizing.

Compact-cruise accessories

Mini-boats have minimum storage space for camp and cruise gear, but most have bow and stern compartments that can hold float bags with backpack-type essentials.

POCKET HOTEL, from Early Winters, needs no rain fly since it's Gore-Tex; it weighs two pounds. From $7\frac{1}{4}$ feet it folds down to $4\frac{1}{4}$ x $15\frac{3}{4}$ inches.

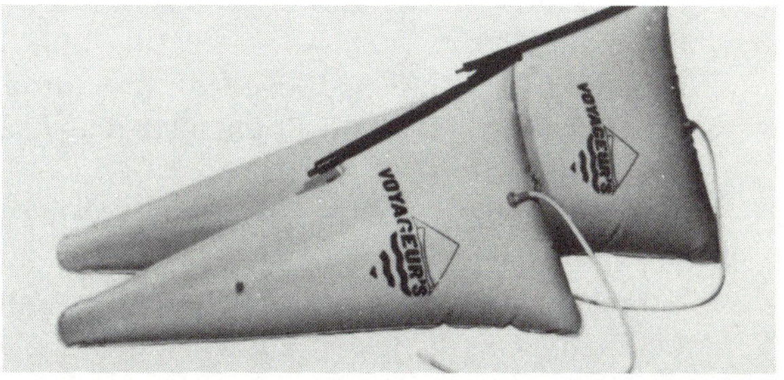

INFLATABLE VOYAGEUR Tour Paks, from Voyageur's, Ltd., open to store a sleeping bag, tent or supplies, and fit in kayak to provide extra flotation.

ADDING ONLY ONE extra ounce to a Coleman Peak 1 stove, the stuff sack for the little cooker can also cushion a camera or binoculars.

BIVOUAC SACK of Gore-Tex that lets perspiration out without leaking rain in, the Early Winters Sleep Inn is a lightweight substitute for a tent.

How to get your boat to pose for better pictures

By PHIL GERACI

THERE'S SOMETHING about a boat that makes you want to take its picture. The sleek, flowing lines and the exciting drama of a rolling sea combine to make boats an ideal photographic subject. The trouble is that boats—like pets and children—can be tricky to capture on film. Their constantly changing angles and the need, usually, to shoot them on the run can make them difficult to pose. They won't sit still—and they shouldn't. You have to let them act naturally, then catch them at just the right instant and angle to get an eye-catching picture.

So specialized is marine photography that professionals who have mastered the art make names for themselves shooting virtually nothing but boats. One such well-known marine photographer is Marion Warren whose open-air studio is the whole of Chesapeake Bay. His distinguished clients have included the U.S. Naval Academy and Presidential families. Warren passes on these tips for shooting better boat pictures based on his years of professional experience:

"First, you must know your subject," he advises. "Watch it in the water. Observe the way the sun flashes on the sails or hull. Note the best angles—head on, off-bow or full astern. All boats have their best side, and that's the side you should photograph."

The biggest single mistake that most amateurs make, Warren believes, is that "they shoot from too far away, so the boat is just a tiny dot in the center of the frame." Ideally, it's best to use a telephoto if your camera takes interchangeable lenses. On a 35-mm camera, moderate teles from 135 mm to 200 mm work well. Longer lenses should be avoided; they bunch up the background too much and cause distortion.

SEE ALSO
**Camera care . . . Cameras . . . Canoes . . .
Night photography . . . Outdoor photography . . .
Panorama photos . . . Photography . . .
Sailboats . . . Underwater photography**

What a telephoto does is let you get up close without actually being that close. You can make a cruiser look like it's about to run you down and still be a safe couple of hundred feet away. If you're shooting with a normal lens, get as near as you can. Make the image of the boat fill the full frame. In some cases, you can create dramatic pictures by including only a portion of the boat—a stern view with someone at the helm or a shot across the bow into a sunset.

Warren prefers his subjects out in open water. Dockside shots are too passive, he believes. Besides, the dock gets in the way, and you can't change the sun's direction if necessary to illuminate the boat's best angle.

To shoot in the open, you need a chase boat to follow your subject. It should be fast and as stable as possible. Get someone to do the driving so you can be free to concentrate on the picture-taking.

"Circle the boat being photographed," says Warren, "to find its best angle and to see which side is best for the sun. Then pick a spot, back off, and signal the operator to move your subject boat to the spot you've picked. When it gets there, start shooting."

Warren says never to shoot a sailboat when it's tacking because the sails go slack. Also, the crew is busy then and may not be in the most photogenic positions. He likes people on the boats he photographs to add reality. Best spots, he finds, are at the helm or tiller. If possible, he likes to use a low angle to silhouette them against the sky.

With 35-mm cameras, filters are seldom needed for rich, dark skies, Warren has found. But he cautions against overexposure, which can block highlights. "There's more light out on the water than most people think. Proper exposure is essential." A good guide is one stop less than needed for the same sky conditions on land.

how to experiment with filters

If you want to experiment with filters, a yellow K2 or deep yellow G will darken a light, colorless

MOVE IN CLOSE for drama, even if you crop out part of the boat. This picture has excitement, fine composition.

sky. Spectacular black-sky effects can be achieved with a red A filter. With color films, you can use a Pola-Screen, which will darken the sky without changing the color of the picture. It will also banish sun glare from the water's surface and kill harsh reflections from windshields, portholes and shiny hulls.

Camera shake can be a serious problem when the chase boat pitches and rolls under the photographer. Warren suggests a shutter speed of at least $^1/_{500}$th of a second, never slower. In heavy seas, $^1/_{1000}$th of a second may be necessary, especially to freeze droplets of spray.

Warren prefers a shooting angle just off the bow for most kinds of boats. Side shots, often requested by clients, are bad because they lack action and perspective, he feels. "They're fine engineering aids, but poor photography."

boat runs from corner to corner

He tries to fill the full negative and to keep the image sharp for crisp enlargements. When composing, he tries to position the boat so it runs from corner to corner, rather than side to side. "Looks more active that way," he says.

ALWAYS TRY for a sense of action, with boat in motion and people on board doing things. Billowing sail below offers a fine photo opportunity.

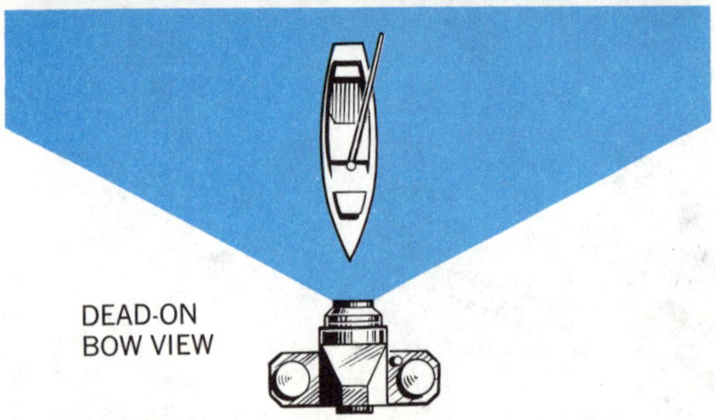

YOUR BOAT OFFERS something different from each quarter of the compass, as shown by these four photos taken head on, from the front quarter, full abeam, and from the after quarter. The head-on shot tends to make the boat appear smaller and far away. Take it as close as possible or use a long lens. Best shot is from a low angle, with camera near the water. The front quarter shot has inherant drama and emphasizes both boat

TIPS ON FINDING THE BEST SHOOTING ANGLES

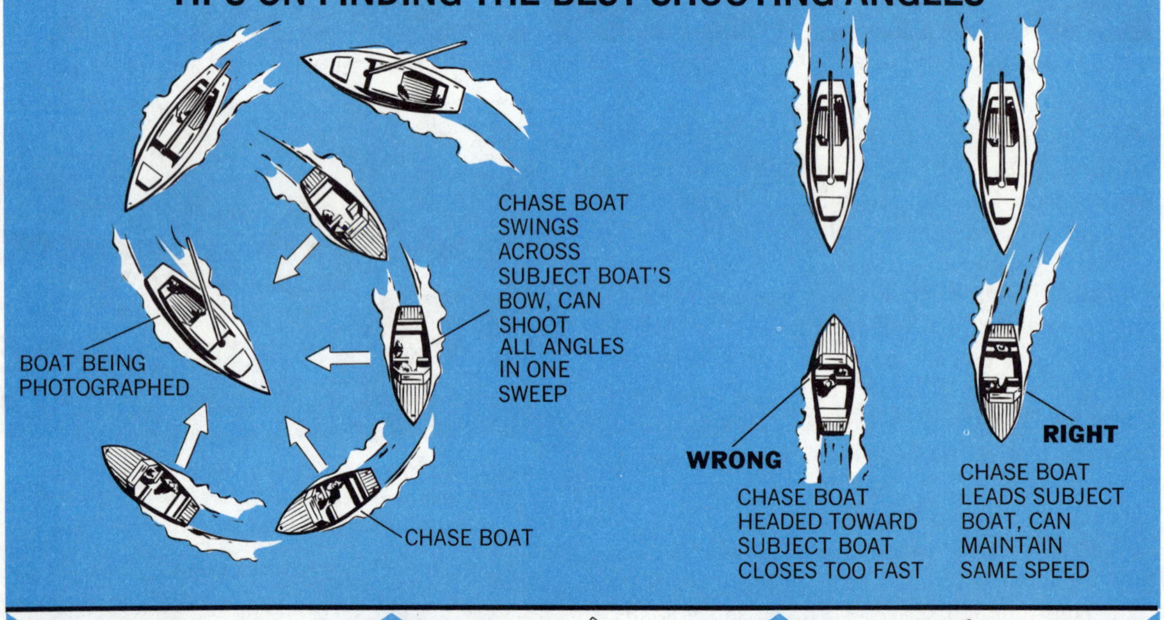

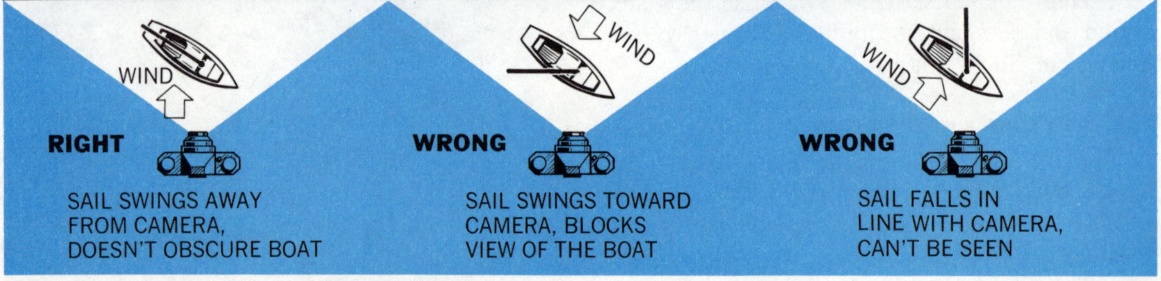

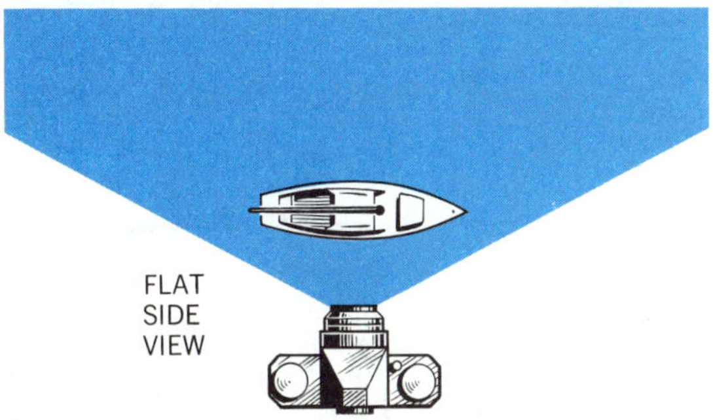

size and action. This shot is most effective when taken from a high angle, looking down into boat. The beam shot makes a good portrait but offers less sense of drama than the front or aft-quarter shots.

Don't be afraid to let some background show. Warren likes to include a portion of shoreline or other boats. He feels that the right kind of background adds credibility to a photograph. He also likes to include a part of the chase boat in the foreground, framing under a sail or over a rail.

Photographing in fog adds drama and often is an effective way to eliminate an offensive background. This calls for caution, however, as there is always the danger of collision with other boats.

Warren prefers windy weather, just after a front has passed through when the air sparkles and the wind whips the water into a frothy texture. Flat, calm water makes a boat look dead and uninteresting.

LOOK FOR special opportunities, such as calm water. Here photo has hull mirrored in water.

Shots from the aft quarter emphasize the hull size and show the spreading wake to great advantage. This angle is good for showing activity on boat and providing viewer with "you are there" feeling.

TRY FOR backlighting, with the boat between you and the sun, for great sparkling water effects.

ALWAYS COME IN CLOSE. Here, close shot allows you to see happy expressions on boater's faces.

PHOTOS ABOVE show advantage of shooting from high camera location. Low camera in top photo caused loss of boat driver. Below, photographer has taken advantage of very photogenic surroundings.

Boats in poor condition pose problems. "You can never really hide a poor paint job. Quickie touchups aren't much help, either." About the only thing you can do with a hull that's seen better days is to use strong backlighting, exposing for the background and letting the boat go dark. This is one of Warren's favorite techniques, even when the boat is in pristine condition. "Backlighting glamorizes the subject, making a pictorial out of what might have been just a routine snapshot."

Cameras require special protection out on the water in windy weather. Warren advises wrapping all but the lens in a plastic bag and keeping the camera under your coat when spray is flying. Check the lens often, drying it carefully with soft tissue and brushing off the lint.

Back on land, dry the camera, then go over metal parts with a slightly oiled, soft rag. Clean the lens with lens-cleaning fluid. Salt water and spray are the nautical photographer's worst enemies.

How to handle a boating emergency

What's the first thing you should do if your boat capsizes? If you're marooned with a dead motor? If you've run aground? Here are some time-tested techniques that could save the day when the unexpected happens

By GEORGE EMORY

THE FIRST LAW of boating safety would probably be: "Do everything you can to avoid an emergency." Know your boat and operate it properly; carry all the right safety equipment and know how to use it; keep your boat, motor and gear in top shape.

But when you *are* faced with an emergency (and it happens to the best of us), the first thing to remember is *don't panic*. Things are seldom as bad as they seem, and for every emergency there's a simple drill. Check the following pages for some important "what-to-do-if" rules.

SEE ALSO

Accident prevention, water . . . Emergencies . . . Fire extinguishers . . . Life preservers . . . Outboard motors . . . Sailboats

YOUR BOAT SUDDENLY CAPSIZES . . .

COUNT HEADS IMMEDIATELY. If anyone is missing, check behind or under the boat. Don life preservers or grab floating cushions. Gather everybody around the boat and make them stay there. (Swimming for shore is risky. It's always farther than it looks.) To right the boat, push down on one side to impart a rollover motion. Be careful: Don't get hit.

ONCE RIGHTED, you can bail out the hull, provided the gunnel is even lightly above water. If the transom cutout is submerged, have passengers bear down on the bow while someone bails the well. Use anything handy for bailing—drinking cups, tin cans, hand splashing or even the bilge pump if it wasn't lost during capsizing. After you've made a little progress, boost the lightest man aboard to bail from the inside. It's slow, but it works.

ROUND-CHINE BOATS can be cleared of considerable amounts of water by rocking them from side to side. Spilled passengers grip opposite gunnels, and those on one side bear down while those on the opposite side let the boat rise so that water spills out over the low side. A few such rolls will remove enough water to allow one man to scramble aboard (over the transom) and finish bailing from the inside.

RIGHTING A SMALL SAILBOAT is easier than righting a runabout. Just place your feet on the centerboard, grip the gunnel with both hands and pull the boat right side up. But if your boat has an aluminum mast that isn't completely sealed at the ends, slip a buoyant cushion under the tip as soon as possible after going over. This will keep the mast from sinking and turning the boat completely upside down, which will make it considerably harder to right. While you're still in the water, empty the hull as much as you can by splashing or bailing. Then reboard over the transom to avoid capsizing (unless you happen to be an old hand at it).

A WATER-FILLED sailboat may flop over again when you're bailing. To help prevent this (and to make the boat easier to right), the sails should be dropped and the centerboard lowered completely before you haul the boat right side up. With some hulls, it's possible to turn the boom into a stabilizing outrigger by lashing it to a cleat at right angles to the boat and placing a buoyant cushion under the end. The important thing to remember in any capsizing is not to exhaust yourself trying to do the impossible. If you can't right the hull easily, hold on and wait for rescue.

YOU'VE HIT SOMETHING AND HOLED THE HULL . . .

IF THE HOLE is forward on a planing hull, it may be possible to keep it above water while running for shore simply by maintaining planing speed. In choppy water, it's a good idea to have somebody crawl up under the foredeck and stuff a rag into the hole or block the opening by pressing a handful of rags over it. Just hold a steady planing speed, avoid sharp turns and you'll have no trouble.

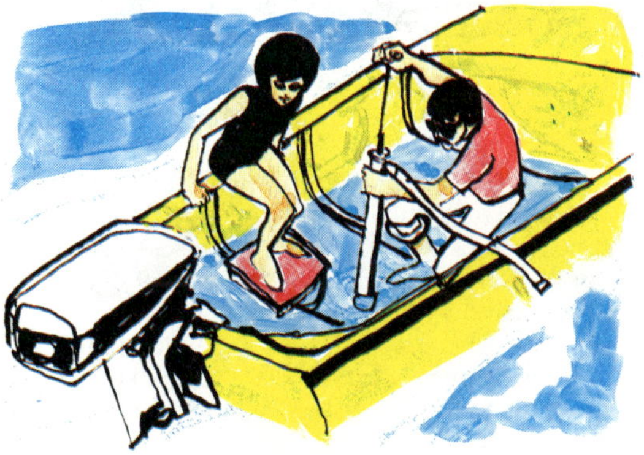

A HOLE IN the cockpit that can be reached from the inside should be plugged with rags or articles of clothing, which can be held in place by having a passenger stand on them. (For that matter, boats have made shore from miles away with a small hole plugged by somebody simply pressing his foot over it.) If the boat has a self-bailer, use it. Have the passengers bail, or man the bilge pump. The boat's speed will depend on the location of the hole. Start slow and check the flow as you increase speed. Aim for the least amount of leakage.

AN EMERGENCY patch for a hole in the cockpit can sometimes be made by wedging gear under a seat to hold the preserver cushion against the leak.

IF YOU CAN'T make it to shore and you're in a boat that can sink completely (such as a sailboat with a heavy keel), get as close to land as you can before going over the side in life preservers. Before you abandon ship, trail a long line astern with a float tied to the end; a plastic oil container might be a likely choice here. This float will serve as a marker for salvage operations. If you have time, also take a "fix" on land objects to help locate the boat.

A HOLE NEAR the chine can sometimes be lifted above the water by shifting passengers and gear to heel the boat. Even if the hole doesn't rise above the waterline, the flow will be reduced by bringing it nearer the surface. As with any hole, block the flow by stuffing the hole with whatever you happen to have at hand—sweaters, jackets, bathing suits or other articles of clothing. Then head for shore at low speed, keeping the hole side up on turns and swinging wide to avoid taking on additional water.

A HOLE UNDER the floorboards that is inaccessible from the cockpit must be plugged from the outside, though shifting weight may also be of some help. Assuming the water is calm and you're a good swimmer, shut off the motor and go over the side. You'll probably have to locate the hole by feel. If it's small, stuff a rag into it. Use a cushion or a pad of rags as a patch for larger holes, holding it snug against the leak by drawing a rope tight around the hull. Then start bailing and make for shore. If possible, head for the nearest beach, since a badly holed boat may sink at dockside before it can be hauled out, especially during off-hours.

YOU'RE HARD AGROUND ON A BAR . . .

KILL THE MOTOR immediately and check for hull damage, fuel-line leaks or spilled fuel, especially if the impact was hard. Then tilt up the lower unit or stern drive and make sure the cooling intakes aren't fouled. Before trying to push off, pump out the bilge to lighten the boat, and move passengers aft (assuming you've grounded at the bow). Use a paddle, boat hook or water ski to pole off, facing to the side or aft to avoid falling overboard.

IF YOU CAN'T pole off, leave one person aboard who knows how to handle the boat and have everyone else who can swim go over the side. This can lighten the boat by as much as a quarter of a ton. To get free, squat with your back against the bow, then push up and back as you straighten your legs. (*Don't* try it in a mucky bottom.) When the boat is free, swim to it.

IF THE BOTTOM is soft, shift passengers to one side to tilt the boat. This raises the deepest point of the hull (especially one with a deep-V) and may free the boat enough so you can pole back to deep water. When free, hand-crank the motor with the switch off and listen for sounds of internal damage that might be worsened by electric starting. If all sounds right, start the motor and check the cooling outlet to make sure the system is working right. If you lost a prop blade and don't have a spare prop aboard, run for shore at the lowest rpm that provides headway.

IF YOU'RE GROUNDED at the stern, use a pole or anything else handy to pry the bow around so you're headed in the opposite direction. Remember that the best way off is almost always the way you came on, since your hull has already plowed the channel. No matter where you're grounded, chances are it rises still higher ahead of you. Use a rag pad over the gunnel to avoid marring it when prying. When headed in the right direction, use the same kind of prying action at the transom to walk the boat toward open water. If you have passengers, of course, move them up to the bow to take weight off the stern while prying.

IF YOU'RE ALONE and grounded on a mucky bottom, there's a good chance you can work the boat free by rocking it from side to side. The safest way to do this is to stand in the cockpit with your feet spread wide apart and rhythmically shift your weight from one foot to the other until you feel the boat begin to rock. Once you've got it rocking, throw your weight into the rhythm to make it rock harder. If you're grounded at the bow and have to rock from the foredeck, tie a lifeline around your waist. When the hull breaks free, pole off.

How to help and be helped

By W. S. KALS

HALF A GALE was building a tough sea the night the motor quit. The 18-foot boat was only 400 yards from the safety of a breakwater. But wind and current were against the skipper. He was being blown out toward the middle of a turbulent sound.

A larger cabin cruiser nosed out of the harbor and spotted the distressed boat. The captain tried desperately to throw a line to the smaller boat. But the seas were running high, and it was impossible to get close enough. How the cruiser skipper finally took the disabled boat in tow is shown in the heavy-sea rescue diagram at the right.

Whether you boat in heavy seas or in calm water, at some time you'll either need a tow or be asked to tow a boat in distress. Everyone should know the basic towing practices, and how to get a line between the boats.

But who throws the line to whom has always worried some boatmen. Some say that if the rescue boat throws a line to the distressed boat, the rescuer becomes liable for anything that happens to the boat in tow. This is not so, according to marine insurance experts. Liability generally rests with the distressed boat. The only time there's a question of liability is when a boat captain attempts to tow another boat without a request for assistance.

A request for help can be given verbally—"I need a hand"—or by signal.

As a matter of courtesy, though, the distressed boat should provide the tow line. Should the line fray or break it's not a loss for the skipper who's helping.

Towing a boat and getting a tow line rigged can be tricky. How to do it in different situations is explained in the next three pages.

SEE ALSO

Accident prevention, water . . . Emergencies . . . Fire extinguishers . . . Life preservers . . . Outboard motors . . . Sailboats

HEAVY-SEA CONDITIONS make it almost impossible to get close enough to a disabled boat to toss a line. There's always danger of the seas lifting one boat and crashing it into the other. The best way to take the distressed boat in tow is for the rescue boat to trail the towline near the stern of the disabled craft. Tie a life ring on the line before trailing it. This keeps the line out of your props and makes it easier for the skipper of the disabled boat to retrieve. Start paying out the towline as you near the stern. Remember to trail the line downwind of the distress boat. You'll have better control of your own boat as you round up into the weather. Besides, the disabled boat will drift down onto the towline, making it easier for the skipper to grab it.

CALM WATER is the best condition for towing. But to avoid colliding at the very first, pull your boat just astern and watch the drift of the disabled boat. Once you know his drift speed and direction, you can pull up alongside and wait for him to drift toward you. You can fend off the other boat just before the two boats kiss. This is an excellent system to use when taking a boat in tow on your beam. Once the two boats are close enough together you can easily attach spring lines. With this system you don't have to jockey your boat around the distressed boat or start horsing the two boats together once lines have been tossed between them.

SHALLOW WATER often traps a boat when the skipper is trying to get a towline to a boat already aground. If you're worried about getting too close to a grounded boat use the drift-back system. Pull your boat into the wind quite a distance out from the shallow water. Judge water depth. Drop your anchor. Let the wind and current take your boat back toward the disabled boat. Remember that your anchor could drag if there isn't enough anchor-line scope. Once you're back as close to the disabled boat as you dare get, secure the anchor line. Then tie a life ring or cushion to the towline. Let it drift on back to the distress boat. Remember, wind and current will often cause your boat to yaw. Watch water depth on either side of your boat.

BEAM TOWING is the best system for getting a disabled boat back to port. But this method is good only in calm waters. It's used a lot in harbors or when lakes or sounds are very still. If the water is calm and you decide on beam towing remember to watch for the wakes of passing boats. Even on calm water a boat wake can cause damage when two boats are coupled together. If the disabled boat has steering control, you can tow him using spring lines attached from your bow to his stern and from your stern to his bow. If he has no steering, attach bow-to-bow and stern-to-stern lines in addition to springs. Remember that with four lines attached between boats, both boats are really locked together. Should an emergency arise, it may be difficult for you to break free of the tow. Avoid trouble spots and high speeds.

CHAFING GEAR is necessary whenever towlines run through chocks or will run on gunwales. A taut towline will fray quickly if not protected.

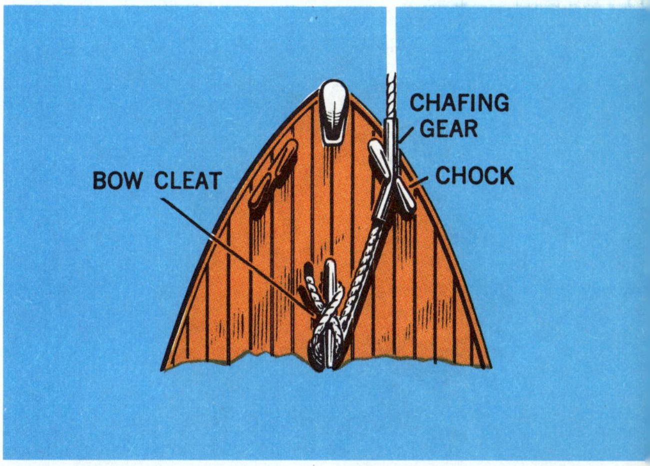

ROUGH-SEA TOWING calls for special techniques. Nothing will break a towline quicker or pull out a cleat faster than a snapping strain on the towline. Nylon line, because of its elasticity, is best. But often the strain is too much even for nylon. To prevent slack-then-strain on line in seas, adjust the towline so the disabled boat is a wave behind you. Both boats will then rise and fall together. Also attach a small anchor to the middle of the towline. This will take up slack—keeping a steady strain on the line. Trailing drags (long lines or a small sea anchor) astern of the disabled boat will also keep strain on the towline and dampen yawing.

SAILBOAT TOWING can be difficult because of weight. Most sailboats, 25 feet long and longer, have deep, heavy keels below the water. There's tremendous strain on the towline when you start pulling a sailboat. Make sure the towline is attached not only to the cleat of the sailboat but to its mast as well. If the cleat pulls out, the mast will hold the towline. Remember, sailboats have low hull speeds. Tow at five knots.

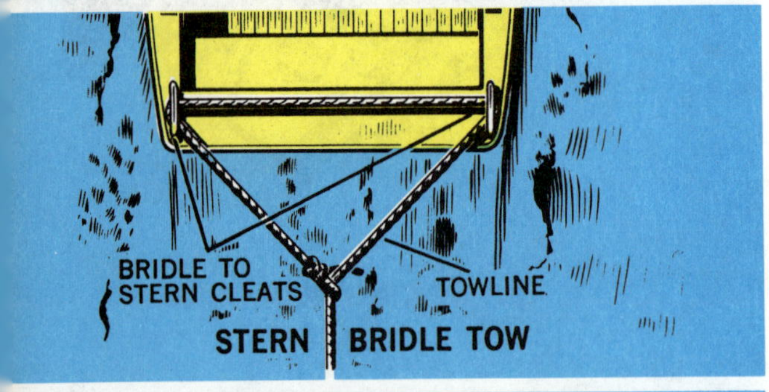

STERN BRIDLE is always better than just snubbing a towline around one stern cleat. The bridle distributes the load between two cleats lessening the chances of cleat failure and providing better towboat control. One danger in towing is a break-away cleat. When the towline is attached to only one cleat, there is nothing to keep the towline and cleat from rifling back should the cleat pull out. Flying cleats have caused serious accidents.

CABIN BRIDLE gives better towboat control. Most pleasure powerboats do not have a mule post in cockpit center. Tying a towline to a mule post (found on Coast Guard boats and yard workboats) lets the tow boat maneuver easily. To get the same maneuverability on a pleasure boat, attach the towline to a line that's snubbed on the bow cleat and that bridles the cabin trunk.

DISTRESS SIGNALS

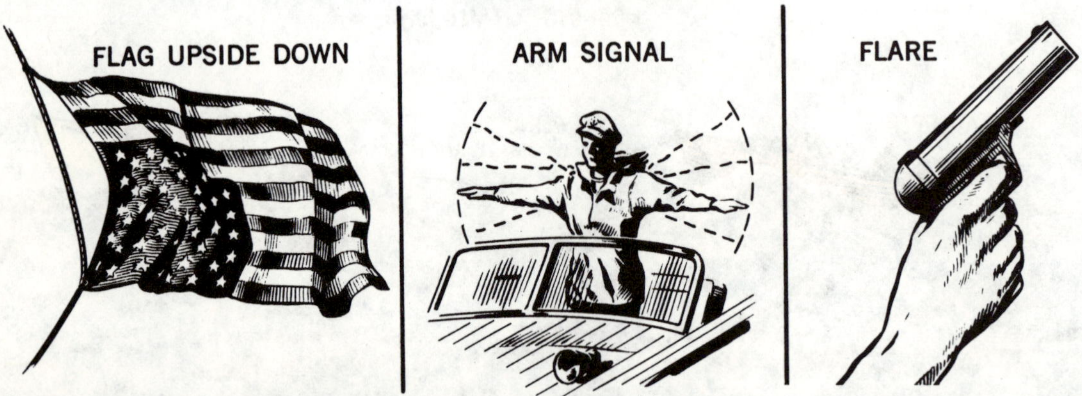

DISTRESS SIGNALS used to summon assistance include an upside-down ensign, slowly raising and lowering extended arms, and flares.

Refinishing a rush seat

I have several rush-seated chairs (not antique). The artificial rush seats show "wear," seeming to be a peeling of the coating. I used a light stain on one seat, but the worn spots darkened so much that they seem worse than before. How can I match the original coating so the repair won't show so prominently?—A.T., N.Y.

From your description, it probably would be best to mix your own stain, using painters' oil colors or, better yet, artists' oil colors. You must be especially painstaking when mixing two or more colors to get an exact match of the old coating.

Squeeze only a small quantity—a little goes a long way—of each color into a suitable container, add a few drops of turpentine and mix thoroughly to a heavy paste. Add a bit of one color or the other until you get a match with the old finish. Apply with a soft cloth. When dry, if the color doesn't quite match, rework the original mix with a trifle more of one or the other color and reapply, successively if necessary, until you get as perfect a match as possible. Allow it to dry thoroughly—48 to 72 hours—then apply a semigloss varnish, preferably spray from an aerosol container.

If the seat is rough, go over the rush with medium steel wool before applying the stain. Brush away all loosened debris.

Do ants damage peonies?

Last blooming season my peonies, particularly the blooms, were covered with black ants. Apparently they did not harm the blooms but do they damage the plants? Should I spray or dust to keep them off?—R.O., Neb.

Ants are present because of the sweetish excretions of the flowers, particularly the developing buds. They cause no damage to buds, blooms or plants so there's no reason to use insecticides.

Wintertime green thumb

I want to grow tuberous begonias next season but I don't know when to start them for the earliest blooms. Some say midwinter, others say later on, some plant directly in open ground after frost. Can you suggest a procedure?—O.L., Ind.

I've only limited experience with these plants, but I've learned that the blooms will be much later in season unless you give the plants an early start indoors. If the season breaks right with an early spring, you should do all right by plantinq directly in open ground.

Loose chair arm

I have a platform rocker on which one arm is loose. The arm is supported by a turning which is attached to the frame by what I think is a single screw with its head hidden by a wooden plug. The exposed head of this plug is rounded and finished. Apparently the plug is glued in place. How can I remove it so I can tighten the screw?—T.A., Ariz.

What you describe is known as a screwhole button, commonly used in furniture construction to conceal screwheads. Usually the only way to remove it is to drill it out, using a drill bit slightly smaller than the diameter of the shouldered portion. If the outer diameter of the exposed head is ½ in., for example, the chances are that the button was driven into a ⅜-in. counter-bored hole. Center a 5/16-in. twist drill and go through to the screwhead. Then break away the waste with a small chisel, taking care not to mar the finished surfaces. Back off the screw a few turns, insert glue into the joint, then tighten the screw and wipe away all excess glue.

You can get a replacement button from any well-stocked hardware store or from Craftsman Wood Service Co., 2727 S. Mary St., Chicago, Ill. 60608. Be sure to give the correct size. However, you may not have to remove the original button. You may be able to drive screws into the loose arm support from the back of the framepiece. Check this first before removing the button.

Dewaxing linoleum

The linoleum kitchen floor at my new address is covered with something that's a dirty, brownish color I simply can't live with. Washing and scouring seems to have no effect. What can I try next?—M.R., Mont.

I'd guess right away that the coating must be either multiple coats of wax or a linoleum varnish that has been neglected, so that the dirt is literally embedded in the coating. This is impossible to remove by ordinary means. What to do next depends on the condition of the linoleum. If it is still good, you may find an attempt to salvage it worthwhile. If the coating is linoleum wax, turpentine applied liberally will remove it. But remember, when using turpentine there's both a health and fire hazard. Have the windows and doors open and, if necessary, place a fan to provide air circulation. As a rule, the turps will soften the wax within a few minutes so that it can be wiped off readily. Treat only a small area at a time. On the other hand, if the coating is linoleum varnish, it will be more satisfactory in the end to replace the old linoleum.

Secrets of successful winter layup

By BOB WHITTIER

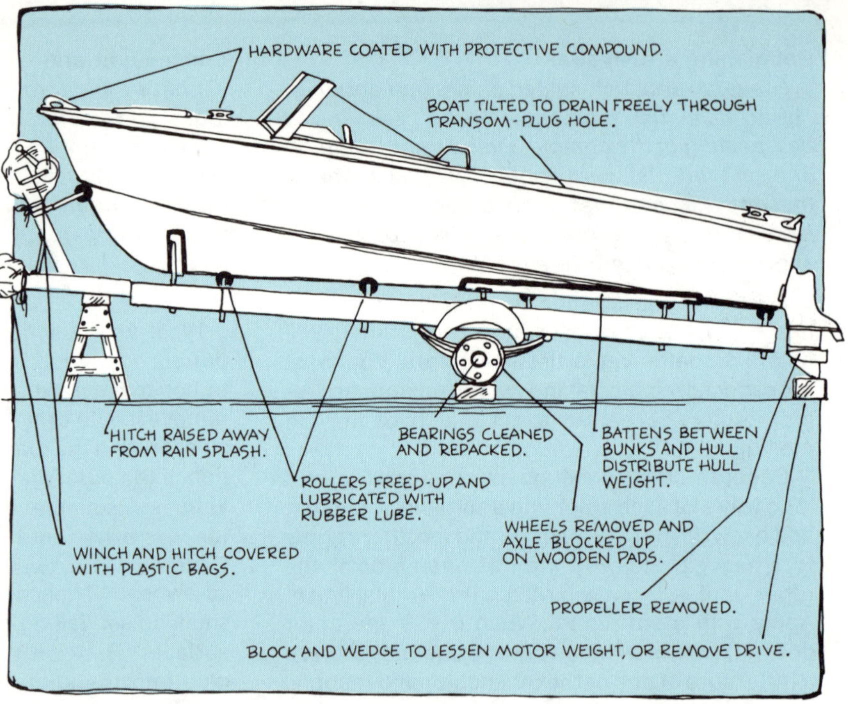

TRAILER BOATS have a ready-made cradle for storage. With additional blocking to support engine weight and hull tilt for proper drainage, your craft is well supported.

Every boat requires tender loving care during the winter months ashore to insure trouble-free days afloat. Here are some tips for protecting your boat during cold weather

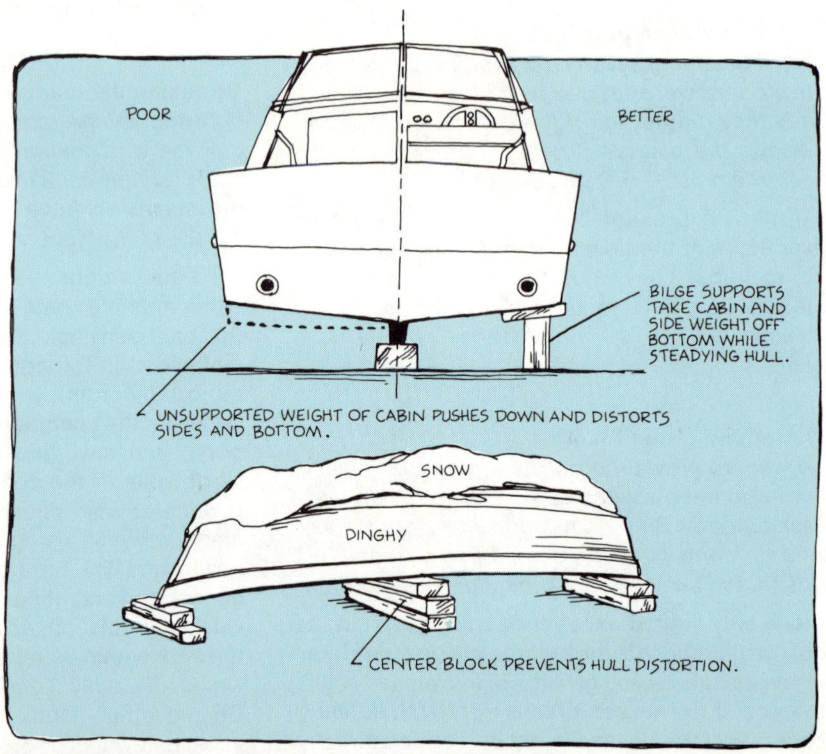

HULL DISTORTION is prevented by positioning supports under load areas of cruiser or dinghy. Craft should be elevated to keep moisture from starting wood rot, or rain and snow from splashing mud on hull.

SEE ALSO

**Boating, trailers . . . Campers . . .
Canoes . . . Kayaks . . .
Outboard motors . . .
Pontoon boats . . . Repairs, boat . . .
Sailboats**

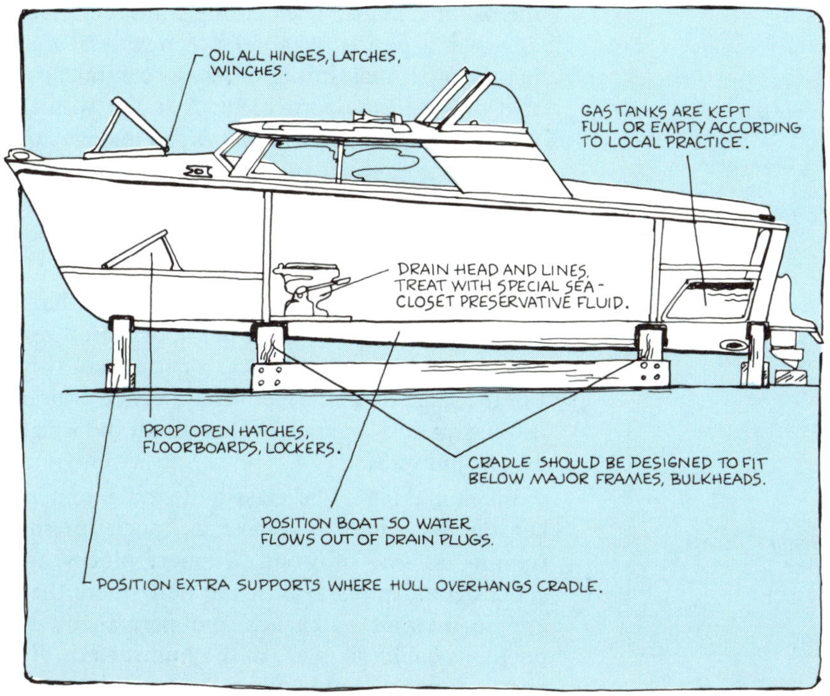

FIBERGLASS hulls, with fewer interior frames and stringers, may need braces positioned under interior bulkheads and strength members but not where supports could dimple the hull. Note all compartments and hatches are left open.

THERE IS STILL no such a thing as a "maintenance-free" boat, but there are many new and easy ways to minimize the work. When most boats were made of wood and needed a lot of upkeep, the early fiberglass builders fighting to gain acceptance for their new material liked to claim that their revolutionary hulls required no care at all.

It's true your fiberglass or aluminum boat does not require the tedious annual caulking, sanding and painting of wooden craft, but it does need attention. Yet the "no care" notion lingers on, and it's depressingly common to see badly neglected boats sitting out in the rain and snow in back yards and marinas.

cleaning

Before haul-out, see if your boat's bilge area is oily or scummy. If it won't pass inspection, use one of the bilge cleaners sold in marine stores. Mix it with bilge water on the season's last cruise. It will slosh around and loosen dirt film, but observe federal regulations against discharging oily waste on waterways.

With a trailered boat, add one of these cleaners to an inch or so of water in the bilge to slosh around on the last trip home. Automotive degreasing compounds in spray cans are safe to use in boats. They will not hurt wood or other structural materials since they are promptly rinsed off, but play safe and keep them off upholstery.

Boats afloat all summer often have algae or other marine growth on their bottoms. Scrub this off before it can dry. Once hardened, it is difficult to get off just by rewetting. Use a stiff-bristled brush or, before hauling out, locate a marina with a high-pressure water wand.

Wash oil from the hull exterior with detergent and a cloth. Flush out the interior with a garden hose. Pockets of sand and silt hold moisture; they can cause wooden members to rot, metal parts to corrode. Even in fiberglass, they can cause stains that are difficult to remove when dry. Brown stains just above the waterline can be removed from fiberglass with a marine stain remover.

If your boat is aluminum, get salt and silt out of longitudinal stringers and other enclosed spaces by running water into them. Any boat that has been dashed with salt spray probably has salt specks on the steering mechanism, switches and wire terminals under the dash or console. Flush there, too.

Most modern boat upholstery is vinyl so check the fine-print warnings on household or automotive cleaning products. Abrasive cleaners can dull the glossy surface. Vinyl cleaners are best.

removing equipment

Depending on storage conditions, some gear can remain aboard while the rest should come

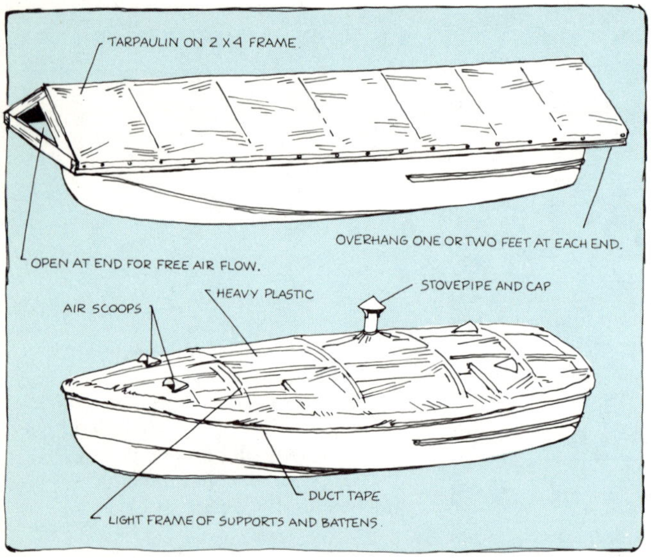

COVER FOR stored craft should provide ventilation. If the overhanging ends (top) tend to catch wind, the cover can be sealed down with duct tape (bottom), but exhausts for damp air should be provided.

ashore. Instruments and electronic equipment suffer from condensation that forms inside with weather changes, and they're tempting to thieves. They're better off safe and dry at home.

Cushions, bedding, curtains and a folding top also do better indoors. Mildew is inactive in cold weather, but mice and squirrels enjoy fabric nests. Sunlight darkens and stiffens synthetic ropes.

Remove and empty portable outboard gas tanks. There's so little oil in the modern 50-to-1 outboard fuel mix that a few leftover gallons can be safely used up in your car. If you see water droplets down on the tank bottom, sop them out with a piece of cloth on the end of a stick. Permanent tanks can be doused with methanol-type gas line antifreeze to remove small water deposits.

Most owners prefer to keep permanent tanks fully filled because condensation can form inside from damp air, and the gas vapor in a partially filled tank increases the explosion hazard. Check with your insurance man and fire department when deciding which way to go.

hull support

The initial curing process of fiberglass resin is so rapid that a new hull is removed from a mold the day it is made. Then curing continues gradually over a period of months. A new boat that's poorly supported during this stage can take a set that may become permanent. A trailer with full and well-adjusted hull supports can make a good winter cradle. Remove outboard motors or press wooden blocks between the floor and lower unit skeg to take some of the weight of a big outboard or stern drive off the transom.

A cradle is desirable for anything larger than a small, light hull. Even on a flat floor, a hull resting on one side could develop a permanent twist. For the same reason, never leave a canoe or pram leaning against a garage wall with all the weight on one gunwale.

When making a fiberglass-hull cradle, remember the boat may not have as much internal framing as one of wood. Support blocks and chocks could press against the hull where there are no internal bulkheads and permanent depressions could be made in the hull surface. If a boat is supported only along the keel, outer sections of the bottom can be pushed down and the V-shape flattened out. To be safe, position supports under internal stringers and bulkheads, and support the chines or curve of the bilge as well.

Wooden boats are traditionally fitted with covers to keep water from seeping into seams where dry rot breeds. Uncovered fiberglass boats will not rot, but the surface gel coat pigment can gradually fade. The more a boat is sheltered from the sun, even by storing it on the shady side of a building, the longer it retains its good looks. Point it one way one winter and the opposite way the next if it must be stored in direct sunlight.

A good winter cover also keeps sunlight off upholstery, varnish and plastics. Marine supply stores sell general-purpose covers to fit small boats.

fittings and gear

Water systems in large boats and cruisers are winterized with special antifreeze that imparts no taste to the tanks. Marine toilets should be treated with a special sea-closet conditioner that keeps valves and packings flexible. Remove storage batteries and leave them at a boatyard or service station where they can be kept in a battery rack and hooked to a trickle charger. Don't leave loose cables dangling in the bilge; electric wires can sometimes act like candlewicks and draw water up into switches and instruments. Remove the bulbs in navigation lights so they won't corrode in their sockets.

Treat your trailer right

By ROBERT D. STEARNS

Expertise and complex tools aren't needed for the preventive maintenance that gives you extra boating fun based on reliable, worry-free trailering

turn the page

SEE ALSO

Boating, safety . . . Boating, storage . . . Outboard motors . . . Pontoon boats . . . Repairs, boat . . . Sailboats

TRAVELS WITH YOUR boat in tow can more than double your fun. The minor maintenance tips shown on these pages can help to minimize any problems with your rig.

After hauling out ashore, tilt your outboard back down into its running position. This puts less strain on the transom, strain that contributes to hairline cracks. Eventually those cracks let in moisture to cause rot in the wood stiffening members imbedded in the stern. Recheck at stops during every trip to be certain your tie-downs are not allowing movement and chafe. Check your own rig for ways you can secure boat to trailer and trailer to car to prevent theft.

Saltwater particularly—even salt-laden moisture in the air—can corrode the exposed metal of your trailer. But periodic touch-ups are an easy way to control rust before it gets a grip. Springs and bearings also need extra attention. Moving parts heat up during high-speed runs, especially with the extra revolutions small wheels must make; bearings may suck in moisture when submerged in cold water.

TWIST TIE-DOWNS before you secure them. This can prevent their whipping in the slipstream—action that can eventually break the straps.

CENTERING THE BOAT to haul it aboard the trailer is easier if your assistant has bow and stern lines to hold against any crosswind.

HUB CAPS TRAP WATER that causes rust. Left off, they make checking lug bolts easy. Replacing them when the trailer's to be sold makes it look like new.

X MARKS THE SPOT: Reflective tape makes your load more visible at night. Such markings are particularly helpful when the trailer carries no load.

LOWER-UNIT OUTBOARD oil can be applied to overheating, dry trailer wheel bearings in an emergency. Keep speed down until the bearing is repacked.

MASHING THE THREADS of the bolt holding the winch handle can prevent it from vibrating loose—or being swiped to replace the one somebody else lost.

HOSING DOWN your trailer extends its life, especially around saltwater. A car-wash attachment with detergent dispenser makes the job easier.

HEAVY SAFETY CHAINS and locks meet state laws just as well as lighter ones, and a free-swinging lock is less vulnerable to a would-be thief.

BOLT THE SPARE tire and trailer jack to the trailer with a length of ½-inch rod stock. A padlocked chain in a cloth sleeve completes the security package.

HEAVY GREASE PAINTED over weld seams and into dips in the trailer frame prevents rust better than paint, and needs re-application only once a year.

PAINTING HEAVY motor oil and mineral spirits or kerosene, mixed 50-50, on the spring leaves can keep them rust-free so they flex more easily.

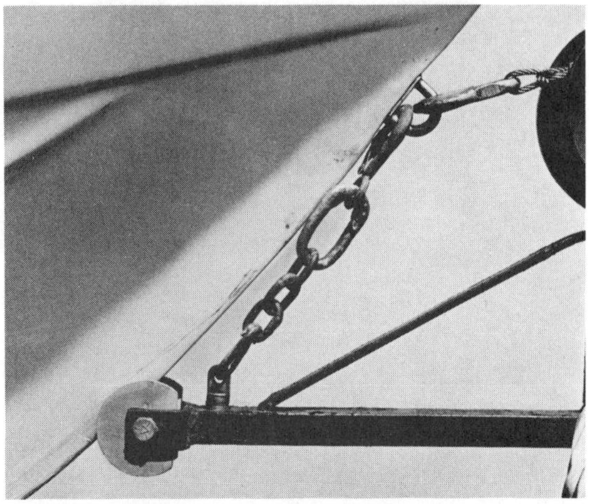

A BOW-STOP CHAIN or cable will keep your boat from climbing the car during an emergency stop. Avoid soft metal hooks to either the bow eye or trailer.

SEE ALSO

Boating, safety . . . Boating, storage . . .
Campers . . . Outboard motors . . .
Pontoon boats . . . Repairs, boat . . . Sailboats

Follow the example of one family which covered more than 3700 miles of beautiful boating country without a single breakdown. Your trip may not be as long, but it should be managed in the same way: First comes choice of the right equipment, then proper maintenance, and finally the use of time-tested travel techniques to ease your way

How to trailer your boat

By PAT PERRETT

WE HAVE TRAILERED our boat more than 3700 miles on a 21-day vacation, and enjoyed every mile of it.

Starting in Southern California, we rolled across scorching deserts, crossed high mountain ranges and followed backwoods roads to camp, cruise and fish in a variety of remote regions.

In the lonely reaches of southeastern Oregon we slept on the shore of Lake Owyhee near sheer cliffs rising straight up for hundreds of feet. We camped in the hushed solitude of Payette Lake in the green wilderness of central Idaho, then loafed through the Salmon River Canyon country, skirted vast Coeur d'Alene Lake and made our way to Indian Creek Campground on isolated Priest Lake high in the Idaho Panhandle.

When it was time to head for home, we took the long way around and swung north into Canada. There we embarked on the longest free ferryboat ride in North America, across Kootenay Lake, and tested our angling skills in its trout-rich waters. Finally, after a lazy sun-soaked campout on the northern shore of the Columbia River's Lake Roosevelt, we turned toward home, arriving late in the evening just 21 days after our departure.

The thing that surprised most of our friends about this idyllic trip was that we had absolutely no difficulties with the boat trailer. This wasn't just luck, of course. Our experiences on previous trips had taught us that the keys to successful longhaul boat trailering are planning, preparation, proper equipment and a few simple driving rules.

Most neophyte boat buyers start out with two strikes against them in trailering. Handicapped by inexperience, lack of knowledge and, sometimes, by an over-enthusiastic marine salesman, they break the cardinal rule of trailering by purchasing a trailer which lacks the capacity to carry anything more than the bare boat. Forgotten are the life preservers, anchor, fuel tanks, fuel, fishing gear, water skis, first-aid kit, canvas top and boat cover, plus that mass of paraphernalia required by the modern camping family.

The capacity of a trailer depends on its structural design, materials, assembly, coupler, axle, springs, hubs, bearings, wheels and tires. It's a complicated engineering equation, so for the most part, the average trailer buyer has to rely on the manufacturer's capacity rating. However, the most likely candidate for weak-link-in-the-chain is tire capacity.

We became acutely sensitive to tire capacity during our first major boating-camping expedition several years ago. Previous trips had included little gear, but this time we were loaded to the gunwales. Though tires fairly groaned, we thought we had capacity to spare.

Following a necessarily careful drive home we discovered the capacity of our 6.70x15 four-ply tires—a standard installation by many trailer manufacturers—was just under 1200 pounds. This meant that the total weight of the rig, with trailer, should not have exceeded 2400 pounds.

Convinced that no one, including ourselves, could accurately estimate our payload, we left the boat loaded and the next morning drove it to a public scale where we paid $1 to find out the true weight. You can imagine our consternation when we received a slip listing the certified weight of our 17-ft. runabout as *3458 pounds!* It was $1 well spent.

The message here is twofold. First, know for sure how much weight you're going to be towing by adding the weight of the trailer, the boat and all conceivable gear, then tacking on an ample safety margin. Second, be positive your tire capacity is sufficient for your load.

You can increase tire capacity by using larger tires or switching to a tandem trailer which has four wheels. Generally, though, it's better to stay with a two-wheel trailer until you're forced to use a tandem. One high-capacity tire is a 7x10.5 tube-type tire designed for use on mobile homes, which has a 2000-pound rating.

long-distance hauling

For long-distance hauling with a boat over 16 ft. long, we suggest automotive-sized wheels and tires. The advantages are many: increased load capacity, greater traction, longer tire life, better road handling, greater clearance, longer wheel-bearing life and easier handling. When practical, it's advantageous to have similar wheels on trailer and towing vehicle.

Tire inflation should be maintained at pressures recommended by the tire manufacturer. Under-inflated boat trailer tires will cause accelerated and uneven tread wear, sway (especially at high speeds) and excessive internal heat.

The most common cause of trailer failure is bearing failure—one problem that's easy to avoid. Few novice trailer boaters are aware of the potential trouble resulting from submerging trailer wheel hubs while launching and retrieving their craft.

When bearings become wet—usually from submersion, but also from condensation—they corrode. This causes excessive friction between the bearings and the bearing race, and the resulting heat melts the protective grease inside the hub. As long as the bearings are smooth, the temperature of bearing grease is about equal to the traveling speed plus the air temperature. That is, at 55 mph on an 85° day the grease temperature would be approximately 140° F. High-quality greases will not melt and lose their effectiveness until the internal hub temperature climbs to 300° F. Around 1500° or 1600°, plastic deformation occurs and metal softens to a buttery consistency. At 2500° to 3000° the bearings melt and then fuse to the axle.

Believe us, it's no fun when you are driving happily toward your launching site and suddenly hear the screech of a bearing which has collapsed for just this reason. We know, because it happened to us during an Oregon boating jaunt. It cost us two precious vacation days and indelibly registered the importance of meticulous bearing care.

The obvious solution is never to submerge the wheel hubs while launching. However, this is impossible on the majority of back-country ramps and, depending upon the boat design and trailer construction, may even be impossible on an ultra-modern ramp.

three ways to protect bearings

There are three basic protective devices designed to keep water from the bearings. They may be classed generally as grease under injection pressure, inflation under pressure and oil bath. We've used them all and, while not completely fail-safe, they all work. Fortunately for boaters, these devices have recently become standard or optional equipment with most major trailer manufacturers.

With the grease system, you fill the hub with grease through a device which replaces the dust cap. A piston creates a slight pressure inside the hub, and there's a pressure-relief device to prevent rupture of any seals. With the hub full of grease under controlled pressure, water cannot enter.

The air-pressure system utilizes air under pressure to do the same thing. The hub is sealed off and, prior to each submersion, air is pumped into the cavity through an air valve, using a hand bulb pump.

The oil-bath system maintains a reservoir of oil within the hub cavity to insure that bearings will remain water-free and constantly lubricated. The dust cap is replaced with a transparent cover which has a filler plug for oil replacement. The level is easily checked by visual examination.

We can't recommend any one system as the best, but we strongly urge every trailer boater to install one of these devices and keep it properly maintained.

During our trip last summer we used a grease-under-pressure system. (There's something very satisfying about being able to fill the hubs with grease prior to each submersion.) We discovered that day-long towing at top speeds caused some grease loss due to wear. However, it was a simple matter to check and add grease as necessary during service station stops.

PROTECTIVE DEVICES which keep water out of the trailer hubs let you submerge wheels without wetting bearings.

It's impossible to emphasize too strongly the importance of good trailer brakes, especially if most of your experience has been in short-haul, flatland trailering. For the light rig, of course, they're not necessary.

There's no specific point where brakes are definitely required, since many factors are involved in the ability to stop. The most important of these are the braking capacity of the vehicle, weight of the tow load, extent of grade, speed and road surface conditions. However, when the gross weight of a two-wheeled trailer approaches 3000 pounds, or exceeds 3500 pounds with any tandem trailer, brakes are not a luxury but a life-saving necessity. One major automobile company even recommends brakes for any trailer weighing more than 1200 pounds.

electric or hydraulic brakes

Most auto manufacturers state that electric brakes are far superior to hydraulic brakes, whether operated by an activator on the trailer coupler ("surge" brakes) or connected directly to the vehicle's hydraulic brake line. The one danger of the direct connection is the possibility of losing all braking power through a malfunction in the trailer's vulnerable external system.

Most electric brakes used today operate automatically when the car's brake pedal is depressed. If desired, the trailer brakes may be applied manually by moving a small lever similar to a turn-signal control. A simple adjustment at the activator switch adjusts the brakes for varying loads. The trailer brakes are applied just before the vehicle brakes make contact, thus preventing the boat from pushing the vehicle forward. This keeps the entire rig on a true course while slowing down.

State laws requiring brakes on boat trailers vary, so check your state's regulations for the exact legal requirements.

As for towing power, you just can't beat a husky pickup camper. We've towed boats with automobiles, station wagons, vans and even our VW sedan, but they all had one common failing—they just weren't designed to go ranging about the countryside with a 3000 to 6000-pound load behind.

inherent advantages of a pickup

The inherent advantages of a pickup are obvious—heavier springs, greater stability, better cooling ability, low ratio axle and better braking. Even with trucks, however, you have to buy one that will match your towing weight requirements. Of course, manufacturers offer optional equipment for both pickups and automobiles to make towing safer and easier. Among the options are higher-capacity cooling systems, four-speed or automatic transmissions, lower axle ratios, anti-spin differentials, larger springs, power brakes, extra-capacity batteries and alternators, flotation tires and dual trailering mirrors.

We think the best all-around outfit for the camping-boating family is a pickup camper and a 17-foot runabout, either outboard or inboard-outdrive. We've driven our Dodge camper thousands of miles and it has almost become a member of the family, just like our boat.

Boat towing generally means slow going, but we make good time with the camper, because of fewer and shorter stops. Meals are quick and easy with the conveniences of a gas range, refrigerator (not an icebox), hot and cold running water, and even a toilet and shower, if you like. You can roll past motel no-vacancy signs without a worry, because your bedroom's right behind you.

At overnight stops the boat's lounge seats and canvas top give us a spare bedroom where the youngsters can be bedded down while the camper is still in use. On the road, the boat functions as a luggage trailer which keeps the camper uncluttered. It's perfect for carrying bulky, light objects, such as a couple of comfortable aluminum chaise longues for predinner relaxation.

Part of our *modus operandi* has been two or three days of traveling to reach the area we're going to explore, and we do the same on the return trip.

plan for a high-mileage day

If we want to get a high-mileage day, we'll let the children continue sleeping in the camper in the morning and drive for two or three hours before stopping to roll up the sleeping bags and prepare the bacon and eggs. Perhaps we'll fix sandwiches to save time at noon. In any case, we always prepare mid-afternoon snacks during this morning stop.

Once you have the equipment, a camping-boating vacation is surprisingly easy on the budget. Our principal expenses for boat-camping, other than for groceries, are limited to gasoline and minimal campground fees. Otherwise, for our gang of six it would cost a minimum of $50 per day for motels and meals.

Driving techniques on a long trip are similar to other towing situations. The main rule is to allow plenty of time so you won't feel a need to hurry. Avoid driving at night. Plan to arrive at your stop with ample time to park the vehicle and get set before dark.

On the road, allow ample distance to stop smoothly and gradually. Let faster drivers have the right of way. You'll find that just plain courtesy pays off. When climbing a grade, use low gears to avoid overheating. Always use the lower gears on down grades of any length or steepness. It's much better to creep down a grade at 25 mph in second gear than to try to save a few minutes by staying in third gear and have to ride the brake pedal all the way.

If you have to drive over a bumpy, unpaved road with your boat, drive extremely slowly (10-15 mph). Boats are designed for water-cushioned bumps and trailers for smooth highways. Both take an unmerciful beating on rutty roads.

The main thing we watch for in launching the boat on a wilderness ramp is to be positive there's a firm footing for our rear tires and that there's enough water depth to handle the boat. We always carry a tow rope, so if necessary, we can unhook the trailer from the camper and push it farther into the water. The same works in reverse. You can push the trailer into the water for loading the boat and then pull the trailer back to firm ground with the tow cable where you can hitch it to the vehicle. Tandem wheels or flotation tires are worthwhile, if you use non-paved ramps with soft footing regularly.

The boat hull or engine installation may dictate the type of hull support. If there's a choice, we favor a roller system over straight padded cradles for easier launching operations and to keep wheel hubs out of the water.

the right kind of hitch

A frame-mounted hitch generally is completely adequate on pickup trucks, but with an automobile most manufacturers recommend using a load-equalizing hitch for loads over 2000 pounds and a tongue weight over 200 pounds. This type hitch redistributes the tongue load in such a way as to prevent all of the load from resting on the ball hitch. Some of the weight is transferred to the front wheels of the towing vehicle and some is shifted back to the trailer wheels. The size of hitch and torsion bars used must match the load.

The above rundown on towing weights, size of tires and other technical features may seem mighty complicated. Actually, it reduces to a very small checklist which is a real headache eliminator.

When it comes to outdoor vacation fun for the entire family we are convinced nothing equals the enjoyment of hitting the road in a camper with a boat trailering merrily behind. At least, that's what we've been doing the past few summers and right now we're studying road maps, camping guides, boating facilities folders and other tempters to decide this year's target.

So, fellow trailer boaters, time's a-wasting. Start plotting your summer safari right now.

BIG INFLATABLES are rapids-running fliers flexible enough to form-fit the drop-offs and bounce off boulders.

Try white-water boating for thrills

With today's equipment and a little practice you can be safe in a modern raft, canoe or kayak—without losing the thrill that comes from high adventure

By DOUG STURGES

IF YOU HAVEN'T been scared and wet—really wet—sliding down a swirling river recently, you're missing one of the best of outdoor adventures. New equipment and techniques make it possible to tackle rougher stretches, or you can pick gentle water and drift along for just about the best in relaxation.

There are three kinds of craft to float you down a fast stream—more like three and a half if you count inner tubes that are so popular for afternoon, not-too-turbulent runs. But for currents that get speedy and rough, your choice should be a modern raft, canoe or kayak.

Best introduction to wild water is available aboard a well-made inflatable raft. For a taste, or a faceful, of white water, it is only necessary to sign up for a raft trip of a few hours or days—no techniques to learn, no river maps to memorize since an experienced outfitter-guide skippers the raft. Boat and equipment will be picked for maximum safety and a river can be an adventure for all the family.

SEE ALSO
Accident prevention, water . . . Boat camping . . . Boat photography . . . Boating, safety . . . Campers . . . Camping . . . Canoes . . . Kayaks . . . Life preservers . . . Map reading . . . Outboard motors . . . Sailboats

THE BIGGEST can carry cargo or passengers through wild water when controlled by experts who know the best path down the river.

blow-up rafts can be strong

Modern rafts, steered by oars, paddles or motor, are not very maneuverable, but provide great abrasion resistance and reserve flotation. Though pioneer trappers and voyageurs managed wilderness rivers aboard logs and timbers lashed together, those rigid models sometimes were pounded to splinters on the rocks. A present-day "rubber" blow-up can slide over without a scratch.

Proper equipment is essential once you decide to try the sport. Good inflatables are not cheap. A "four man" raft (suitable for two on a river run) rugged enough to bounce off boulders and branches could cost over $500; larger craft over $1000. Light thin-skinned models, fine for paddling or fishing, are considered swimming-pool toys by experienced river rats. Strong, neoprene-coated synthetic fabrics are more durable, and experiments are now being made with DuPont's Kevlar 49 aramid plastic filaments, superior strength-to-weight materials.

Big rafts used commercially for group river-runs may also be headed for legal shoals. Most are imported, making them "foreign-made vessels trafficking between U.S. ports," which the Coast Guard can't certify as safe until laws are passed to cut through the red tape.

must learn some tricks and skills

No special training or permits are required on many rivers to run rafts on your own, but training and experience are highly advisable. Rafts can turn over, swamp, hang up on submerged trees, slam into underwater rocks, be trapped in suction-hole eddies or be spun out by the helical flow of a bend in the river. The white-water skipper must learn the hydraulics of river currents. He must study charts, learn how to read the water and know how to scout conditions ahead—sometimes it makes better sense to get out and walk while lowering the boat downstream by line.

canoes

One step up in speed and difficulty for running rapids is the Indians' double-ender. When water starts showing white patches, however, decking is necessary to keep the water out, and special skills required to keep the canoe upright. A 17-footer is a good average size for two paddlers with spray-skirt decking added and a shallow shoe keel to make maneuvering easier.

More specialized decked canoes are called C-1s and C-2s (for competition). The one-man C-1 slalom model is 13 feet long and weighs 40 pounds or less. The speedy C-1 down-river model is a foot longer. For two paddlers, the C-2 slalom and down-river models are about 16½ feet long and weigh 50 pounds.

Wilderness canoe campers can run into white water in an open-decked canoe without expecting it. Probably the best advice around for this sport is in *The Complete Wilderness Paddler* by Davidson and Rugge. It's considered the first and last word by many canoeists.

kayaks

Fastest and most maneuverable of all, the Eskimo invention looks much like the new decked canoes. You will be paddling seated rather than kneeling, however, and you'll use a double rather than a single-bladed paddle. You'll have fewer paddle strokes to worry about, but will need to learn the Eskimo roll and get used to wearing a helmet so that if flipped in a suckhole you can roll back up with your head intact. I found the roll difficult to learn until an experienced paddler taught me in a shallow pool; but the confidence it gave me was worthwhile when I rounded a bend into a chute one day, capsized coming out of a haystack and quickly rolled upright rather than having to bail out in the boil.

YOU CAN CONVERT from calm-water canoe to rough-water special with Grumman's nylon spray cover for its 17-footers. Decking has openings for three.

SMALLER BOATS are a bigger challenge, but small size is necessary in narrow cuts. Four-man boat is the right size for two in rapids.

The most popular kayak today is the fiberglass slalom model—13 feet, 2 inches long by 23 inches wide and 20 to 35 pounds in weight. With it you'll want the double-bladed paddle, helmet, a quality life jacket, flotation bags for underdecks and probably a wet suit. You also need good instructions; river running clubs are often a good source. Ski resorts frequently switch to kayak lessons during the summer. Aspen, CO, has several schools, as well as eight different outfits offering group river raft runs that include lunch. The Aspen Chamber of Commerce can provide a list.

where to go

Excellent books, like *White-water!* by Strung, Curtis and Perry and *The All-Purpose Guide to Paddling* by Norman, tell of rivers, clubs, associations and waters where the action is rated from Class I, easy, through Class VI, too dangerous to be passable. With experience and courage you can work your way up.

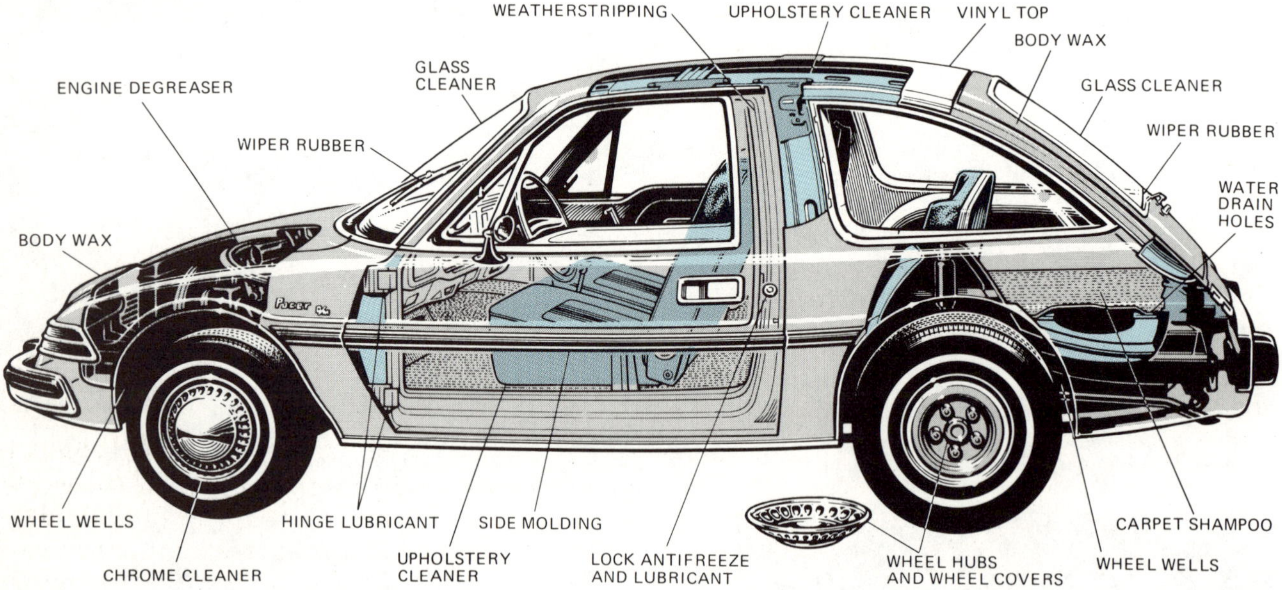

Every car ever built seems to come equipped with its own particular rattle or squeak that's impossible to find. Sometimes the source is so mysterious you're inclined to live with the annoyance. Well, here's a systematic way of finding that rattle or squeak, then eliminating it. Here are tips, too, on finding water leaks, protecting the car's finish, and taking care of vinyl tops.

Car care inside and out

SEE ALSO

Autos, body repair . . . Autos, maintenance . . . Autos, ramps . . . Belts, auto . . . Engines, auto . . . Fuel systems, auto . . . Leaks, auto . . . Noises, auto . . . Power-train noise, auto . . . Ramps, auto repair . . . Rust, auto . . . Tune-up, auto

NOISE, RADIOS, body leaks, paint and finish are the problems most owners have with their auto bodies. Each of these areas can be of major concern to an owner who annually puts many miles on his car.

Some cars have annoying rattles from day one. Nobody seems to be able to pinpoint the exact location of some rattles. Finding the source may be one of the toughest tasks you face. Fixing the rattle, squeak, groan, whistle or whatever is usually simple.

Drive the car on different road surfaces, over bumps and at different speeds to establish whether noise is coming from the body or chassis. Once you have settled on the body (you've ruled out such chassis areas as engine, suspension and exhaust), establish if noise is being caused by loose body bolts (nonunitized body), broken weld (unitized body), or a loose door or window.

If the car has a nonunitized (or partially nonunitized) body, loose body bolts will cause rattles that are more pronounced when the car goes over bumps. Tighten bolts with a torque wrench to manufacturer specifications, which is usually 25 to 30 ft.-lb.

If the car has a unitized (or partially unitized) body, a weld that has broken loose will produce a groan or squeak that's amplified when the car goes over bumps. The broken weld should be found and repaired by a repair shop that has a spot-welding facility.

TRACKING DOWN LOOSE BOLTS AND PARTS

Most times body noise is produced by something that's come loose. To find the rattle, start at one end of the car and gently tap every spot from top to bottom with a rubber mallet. Take your time and tap every inch of the fenders, doors, hood, trunk lid and windows.

When you hear a rattle, stop and tighten bolts in the area. Test again. If a part is held by a catch or rides on hinges, lubricate the catch or hinge and test again.

If you hear a rattle when striking the center of a door, there might be something lying inside the door—maybe a bolt that's dropped from place or even a tool left in the door during assembly. Remove the trim panel and investigate.

Rattles from a window are caused when channel weatherstripping comes loose or wears out, or a window regulator goes bad.

There's another possibility that exists when a door rattles: The door may not be aligned correctly. One way to find out is to look at the gap between the door and the adjacent fender. Now check the gap between door and fender on the other side of the car. If there's an appreciable difference between the two gaps, it indicates that the rattling door should be realigned. Here's how:

- Loosen door hinge bolts.
- Using a pry bar, move the door until the gap between the door and adjacent fender is equal to the gap between the door and adjacent fender on the opposite side of the car.
- Tighten hinge bolts securely.
- Realign the door striker plate by loosening striker plate bolts and taking the plate off. Insert (or remove) metal striker plate shims behind the plate until a clearance of 3/32 to 5/32 inch between striker plate and door lock is obtained. Shims may be purchased from an auto supply and accessory dealer, or from the parts department of a dealer selling your make car.

To get a clear shot at measuring that distance between the striker plate and door lock, clean off both parts and apply a layer of grease or graphite to the striker plate bolt. Open and close the door once or twice. A pattern from the door lock will impress itself on the grease or graphite. Measure from the pattern to the tip of the striker plate bolt to establish the clearance between striker plate and door lock (remember, it should be 3/32 to 5/32 inch).

Excessive distance between the two components causes a door to rattle. Insufficient clearance interferes with locking action.

TRACKING DOWN CHASSIS NOISE

Suppose during your road test you determined that noise was coming from a chassis part rather than the body. Chassis parts that produce noise most often are the alternator when it comes loose on its mounting bracket; power steering and airconditioner mounting brackets; motor mounts; suspension parts, such as loose shock absorbers and sway bars; and exhaust system components.

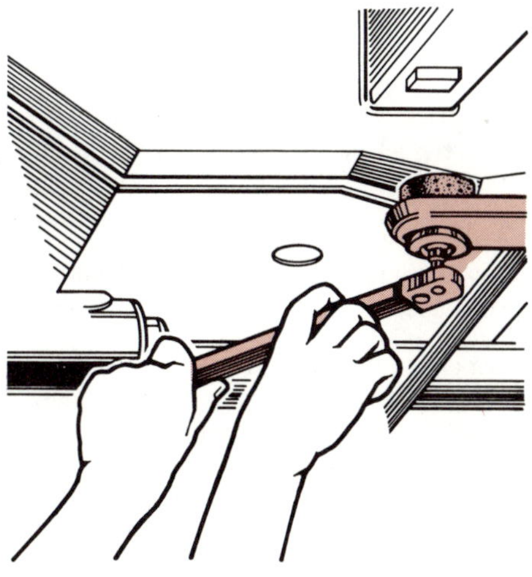

TIGHTENING body bolts with a torque wrench may eliminate an elusive rattle.

Each should be inspected closely. The toughest noise to find is one produced in the engine compartment. A handy tool you may want to consider buying to help you isolate noise is an auto stethoscope. When placed against a part, it amplifies any noise the part may be producing, leaving no doubt about the noise source.

A FEW WORDS ABOUT RADIOS

"Cutting in and out" is defined as a radio that is playing normally and suddenly dies—and then comes back on. Don't confuse it with station fade which occurs when you drive away from an area served by a particular station.

Cutting in and out is caused by loose connections or by wires that ground themselves out as you drive along.

Connections to the radio's ground, and connections to the battery, antenna and remote speakers (if any) should be tightened and inspected for integrity. Broken wires should be replaced or spliced together.

Incidentally, if the radio is dead (dial light out) don't rush to have a radio repairman pull it from the car—not before you replace the fuse serving the radio in the car's fuse block and try the radio.

Interference is normally produced by the car's ignition system. Every car with a radio has a means of suppressing this interference. Some have RF (radio interference) shields in the distributor; some have resistor wires as part of the ignition wiring; still others call for using resistor-type sparkplugs. Resistor wiring is the method that goes awry most often. When it happens, replacing the resistor wire is in order, or you can always use resistor-type sparkplugs.

By the way, if you have a stereo tape player in your car, don't forget to clean the player's head periodically—every 100 hours of operation is the recommended interval. Follow cleaning instructions in the owner's manual. Normally all that is required is cleaning the player head with a cotton swab that's been dipped in alcohol.

REALIGNING a car door requires an adjustment to door striker plate.

Important: Never apply any lubricant to a stereo tape player, and don't bring any magnetized tools near the head. If the head becomes magnetized, every tape you insert into the player will be ruined.

STOPPING BODY LEAKS

The procedure to follow if water is leaking into the car's interior is: **1.** find the source of entry; **2.** seal it up.

To find a water leak, the first thing to do is tape a garden hose minus its nozzle to the roof of the car. Put a tin can right ahead of the spout so water coming from the hose overspreads the entire windshield or rear window.

If the leak has been showing up in the front of the car, test the windshield. Chances are the opening is there. If the leak has been showing up in back, waterdown the rear window. Be sure the entire expanse is covered with water. Then get inside the car and wait to see where the water starts leaking in.

Have patience. A leak may not show up for a while.

Very important: Every 5 or 10 minutes, get out of the car and rock it from side-to-side. This action allows water which is leaking through the windshield and collecting in a seam to untrap itself so it can start dripping into the car's interior.

When you establish without doubt where water is leaking into the car during this test, you should apply windshield sealer around the glass.

But this is important: Do **not** apply windshield sealer over chrome molding strips. You won't seal the leak, but instead you will "seal" the molding in place. This means that when you finally remove molding to make the repair properly you will have to exert extraordinary pressure behind the strips to pop them loose. This pressure will probably be strong enough to crack the expensive windshield.

To correctly seal a leak through a windshield, remove chrome molding with a professional-style windshield molding removal tool, which may be obtained from an auto parts and accessories dealer, or from an auto body repair shop.

Slide the tool under the molding until it hits a clip holding the chrome in place. Twist the tool gently until the molding pops loose from the clip. As you get to each clip, mark its location with chalk to facilitate replacement.

Never try removing molding strips with a screwdriver or pry bar. You will crack the glass.

After all strips have been removed, take one of the holding clips to an auto body shop or auto supply and accessories store and get a number of new clips. You should not reuse the old ones, which will become distorted when you remove the molding.

Place a new clip in each spot where an old clip had been. Then apply a generous bead of auto windshield sealer as directed on the package. Make certain that every inch of the perimeter is covered with sealer. Leaving a bare spot offers a gap through which water may enter.

After applying windshield sealer, reinstall molding. Place the strips over the edges of the glass and pop them back on the clips.

CAR WASHING should be a weekly job—less often if you garage your car.

OTHER AREAS OF LEAKAGE

Water can leak through windows, doors, windshield wiper bosses, holes in the firewall, drip rails over doors, and fender joints.

Play a heavy stream of water from a hose on every cranny and crack as someone in the car keeps his eyes peeled. If water leaks into the car, seal the particular spot being doused. If water is entering the car through a window or door, the weatherstripping is either loose or worn. Fix or replace it.

GETTING RID OF BODY RUST

There are four methods to remove rust spots:

1. Grind the spot down and/or cut away rusted metal as necessary. Back up the repair with the screening material included with the body-repair kit you're using, and apply body filler. Sand and paint.

2. Grind the spot down, making sure you get rid of all loose, rusted metal, and cover the area with aluminum tape, which comes in four-inch-wide strips. See that the tape extends at least one inch beyond the damage and adheres tightly at all of the edges.

Roughen up the tape with 100-grit sandpaper, apply plastic body filler, shape and sand, then paint.

3. Grind the damaged area and attach a piece of 20 to 22-gauge sheet metal with a riveting tool. Roughen the metal, apply plastic filler, shape and sand, then paint. Pay particular attention to edges. Make sure body filler is feathered into the car's body so edges are sealed.

4. Weld or braze sheet metal to the car's body. This is the permanent way of making the repair.

MINIMIZING PAINT PROBLEMS

Today's car finishes are better than ever, so there's no reason why the paint on your car shouldn't sparkle for the life of the vehicle. The easiest and least expensive way to preserve the original luster is to wash the car as often as you can. Washing gets rid of tree sap, road tar, insects and bird droppings, gasoline, industrial fallout and other harmful agents. Always use cold water, never wash in the direct rays of the hot sun, and wait until the metal is cool. Your auto parts and accessories dealer has available car wash compounds and agents which will remove stubborn tar and other contaminants.

After washing and cleaning—and once a week isn't too often for this important car-care job—you should inspect your car's finish closely. Oxidized paint looks chalky, or gives the appearance of a film hiding the true color of your car. You'll have to use a cleaner to remove the dead paint and a wax to lay on a new protective coating—or you can use a combination cleaner/wax that will do the job in one step.

You've got your choice of a wide range of cleaners and waxes to do the job—from wax-impregnated cloths to sprays, liquids and presoftened pastes. Many car owners have tried all of these types at one time or another looking for the best one to suit their needs. Many car buffs stock several different types of waxes so they can do a quick job or a real elbow-grease job depending on how much time they have.

CLEANING AND POLISHING removes dead paint and lays down protective finish.

You should polish one section at a time using a circular motion to apply the wax and making sure to overlap sufficiently. Your cloth will slowly become the color of your car as you rub off dead paint, so turn over the cloth frequently. When the wax is dry, it will haze on the surface and is then ready to be removed with a clean cloth and the surface buffed to a high shine. Again, fold the cloth frequently, as it becomes glazed with dead paint.

Vinyl tops need their own special care. Frequent washing is as vital for a vinyl top as it is for the car's paint finish—maybe even more so. A soft-bristled brush is a help in thoroughly cleaning with mild soap. When the surface is clean and dry, you can use vinyl top dressing on the roof. You can use the neutral, or colorless, product or get the color that matches your vinyl top.

Scratches or cuts in the vinyl can also be repaired now, using one of the repair kits made for the purpose.

Important: Wood-grain applique should be washed only. Do not polish.

When cleaning a car, take time to spiff up the interior. Here are some tips:

■ Thoroughly vacuum carpeting. If there is a soiled spot, it may be removed with carpet cleaner. Make sure carpets are dry before closing windows and doors.

■ Wash bright metal parts with lukewarm water and a mild soap. Rinse. Do not use metal polishes.

■ Remove dust and loose dirt that accumulate on interior seat fabrics with a vacuum cleaner or whisk broom. Soils, stains and spots can usually be cleaned away with a good-quality fabric cleaner.

■ Clean seat belts with a mild soap solution and lukewarm water. See that they're not frayed—and use them.

TIPS ABOUT OTHER BODY AREAS

Here are a few other points about problem body areas that you may find valuable:

■ If new windshield wipers streak, it probably means that arm tension is excessive. You may be able to relieve tension yourself by gently bending the arm, but don't go to extremes. If this doesn't work, tension should be tested with an ounce scale and reset to manufacturer requirements.

■ If windshield-washer reservoir is full, but you're not getting a solid squirt of fluid, be sure the little nozzles aimed at the windshield are clear, and also see to it that the filter in the windshield washer reservoir is not clogged. You'll need a pin or small stiff wire to clean out the washer nozzles.

■ Window smog is a problem in many cars having vinyl and imitation leather interiors. These plastic coverings give off an agent that coats windows. Try cleaning smog away with a good-quality windshield cleaner or a strong solution of ammonia and water.

■ Hub caps that creep and make noise may be silenced by having another two or three lugs welded on them to hold them still.

■ Speedometer cables seldom need greasing, but if one begins making noise you will need a service manual to find out how to remove it for lubrication.

How often should you wax your car?

■ PREVENTION IS the best cure for chemical or other damage to your car's finish. The best prevention is frequent washing with a good-quality nonalkaline car-wash detergent. A heavy coat of auto wax applied at least once every six months will help. Furthermore, if your car is left outdoors rather than garaged, you might want to consider covering it overnight with a heavy plastic dropcloth.

Also keep in mind that any chips in the paint should be touched up immediately in order to prevent damage from spreading. An auto-parts supply dealer has touch-up paints available to match your car's finish.

To touch up all minor flaws such as scratches, localized blisters, pitting and peel, apply baby oil to the flaw and very carefully sand the area with 600-grit *wet* sandpaper. Wash off the sanding sludge and wipe the area with a clean, soft cloth.

If the defect is removed before you get to bare metal, buff the area with a fine buffing compound. If you can't get rid of the flaw without removing paint to bare metal, touch up the spot with touch-up paint, let dry, then buff and polish.

There are shelves of other body and cleaning supplies at a local auto supply dealer to help you rectify tough conditions that ordinary products can't touch. What you need for hard-to-remove scuff marks, on tires, for example, is a commercially available white sidewall cleaner and a stiff-bristle brush or soap pad. Do not use any makeshift cleaning substance containing any petroleum, such as gasoline or kerosene. Petroleum is harmful to rubber.

industrial chemicals

Cars that suddenly develop "freckles," especially in heavy industrial areas, have probably been infected by chemicals in the air, specifically acid or alkali.

When acid or alkali on paint gets wet, it can change color pigment, like blue spots in red, dark blue spots in metallic green and bleached-out areas in yellow.

SEE ALSO

Autos, body repair . . . Autos, maintenance . . . Belts, auto . . . Engines, auto . . . Leaks, auto . . . Noises, auto . . . Power-train noise, auto . . . Ramps, auto repair . . . Rust, auto

Hopefully, chemical damage will be spotted before it eats into the finish and extends below the surface. If so, it can be removed using the method described here. If the damage has gone deep into the paint film and won't polish out, refinishing will be required to get rid of further chemical injury.

Here is how to restore your car's complexion.

■ Wash the finish thoroughly with a good-quality commercial car-wash detergent. Let the finish dry.

■ Taking a small area at a time on the car's flat surfaces, apply a medium-grit polishing compound.

■ With a variable-speed drill equipped with a buffing pad, polish off spots. The drill should be operated at low to medium speed. Concentrate on spotted areas only. Repeat until spots are removed.

■ Over curved surfaces and near edges and metal trim, the procedure will have to be done by hand. Form a cotton cloth into a ball and rub the spots vigorously.

■ Wipe off excess compound with a clean, dry cloth and buff out the area with a clean, dry lamb's-wool pad to get rid of polishing marks and to bring up the gloss.

iron-particle fallout

If those rust spots feel rough to the touch and are hard to get off by simply washing the car, then the finish has been infected by iron-particle fallout. To get rid of iron-particle damage, proceed as follows as soon as possible:

■ Wash the car thoroughly with a good-quality commercially available nonalkaline car-wash detergent.

■ Mix 6 to 8 ounces of dry powder oxalic acid (available in hardware stores) in one gallon of warm water. Add one or two tablespoons of car-wash detergent.

■ Using a large sponge, apply the solution freely to all affected areas. Keep the area wet and run your hand over the surface occasionally. When you no longer feel roughness, you can stop the treatment.

■ Rinse the area with clear water thoroughly. This must be done to prevent corrosion, which remaining traces of oxalic acid will cause.

Wax your car at least twice a year under normal conditions, oftener if you detect surface damage.

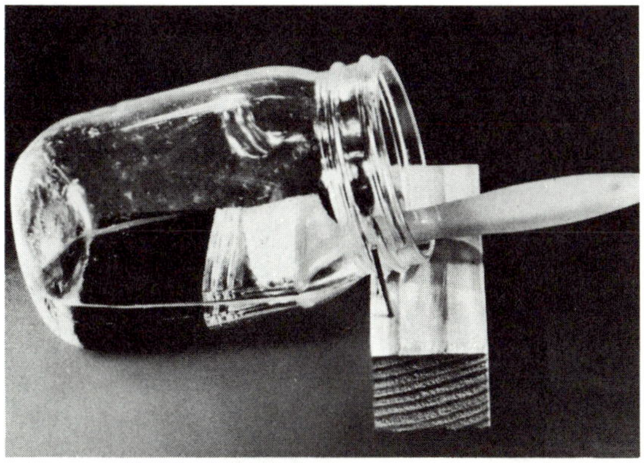

YOU'LL USE less turpentine the next time that you have a paintbrush to clean if you tilt the jar as shown. Place the dirty brush in the container, then pour just enough turpentine to cover the bristles.

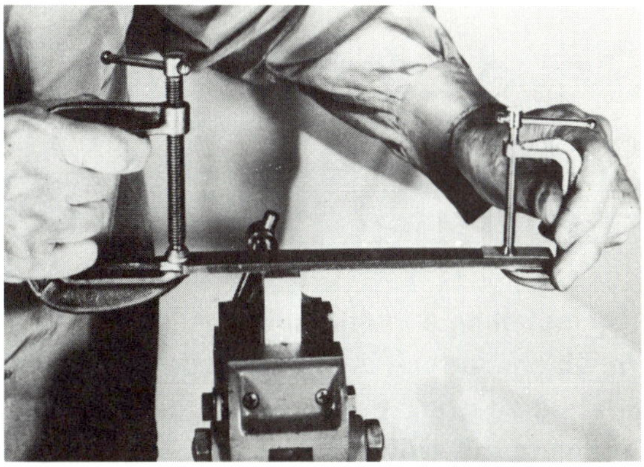

YOU CAN IMPROVISE file handles by clamping both ends of a file securely with a pair of C-clamps. This way, your hands will be protected from accidental bumps against the vise.

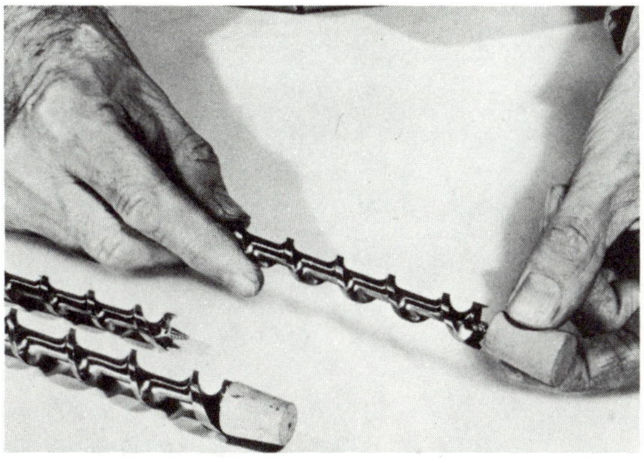

AUGER-BIT SCREW POINTS will stay sharper longer if they are protected before being parked in drawer or toolbox. A rubber bumper or bottle cork slips on and off quickly, yet absorbs the bangs and bumps.

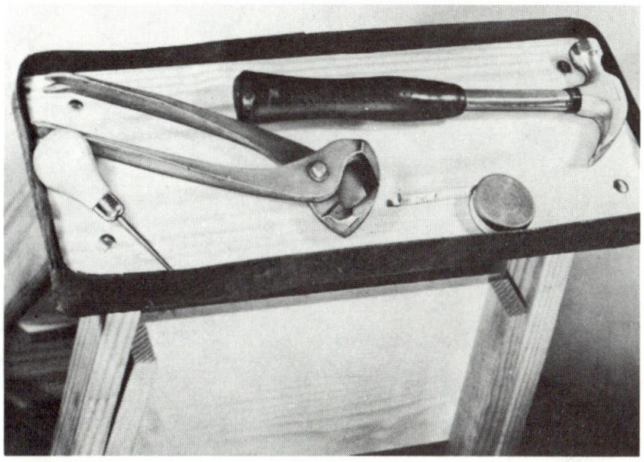

HEFTY STRIP of inner tube tacked around the perimeter of a stepladder's top step will keep small tools and round objects fenced in. Then, when you move the ladder, it's not necessary to unload tools.

USED FLASHCUBES can add gaiety to your next Christmas tree at no cost. Once they have been flashed, the cubes will effectively reflect the array of colors hanging near them. Use ribbon to tie bulbs to limb.

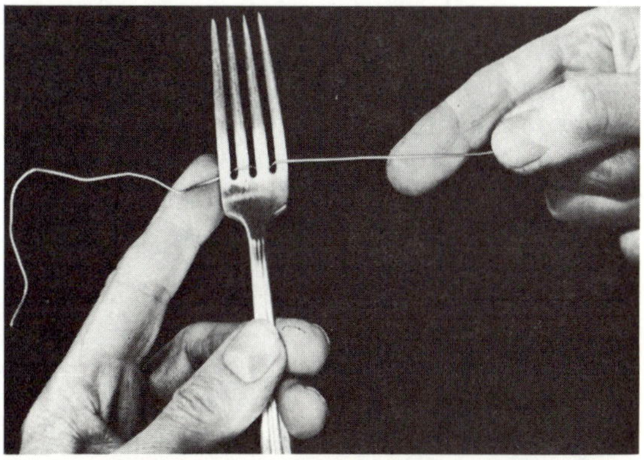

STRAIGHTENING KINKED WIRE is a snap if it is passed through the tines of a discarded fork as indicated. After positioning one end of the wire, draw the entire length through, using a firm and even pressure.

Save money and energy with a multifuel boiler

By installing a multifuel boiler, you can burn whichever fuel is cheapest during any heating season. Here's what it takes to make the switch

By JOSEPH R. PROVEY

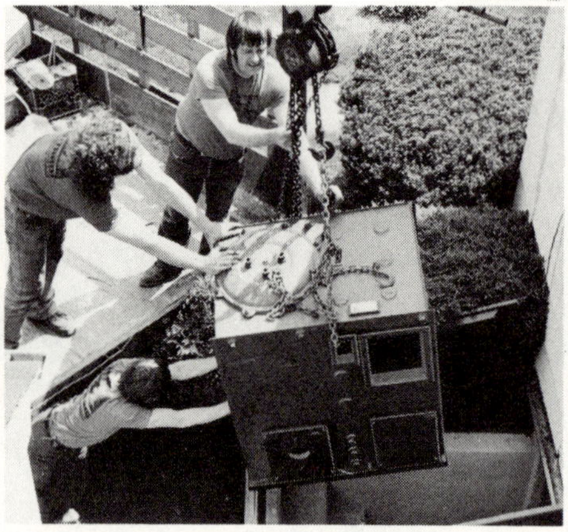

MULTIFUEL UNIT (right) operates at efficiency of 84 percent (oil) or 62 percent (wood). Old oil burner (left) was 68 percent efficient. Basement entry eased the task of getting the new unit in and the old one out.

■ THE FIRST TIME I fired up my multifuel boiler with a load of wood, it struck me that it was also the first time in my life I was taking full responsibility for providing heat for my family. It felt good, but also a little scary—a contract with the oil company had always taken care of everything. The burner fed itself and deliveries were automatic. In recent years, however, so were the price-per-gallon increases.

Now I can call the shots—without giving up the admitted convenience of oil. The HS TARM unit I chose will burn oil, gas, coal, coke or wood, and even operate on electricity. I ruled out gas and electricity since the former is not available to me and the latter costs too much. Coal is a last resort even though its cost per B.T.U. is about half that of oil.

We scheduled and completed our installation in the spring, when a service interruption was not critical and installers weren't completely booked.

The initial cost was about $3400. The payback period is relatively short. In my case, I am using oil to heat my domestic water during the mild-weather months and will use wood for both domestic hot water and space heating during the winter. The wood, even in my well-populated suburban area, costs only sweat. My oil savings will be about 600 gallons, which converts to

SEE ALSO
**Energy, saving . . . Furnaces . . . Heat pumps . . .
Heating systems, home . . .
Heating systems, solar . . . Humidifiers . . .
Radiator covers . . . Solar energy . . .
Stoves, wood-burning . . . Winterizing, homes**

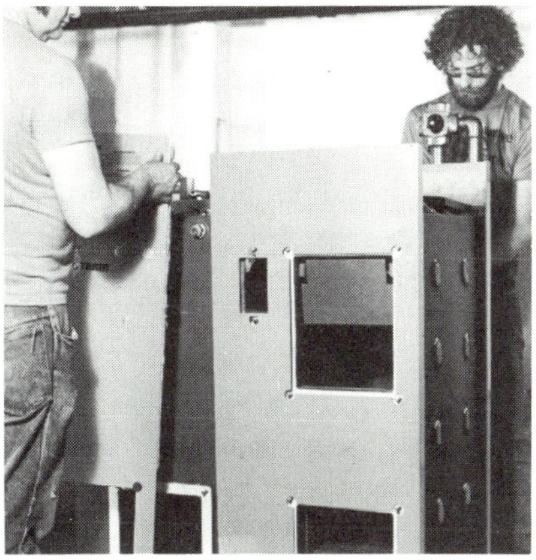

INSTALLATION of boiler jacket and mounting of doors and components can be done by the homeowner.

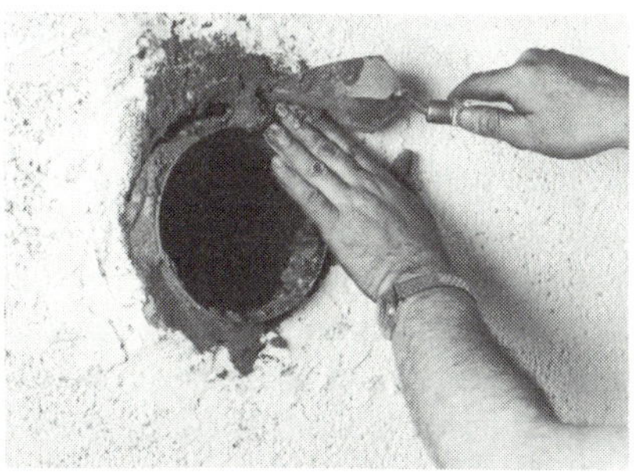

BEFORE FLUE pipe was installed, thimble was mortared in place. Then flue pipe was inserted and joint sealed.

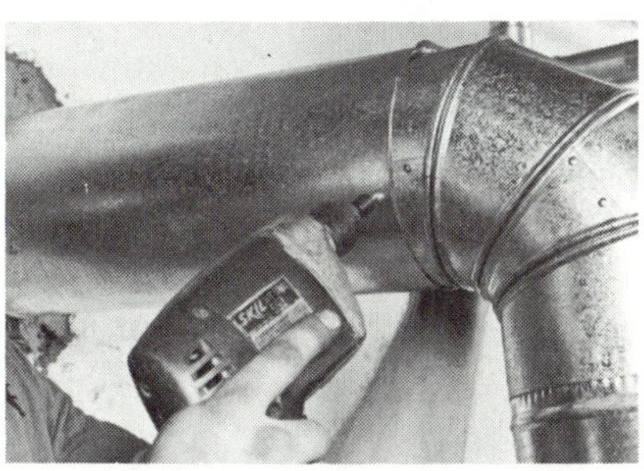

FLUE PIPE sections were fastened with sheet-metal screws to keep them from separating due to vibration.

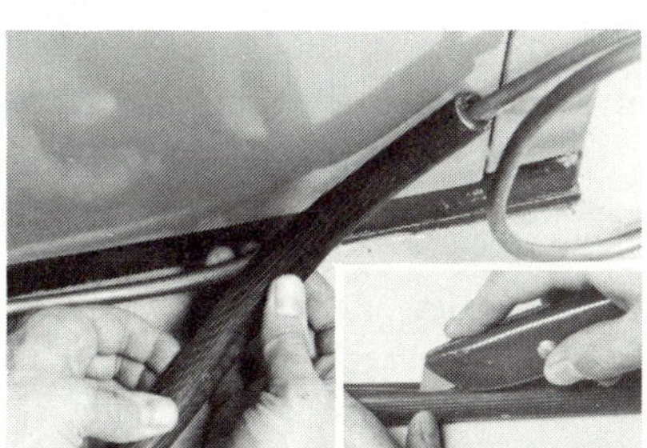

OIL FEED LINE to burner was protected by slipping an old garden hose over the exposed tubing.

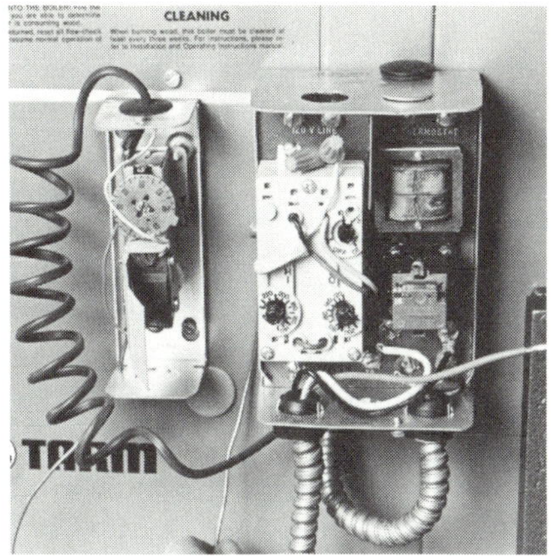

CONNECTING overheat control (A) and master hot-water control (B) normally requires professional help.

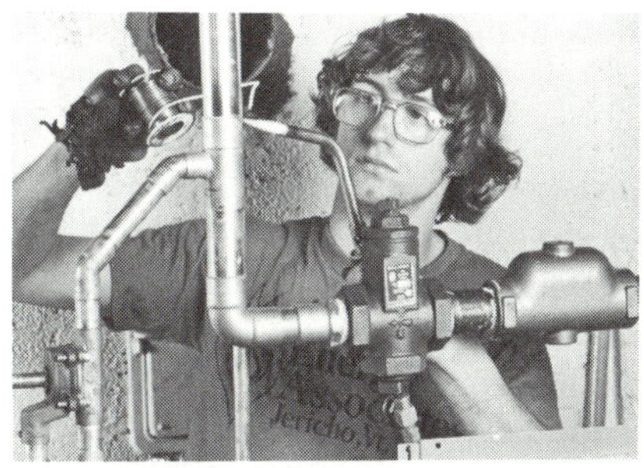

AIR PURGER, valves and copper pipes were plumbed and soldered according to the manufacturer's recommendations.

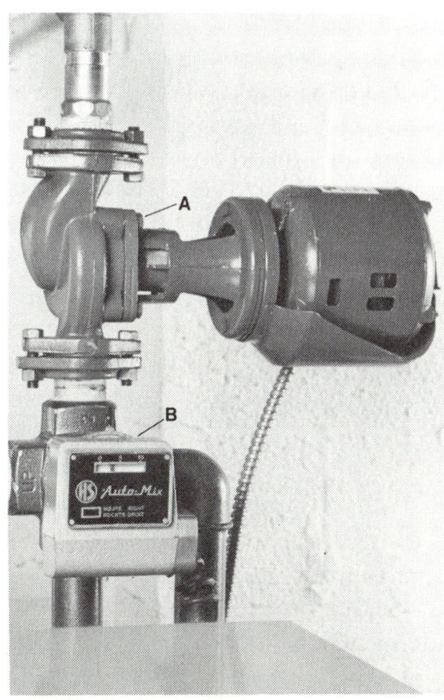

CIRCULATOR PUMP (A) on return line operates constantly during heating season. Auto mix valve (B) feeds more—or less—hot water from boiler to radiators, depending on thermostat's call for heat.

BOILER MAINTENANCE

If you are accustomed to low-maintenance fuels like gas or oil, be aware that alternative fuels (coal and especially wood) will demand more of your attention. Chimneys, for instance, must be cleaned once a year. The stovepipe between the boiler and the chimney must be removed and inspected for corrosion, creosote and soot at least twice during a heating season. The oil or gas burner should be adjusted, and the burner firebox cleaned, once a year. Cleaning of the inside boiler walls and flue passages must be done at least every two months during the heating season. Otherwise, a buildup of creosote will slow heat transfer.

SCOOP IS USED for emptying ashes. They should be removed before they touch grates and restrict airflow.

WIRE FLUE BRUSH and long-handle scraper are provided with unit for cleaning creosote from boiler.

METER reads 23-percent moisture content in logs seasoned 10 months—slightly high for burning.

nearly $500 at 82 cents per gallon. Conservatively projecting the price of heating oil to rise 10 percent a year, my multifuel unit will pay for itself (beyond the cost of a new oil-fired unit) in three to four years.

We began planning our installation by looking at available units and sending for manufacturer's literature. After choosing the unit which suited my needs, I checked the dimensions of access to the basement, condition and size of my chimney flue, and the size of the area where the unit was to be installed. I had to be sure I could get the unit into my basement without removing a wall or floor section, that my chimney was the right size, in good repair and tile-lined, and that there was adequate space for recommended clearances. Once satisfied, I visited my local building department to get a heating permit.

Codes vary from state to state and even from city to city. A few city codes have not approved multifuel units, so check before you buy. Don't chance an illegal installation—it may lower the resale value of your home. And if you should have a fire, the insurance adjuster will be the first person to find out if you had a valid heating permit.

When it came to actual installation, I was pleased to find that Tekton Corp., distributor of HS TARM boilers, encourages homeowners to participate. Depending on the dealer, you can assemble or trim out the unit yourself and save part of the installation cost ($400 to $1000 depending on where you live). I chose to work with a top-notch crew of professional installers and found this gave me invaluable knowledge of the unit.

In my opinion, connecting the electric controls, circulating pump and valves is best left to *licensed* professionals familiar with your unit—unless you are blessed with plenty of time, can acquire a good installation manual and have a background in plumbing and electrical work.

differences and advantages

Since solid-fuel burning is inherently different from burning gas or oil, the heat distribution and safety systems we chose are more sophisticated than conventional systems. Our installation utilizes a mixing valve and a circulator which runs continuously—instead of a typical hydronic system that periodically circulates fairly high-temperature water. The four-way mixing valve adds more or less return water to the supply being pumped to the radiators and is controlled by the house thermostat. Aside from using heat more efficiently and eliminating costly short cycling of the oil burner, other advantages you will obtain through continuous circulation include:

- Longer boiler life due to elimination of thermal shock to the boiler caused by surges of cold return water every time the circulator is started.
- Longer circulator life, since most wear in circulators occurs during motor start-up.
- A quieter house during the heating season.
- A more comfortable house since the heat is more even.

Continuous circulation of water to radiators also acts as a safety feature for our wood-fired hot-water heating system. Since the wood fire is always generating heat (it can't be turned off like my old oil burner), the system will dispose of the heat efficiently. In a conventional system, there is a greater possibility of boiler overheat (when there is no circulation) and creosote formation (caused by the fire burning too slowly between sporadic calls for heat).

Other safety features on our unit include a high-temperature overheat control which causes overheated boiler water to circulate to radiators—even if there is no call from the house thermostat.

Both the domestic hot-water coil and the boiler have pressure-relief valves piped down to near the floor or to a drain.

A backflow preventer was installed on the feed line to the boiler to prevent the contaminated water in the heat distribution loop from entering the domestic water supply.

in a power failure

Even with the electricity off, my multifuel boiler will keep our house warm. When an outage occurs, a special solenoid valve opens and allows hot boiler water to gravity-feed to the radiators, bypassing the check valve. The fire during such an outage would have to be fueled carefully and in moderation to prevent overheating the boiler. The automatic draft regulator will continue to control the fire even without electricity.

the answer: renewable fuels

The increasing frequency of oil and gas shortages will inevitably force us to depend on safe, renewable energy sources instead of nonrenewable and species-endangering ones. During the transition, a smart homeowner will leave open as many options as possible—a multifuel boiler or furnace fills the bill.

By W. CLYDE LAMMEY

What you should know about bolts

Bolts hold things together—make them perform as a unit or as an assembly of functional parts. Here's how to choose the right one for the job

■ WHEN THE JOB calls for use of a bolt rather than a screw or other type fastener, the homeowner must decide what type and size of bolt is best adapted to the purpose. If the parts to be joined are of metal, then a machine bolt with either a square or hex head usually is best. If the head bears on metal, then no washer will be required under the head in average work. But if the parts are subject to vibration, shear or shake, use a lock washer under the nut.

On the other hand if the parts are of wood, or if the part against which the head must bear is of wood, then it is generally best to use a carriage bolt. The head of the latter is relatively larger in proportion to the body diameter and is crowned in a manner similar to that of an oval-headed screw. The body has square shoulders just below the head. When it is tapped into a hole, the squared portion of the head prevents the bolt from turning when you tighten or loosen the nut. When the nut is turned down on wood, always use a flat washer under it to prevent crushing or other defacement of the material.

Machine screws differ from machine bolts in that they usually are threaded the full body length and the heads are available in a range of shapes, or types, commonly known as flat, round, oval and fillister, also in the socket (Allen) and Phillips types. The flat and oval heads are much the same as those of ordinary wood-screw heads of the same types, the heads being shaped to seat in countersunk holes in the same manner as flat-head wood screws. But round and fillister-head machine screws are designed to seat directly on a flat surface or onto a lock washer. All machine-screw heads are slotted so that they may

SEE ALSO
Drapery rods . . . Fasteners . . . Moldings . . . Nails . . . Screws

SIZES ARE designated by length in inches, by diameter in numbers of the American Screw Gauge for diameters less than ¼", and in fractions of an inch for diameters ¼" and larger. Designations are for sizes commonly used.

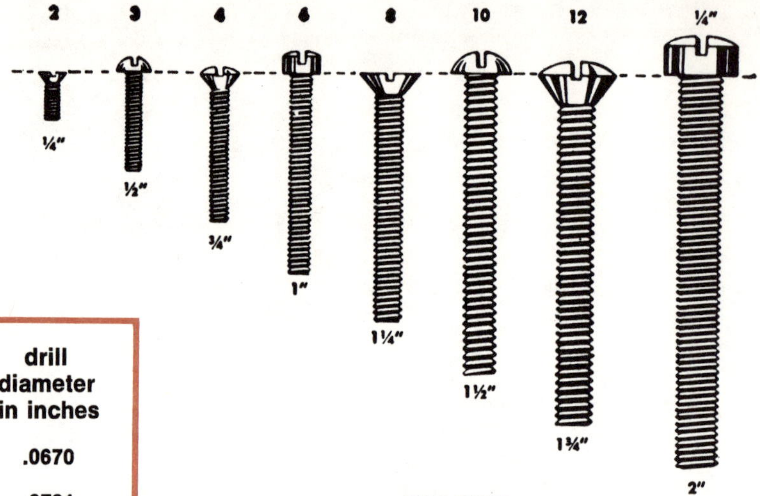

HEAD STYLES

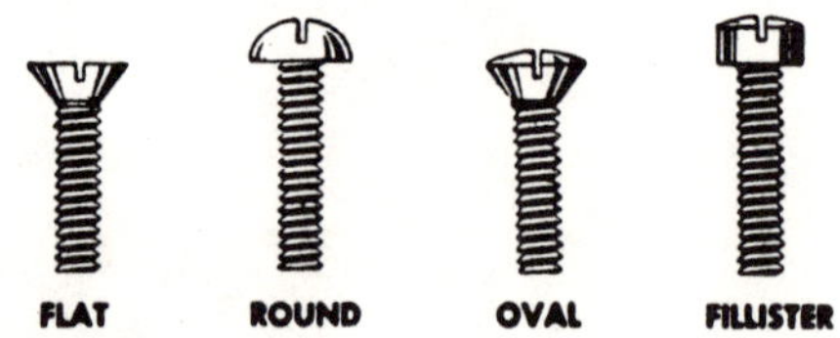

tap size diameter	threads per in.	drill size no.	drill diameter in inches
2	56	51	.0670
3	48	5/64"	.0781
4	40	43	.0890
6	32	36	.1065
8	32	29	.1360
10	24	25	.1495
12	24	17	.1730
¼"	20	8	.1990
5/16"	18	F	.2570
⅜"	16	5/16"	.3125
½"	13	27/64"	.4219

MACHINE SCREWS—the commercial term for screws to be driven in drilled and tapped holes—are used for assembly of metal parts. Machine screws are regularly made in mild steel and brass, with four types of head—flat, round, oval and fillister. Furnished plain and also with commonly used platings and degrees of finish—nickel, brass, copper, cadmium, electrogalvanized, Parkerized and zinc-plated.

be driven with an ordinary screw driver, excepting those with Allen and Phillips heads, the former to be driven with an Allen wrench and the latter with a Phillips driver.

Machine screws are designed mainly for assembly of metal parts, where they usually are driven into tapped holes rather than being drawn tight with nuts. They are widely used in the assembly of small machines, household appliances, models and experimental apparatus, instruments and in units having parts that must be easily assembled and disassembled in use, or for substitution or replacement. Machine screws come in a wide range of sizes from 0-80 up, are threaded both coarse and fine, and lengths and diameters are held to close dimensions.

CARRIAGE-BOLT DIMENSIONS (in inches)

AMERICAN STANDARD CARRIAGE BOLTS, ROUND HEAD, SQUARE NECK

BOLT SIZE diameter of thread and width of square	diameter of head	height of head	bolt length and shorter	depth of square	bolt length and longer	depth of square
No. 10 (3/16")	7/16	3/32	1⅛	⅛	1¼	7/32
¼	9/16	⅛	1¼	5/32	1⅜	¼
5/16	11/16	5/32	1¼	3/16	1⅜	9/32
⅜	13/16	3/16	1½	7/32	1⅝	5/16
7/16	15/16	7/32	1½	¼	1⅝	11/32
½	1 1/16	¼	1⅞	9/32	2	⅜
9/16	1 3/16	9/32	1⅞	5/16	2	13/32
⅝	1 5/16	5/16	1⅞	11/32	2	7/16
¾	1 9/16	⅜	1⅞	13/32	2	½
⅞	1 13/16	7/16	1⅞	15/32	2	9/16
1	2 1/16	½	1⅞	17/32	2	⅝

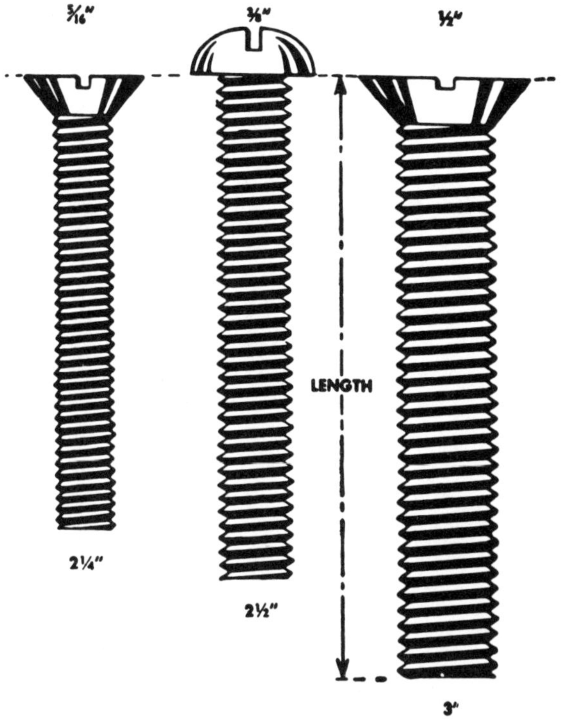

BELOW, methods of determining diameter of body and number of threads per inch with ordinary rule.

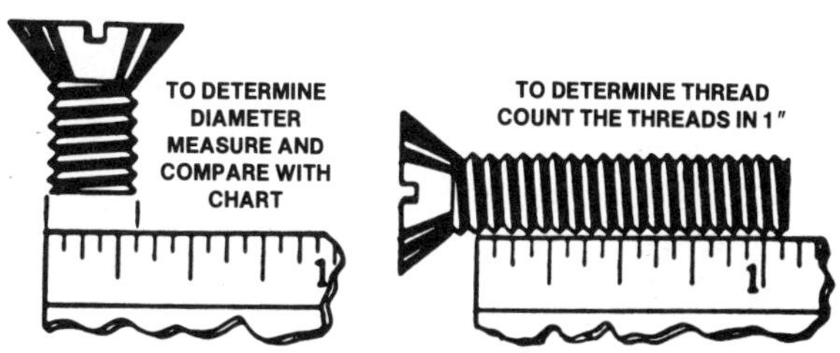

ILLUSTRATIONS SHOW MEASUREMENT OF A 5/16"-18 MACHINE SCREW

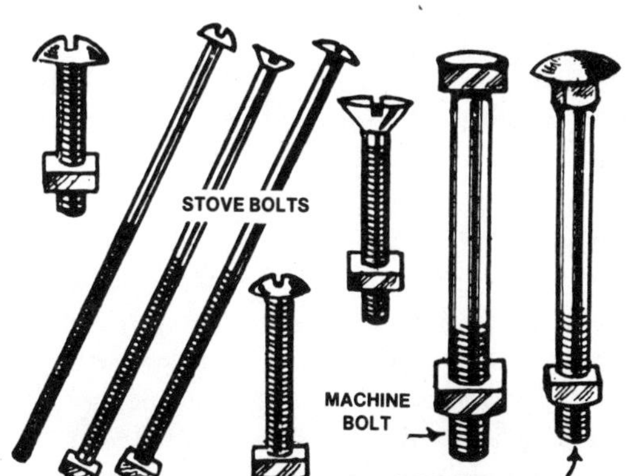

STOVE BOLTS usually are carried in stock in standard sizes. Intermediate or extra-length bolts are often available on special order if not stocked. Machine and carriage bolts are ordinarily made with full-diameter shanks. The standard sizes generally are available at any well-stocked hardware store.

stove bolts

"Stove" bolts acquired the name a long time ago and it stuck, even though their use has diversified widely from the purpose for which they were originally designed, that of fasteners in the assembly of stoves. Now they are perhaps among the most widely used fasteners where it is necessary to hold parts together with small bolts. They have slotted heads, like common wood screws, which come either flat or round. They are available in diameters from 5/32 to ½ in. and in lengths from 3/8 to 6 in. Stove bolts are not precision-made, being manufactured by upsetting and swaging processes, and the threads generally are rolled rather than die-cut. On the shorter lengths the threads are rolled the full body length. On longer bolts threads may vary from 1 to 2 in. in length. Nuts furnished with stove bolts are ordinarily square, but, any nut tapped with a coarse thread may be used.

hole size

In wood the diameter of the hole should be the same as that of the bolt. This assures a snug fit and offsets any tendency of the parts to work loose. In metal it is a common practice to drill bolt holes about 1/64 to 1/32 in. oversize so that when the holes are brought into register the bolt will slip easily into place. If holes are drilled the same size as the bolt it may be necessary to tap it rather forcefully. This can swage or upset the threads, making the nut difficult to start.

length of bolt

Length of the bolt ordinarily should be such that all the threads of the nut engage—with perhaps two or three threads over—when the nut is drawn tight. Of course, you may not always have at hand a bolt, or bolts, that meet this ideal specification. But don't use a bolt of any size that's a thread or two short of full engagement with the nut when the latter is tightened. It might loosen or strip and let you down at some critical time later on. Better to use a bolt that's too long, cutting the excess off the threaded end if clearance is a problem. If you do have occasion to reduce the length of a bolt by cutting off a portion of the threaded end, cut it as nearly square as possible freehand. Then file the end smooth and bevel, or "break" it slightly with a file so that the nut will "take" the threads easily. Avoid use of bolts with damaged threads.

IN THIS system by Knape & Vogt, aluminum standards and brackets are combined with prefinished boards.

YOU CAN use Masonite Pegboard almost anywhere. Special brackets support shelves of various sizes.

All kinds of book shelves

By DAVID WARREN

■ SAGGING BOOK shelves make a whole room look tipsy, as though it somehow is out of kilter with the rest of the world. And sagging shelves also give an air of impermanence, as though the owner were only camping out for a few weeks.

Sagging shelves are relatively common, and are the result of a poor choice of shelving systems. You must consider the strength of the system versus the task you'll be asking it to perform. Usually a shelving system is acquired because it looks good. But time and gravity sometimes take their toll.

For example, a 1-in. (nominal) pine shelf with brackets spaced 12 in. apart will support 670 lbs. per square inch. But the same board bridging brackets spaced 36 in. apart will support only 38 lbs. per square inch. Spread the brackets to 72 in., and the shelf will hold only 5 lbs. per square inch.

Another factor in the strength of book shelves is the method used to attach them to the wall. A screw turned into plasterboard will pull out easily; a good wall anchor will support a tremendous load.

college student's standby

Perhaps the simplest and least expensive system of book shelves is the college student's old standby: stacks of concrete blocks with shelf boards between. It's a strong, durable and cheap system, but the blocks themselves take up a considerable amount of room, and the shelving setup is not exactly a decorator's dream.

Another possibility is utility shelving made of perforated steel. A good utility shelving system is about the strongest system made, but most of us don't need *that* much strength in our living room or study. And again it's not very attractive.

HOW ARE THESE massive oak-plank shelves anchored? Lag bolts enter the oak from the other side of the wall, passing totally through the studs. Lagbolt heads were countersunk and plastered over.

decorative utility shelving

However, Hirsh Company and Quaker Industries are two manufacturers of utility shelving who are extending the limits of their products into the area of interior decor. They've done this by adding bright colors to lightweight utility shelving. The color selection is wide, including red, blue, yellow, brown, green, white and almond. Low in cost, these smart-looking shelves make attractive book shelves and utility storage space in student study rooms, home offices, laundry rooms, and other areas where strong but attractive shelving is required.

When most of us think of book shelves, though, we think of what has become the standard system in most homes: slotted steel wall supports, with thin steel brackets that hold wood, plywood or particle-board shelves.

many choices

You have a wide choice of systems, and usually a choice of colors and finishes within each system. Among the well-known manufacturers are Stanley, Knape & Vogt, National Manufacturing, Pluswood, Weyerhauser and Flair Fold.

Prefinished shelf boards are marketed in standard lengths and widths from 8x24 to 12x72 in., though not all sizes are available from every manufacturer. You can buy boards prefinished in walnut, butcher block, pecan, black, white and several solid colors. Most surfaces are melamine, which is handsome and stands up well under regular cleaning. But note that it does not have the durability nor scratch resistance of plastic laminate.

shelfboards for your own system

Weyerhauser markets "Appearance Boards" in lengths to 12 ft. They are available in plain or wood-grain finishes. They not only are applicable to standard shelving systems, but are well suited to the construction of a shelf system of your own design.

These standard shelf systems are supported by hardware consisting of steel (or aluminum) slotted standards. Brackets are keyed to fit the slots. In such a system, if the wall is vertical the shelves inevitably are horizontal, back to front. If you are careful to mount the supports at exactly the same height, the shelves are flat and level.

Make a mental note that in most of these systems there is a top and bottom to the supports. Many a homemaker has carefully screwed his supports into the studs, only to find that one or more of them are upside down. The slots look the same no matter which end is at the top, so be careful.

HERE'S THE richness and warmth of real wood. Brackets have steel strips that key over wall screws.

SHAKER STYLE shelves, crafted in cherry, are ideal for books, collections, even house plants.

You don't have to buy prefinished boards in order to use these handsome standards and brackets. You can cut your own shelves of plywood and cover the edges with pine strips. Or if you want especially attractive and durable shelves you can apply a plastic laminate to particle-board shelves. The result will be the most attractive shelves you can build, and you have your choice of a tremendous number of patterns.

In fastening the standards to the wall, keep three things in mind:

First, the standards should be located so shelves will not protrude very far beyond the brackets. Three inches is a good measure of thumb. This assures that a heavy object on the end of a shelf will not tip up the opposite end. Naturally the location of the appropriate wall stud may affect how far the shelf extends beyond the end bracket.

Second, be sure that the screws provided with the standards do indeed penetrate into studs. Magnetic and electronic stud locators are available. Usually the simplest way to locate studs is to examine the baseboard. The nails that hold it in most cases are driven into studs.

Occasionally it is impossible to locate a support over a stud. In such a case use a suitable wall anchor.

Third, make certain the shelves are level. The first step is to attach one standard to the wall with the brackets at exactly the right heights. Then rest one end of a level atop the standard (or against the bottom), center the bubble in the glass, and then hold the level tight to the wall. Now press the second standard against the wall at the desired distance, and mark the position of the top screw hole. Bore a hole for the top screw and drive it in place, drawing the standard tight to the wall before marking other hole locations.

Now install the brackets. Don't forget to take the thickness of the shelves into consideration as you determine the spacing of the brackets. Once you have located the brackets in one standard, you can "count slots" to make sure all the other brackets are properly positioned.

tap brackets into place

As you install each bracket, tap it on the top, close to the standard, with a hammer to make certain that it is well seated in the slots. The design of the bracket does not allow you to see whether it is seated properly. A tap with the hammer assures that the bracket is securely locked in its designed position and will not slip out from normal home vibrations.

There's one trick you can use if you want particularly attractive shelves. This eliminates the gap all along the back of each shelf (the protruding standard prevents you from installing the shelf flush with the wall). If you want to solve this problem, and at the same time eliminate the protruding ends of the shelf brackets, buy brackets the next size smaller than your shelf boards.

After installing the hardware, place each shelf in position. Mark the rear edge of each shelf for notching for the standards; mark the bottom side for the projecting front tip of each bracket. Cut the notches and drill ⅜-in. holes for the bracket tips. Reinstall the shelves flush with the wall.

This kind of installation requires considerably more work, but it is neater, slightly stronger, and somewhat cheaper. The smaller size brackets are less expensive, and if you need a good many of them for your particular installation, you'll save a significant amount of money.

The standard system of wall shelving offers great versatility. You set up your own system of shelves just the way you want it. You are not locked into a specific shelf spacing or arrangement; indeed you can also have shelves of various widths by buying brackets of various sizes. Frequently homeowners will install a wider shelf at the bottom or the top to hold those highway atlases and photo albums that seem to fit nowhere else.

You can also change the arrangement anytime you wish simply by moving brackets to new positions. And for a thorough cleaning, you can lift the shelves right off the wall.

If you prefer the look and warmth of real, all-wood shelving, you have a couple of options. You can buy handsome, ready-made, prefinished shelving in one of several styles, or you can build your own shelves, perhaps copying an authentic period piece. Flair Fold produces solid wood shelves and brackets in five distinctive styles to harmonize with Tudor, Colonial, Early American, Provincial, Traditional and Contemporary interiors. Each bracket has a hardware strip attached, which keys over the heads of screws driven into wall studs. Installation is simple and easy. The same brackets can be attached to matching wood standards to visually unify several shelves. Bracket-supported mantel boards are also available with this system.

wall anchors

Whenever you hang book shelves on a wall you must be certain your screws have a solid hold. Books on even a short shelf have tremendous weight. Wall anchors help assure a solid grip on the wall.

The best anchor of all, of course, is a 2x4 stud inside the wall. If you can screw into a stud, whatever you hang will almost certainly stay in place. But in hanging book shelves it's not always possible to find studs exactly where you need them because the spacing is wrong. And of course a solid masonry wall presents still another and more difficult problem.

plastic sleeves

The simplest and most economical wall anchor is a plastic sleeve that has a slight taper to it. Sleeves vary in length from ¾-in. upward. You drill a slightly undersize hole in the plasterboard, tap a sleeve into it, then drive your screw into the sleeve. As the screw penetrates the sleeve it expands it, forcing it tight into the plasterboard.

With plastic sleeves you can use the matching wood screws furnished with your shelving standards, but any sheet-metal screw will work with this type of anchor. A similar anchor made of lead is designed for solid masonry walls.

Of course you must drill holes to use these plastic or lead anchors; the packaging usually tells you what size drill bit to use.

If you ever decide to relocate your shelves, you can lift out the anchors with a screwdriver blade. Plug the holes with patching plaster, sand lightly, and the wall will show no sign that it once supported a system of book shelves.

Plastic wall anchors should be used to hold only relatively light weights. If you plan an extensive system of book shelves, or want to display particularly heavy objects, use toggle bolts or expansion anchors usually called Molly bolts.

A toggle bolt is easily identified by the pair of spring-loaded wings threaded onto it. It is a heavy-duty anchor for hollow walls. Sizes range from 2 to 6 inches.

To install a toggle bolt, drill a hole through the plasterboard large enough to accommodate the toggle with its wings folded back. When you push the folded wings through the plasterboard, they spring open inside the wall. Then, as you tighten the bolt, the wings are drawn tight against the back side of the plasterboard to grip over a relatively large area.

Important: Be sure you install the bolt part of your toggle bolt through the shelf standard or bracket *before* you push the wings through the wall. Once the wings spring outward, you cannot remove the bolt without losing the wings inside the wall.

expansion bolts

An expansion bolt is another heavy-duty anchor for hollow walls. Instead of wings, it has a slotted metal sleeve around the bolt. When you insert the anchor in the hole in the wall and tighten the bolt, the slotted sleeve bends and spreads open like the legs of a spider to press against the back side of the plasterboard. Once the anchor is in position you can remove the bolt because the anchor is permanently in place. Then use the bolt to attach your bracket or standard.

Expansion bolts are sized to fit the thickness of the plasterboard, so it is important that you buy the proper size. They are available in *short,* for walls ⅛ to ⅝-in. thick; *long,* for ⅝ to 1¼-in.; and *extra long,* for 1-¼ to 1-¾-in. thick. The thicker walls, of course, are masonry walls.

Whatever your book-shelf system, take time to anchor it properly. It's likely to be there for a good many years.

THE SHELF unit shown above was built along an inside wall of a family room. At the corners, paneling edges are concealed by a matching metal molding that was nailed to the framing, as shown at the right. At the far right is pictured a built-in planter at the end of the bookcase wall, added to help relieve the "sawed-off" look of the extra-wide divider wall.

Build an inside-the-wall bookcase

By WAYNE C. LECKEY

Shelves built flush in the wall can turn a dull surface into a conversation piece, and they don't get in the way of furniture

■ WHEN FLUSH in the wall, bookshelves not only take on a built-in look but have a way of transforming an uninviting wall into a dramatic center of interest. More important, perhaps, they're not in the way to interfere with room furnishings.

Almost any wall will lend itself to built-in bookshelves, but an inside wall presents fewer problems.

The bookshelf wall you see in the photo at the left was built along an inside wall of our family room which separates the room from the foyer. Since it was a divider wall in a sense, I went farther and built a planter at the end, filled it with greens and spotlighted it from above. Whether you can borrow this idea depends on your wall.

Where the wall concerned is plastered, it isn't necessary to remove the lath and plaster. In my case, the wall was paneled to begin with and it was no problem to pull off the plywood. However, exposed studs do make it easier to get at any wiring and bring it out to the new wall.

You can make the niche any size you want, of course. I started out by nailing a 44¼ x 67¼-in. sheet of Masonite's "Travertine marble" hardboard horizontally (and level) to the studs 34 in. up from the plate and then blocking out the ends with 2x4s. Next I framed the panel all around the edge with 1x2s and nailed them at points where they crossed the studs.

SEE ALSO

**Bookends . . . Bookracks . . . Bookstands . . .
Built-ins . . . Family rooms . . . Fasteners . . .
Paneling, hardboard . . . Paneling, plywood . . .
Paneling, wood . . . Racks, book . . . Storage walls**

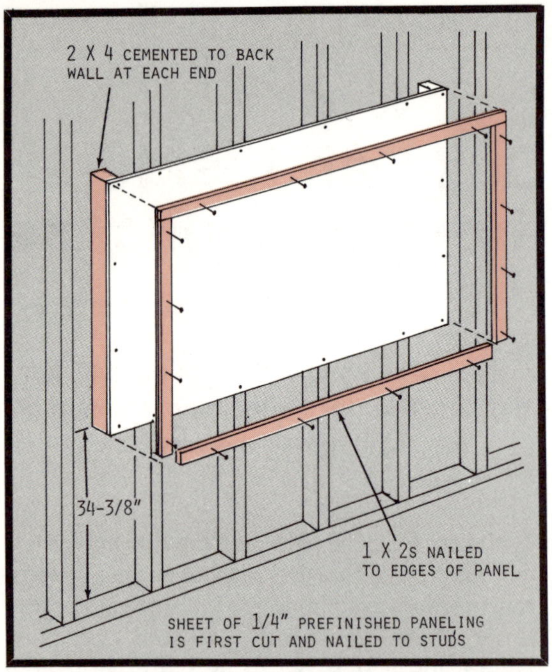

If wall size permits, make the recess equal the size of a 4x8-ft. panel and you won't have to cut it. Where the bookcase wall is to match a painted room, plasterboard would be used to line the recess and face the wall. Here, regular plaster bead would be used to frame the outer corners of the recess.

THE HEADER and plate of the bookcase's recess must be level and even with the back-wall 1x2s.

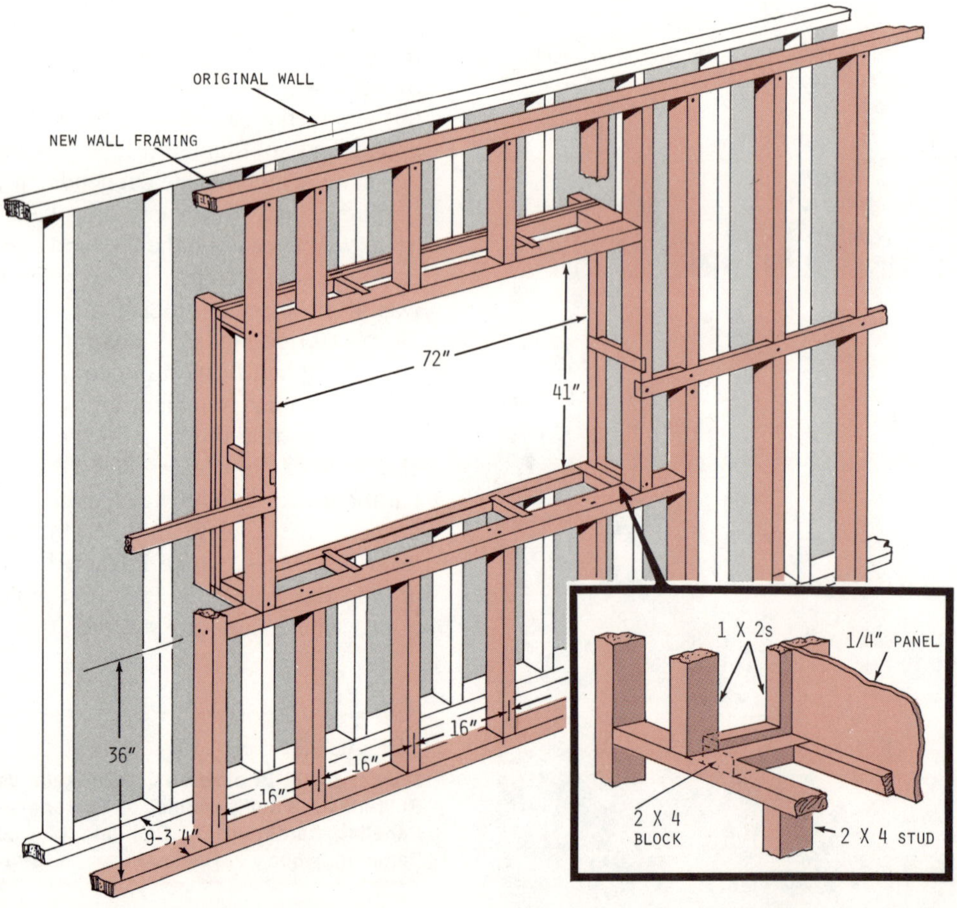

PLANTER FRAMING is a continuation of the new wall. Top is left open to receive 4-in.-deep sheet-metal pan.

STICKS ARE USED to hold top and bottom panels in place when cementing lining in the bookcase's recess.

This done, I started to frame the second wall. First you nail a 2x4 soleplate to the floor, locating it 9¾ in. out from the first wall. Next you nail another 2x4 plate to the ceiling. Here you will need to prop this against the ceiling with a couple of studs and then plumb it so it aligns with the bottom plate. If you're lucky to have the ceiling joists run at right angles to the wall, you can spike the top plate to them. If they run parallel and miss the top plate, you'll have to anchor it with toggle bolts.

The front opening of the niche is framed to coincide with the 1x2s at the back; whatever they measure from inside to inside, the opening at the front is made to measure the same. In my case it was 41x64 in. Your particular framing may vary somewhat from that shown in the drawing, but essentially it's framed as detailed.

STARTING PANEL is inserted in channels of molding. Work from left to right; leave ¼-in. space at floor.

A 2x4 header is placed across the top of the opening, a 2x4 plate across the bottom and short studs installed above and below.

Now short blocks are cut to fit between the back and front wall for support. These are 2x4s at the corners and 1x2s elsewhere. I dadoed the latter into the front wall, but you can simply butt them—it's not that critical. If you want to notch them, do it when cutting the framing members. Finally, 1x2 blocks are added to the four 2x4 blocks to create gluing surfaces.

I used Marlite's plastic-finished paneling in Italian cherry to line and face the wall. It's ¼-in. hardboard, comes in random plank 16 in. wide for easy handling, and has tongue-and-groove edges to assure perfect fitting joints. There are any number of prefinished plywood panels from which to pick. If you're going to paint the wall, you'll want to line and face it with plasterboard, then tape and fill the joints.

Assuming you are using the same or similar paneling as I did, the narrow pieces which line the niche are ripped 9⅝ in. wide to allow ⅛ in. for expansion. Cut and install the end pieces first, sawing them a trifle short. I used a panel adhesive to cement them in place. It's a sticky mastic that bonds in minutes once the panel is pressed in place.

Next, cut and cement the top and bottom pieces in place. Like the ends, they're butted against the back wall and cut to fit nice and snug against the end panels. Sticks wedged between them, at front and back, hold them in place while the cement sets. Any adhesive smears can be easily removed with a cloth dipped in regular rubber-cement thinner.

You're now ready to panel the wall. First you must cover the exposed edges of the lining with an aluminum outside-corner molding which you miter at the corners like a picture frame. It saws easily, comes in 8-ft. lengths and matches the color of the paneling. A flange permits the molding to be nailed in place so that the nails are later concealed by the paneling. Applying the paneling involves cutting the planks to fit and cementing them to the studs. Although I didn't use them, special metal clips are provided to self-space the joints, since they should not be forced tightly together. I watched this carefully in cementing panels, using the thickness of a dime to keep them properly spaced.

I used Masonite's new shelf brackets, which need no vertical standards. They're designed to hook in slots in their Royalcote Living-Wall paneling, but I simply cut identical slots in the marble-textured hardboard, using a tiny burr in a hand grinder and a template to space the slots evenly. You can arrange the shelves as you wish. I found that two 10x48-in. ready-made shelves, staggered as shown, provided ample room for books, plus tall bric-a-brac.

FLANGE OF MOLDING is first drilled every 4 in. for l-in. nails that are used to fasten it at the corners.

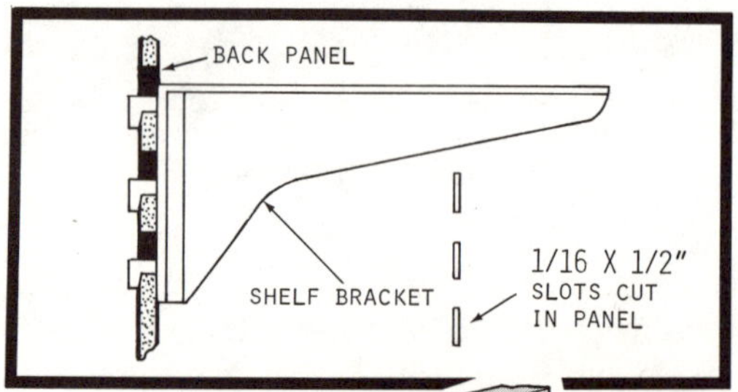

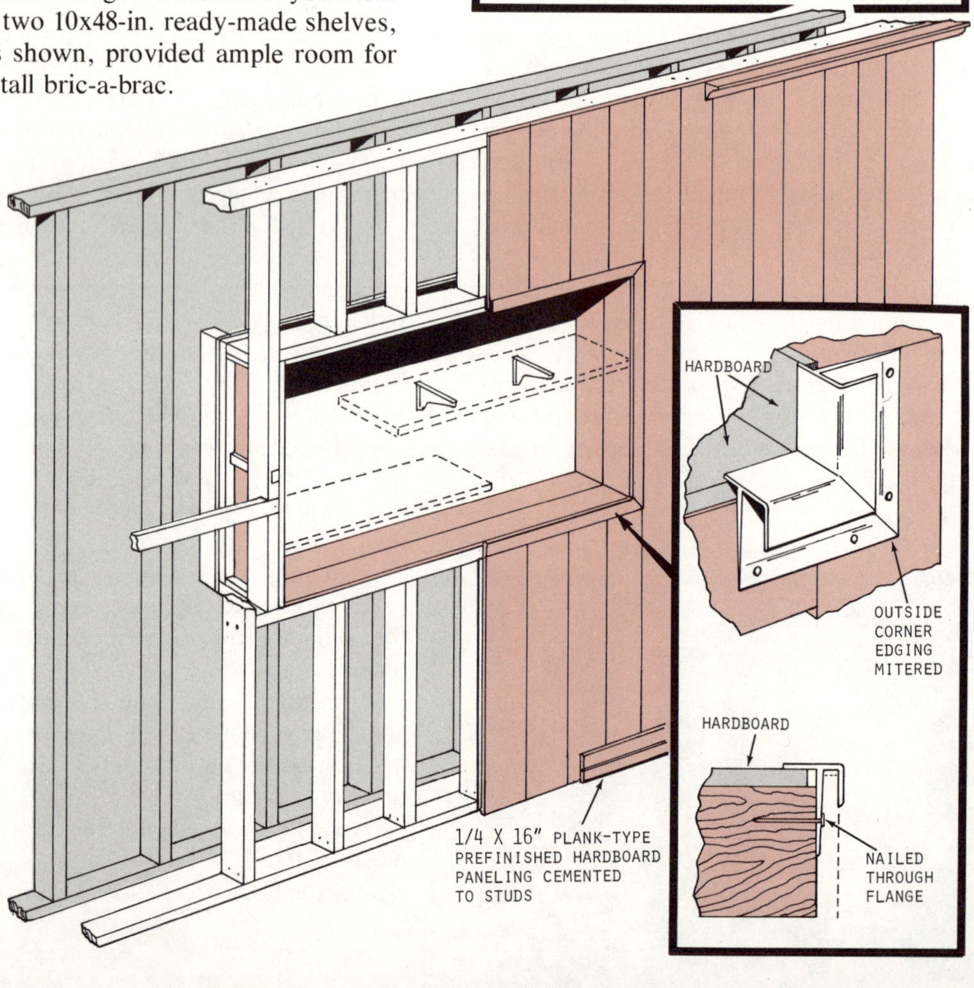

Walk-in bookcase closet

By JAMES PLAKE

BUILT IN A CORNER, the bookcase closet takes little space, yet provides shelves, hidden storage.

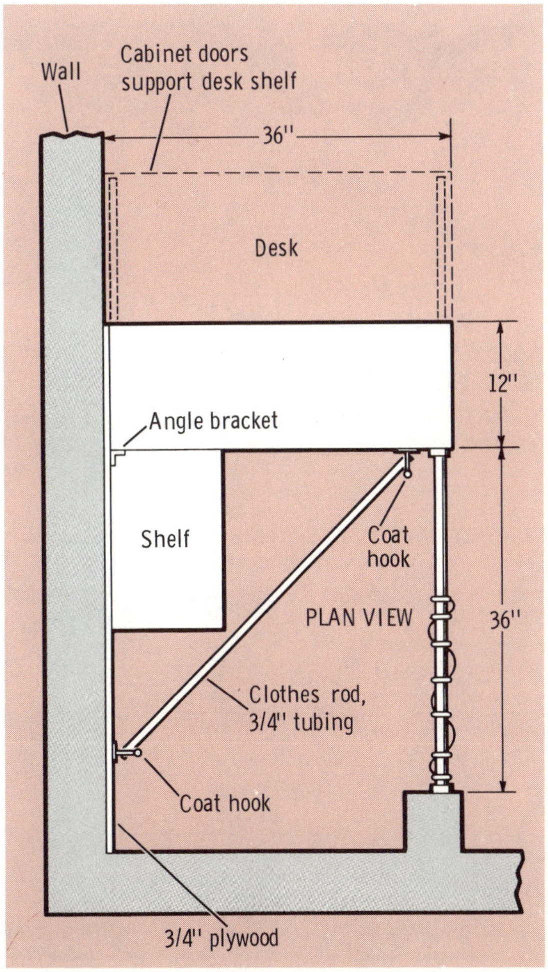

■ IF YOUR LIVING AREA seems to shrink before your eyes, it's no illusion—you've just become short of storage space. This is especially true if you're renting an apartment, since your rental contract likely prevents you from making any permanent changes.

A novel solution to such a storage shortage is this free-standing, combination walk-in bookcase closet which fits in a corner. Construction is easier than it looks, and although the unit takes up only 9 sq. ft. of floor space and is inexpensive to build, it can store quite a few items of clothing and many volumes from your library.

What's more, you can increase its portability by fitting small casters on the bottom. With these, you could move it from wall to wall or from room to room depending on your need.

SEE ALSO

Book shelves . . . Bookends . . . Bookracks . . . Bookstands . . . Cabinet furniture . . . Closets . . . Entryways . . . Modular furniture . . . Room dividers . . . Storage walls

Here is a clever gift idea for a friend or relative. With a minimum amount of equipment almost anyone can make these unique bookends

Personalized bookends

By ROSARIO CAPOTOSTO

1. MATERIALS AND TOOLS used: pictures, plywood, electric iron, scissors, kraft paper, mounting tissue.

■ PHOTOGRAPHIC bookends will add a novel touch to your bookshelves, particularly when they are cutouts of members of the family or friends. And they're ideal for Christmas gift-giving.

Though children make great subjects, grown-ups can get into the act, too. It is easy to photograph your subject posed in a holding or pushing position, and any background will do because it will be cut out. Pose the person against a wall or other vertical prop to represent the books. This helps to obtain a convincing, natural stance. Enlargements can be single or double weight, glossy or matte; it's not too important. Mounting can be on hardboard or ordinary fir plywood.

For permanence, use contact cement to mount the prints, but avoid lumps or bubbles in cement because they show through on the print surface. A better way to mount the pictures is with dry-mounting tissue.

Standard photo dry-mounting tissue doesn't work too well for mounting pictures on materials

2. SPOT-TACK TISSUE to back of the photo using point of the iron. This will keep pieces from shifting.

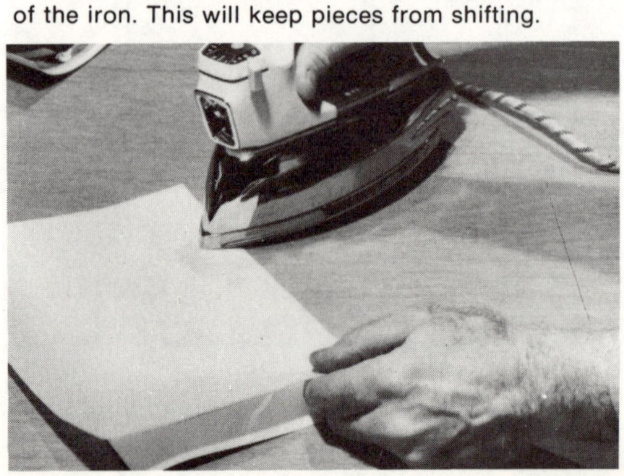

SEE ALSO

Bookcases . . . Bookracks . . . Bookstands . . . Close-up photos . . . Copy photography . . . Desk accessories . . . Frames, picture . . . Outdoor photography . . . Photography . . . Prints, photo . . . Racks, book

3. **USE LOW-HEAT IRON** and wrapping-paper buffer. Hold the paper and slowly pass iron over the "sandwich."

4. **MARK OFF** an outline for proposed base of the picture. The author found a ballpoint pen best here.

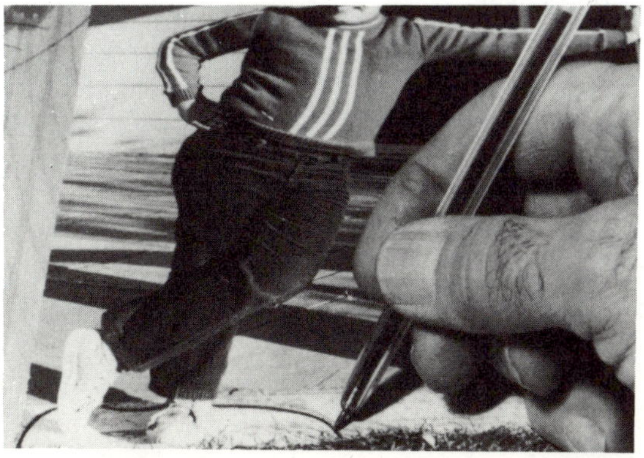

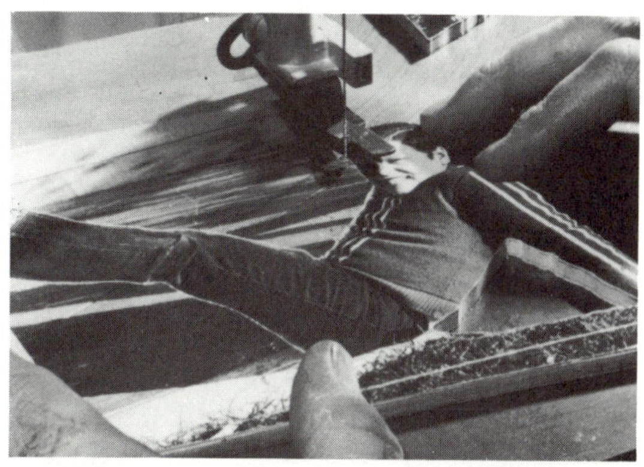

5. **SET JIGSAW** tilting table at a slight angle so the cutout edge bevels slightly to back (i.e., undercut).

6. **EXPOSED PORTION** of the groove for photo cutout is easily concealed by a glued-in wood spline.

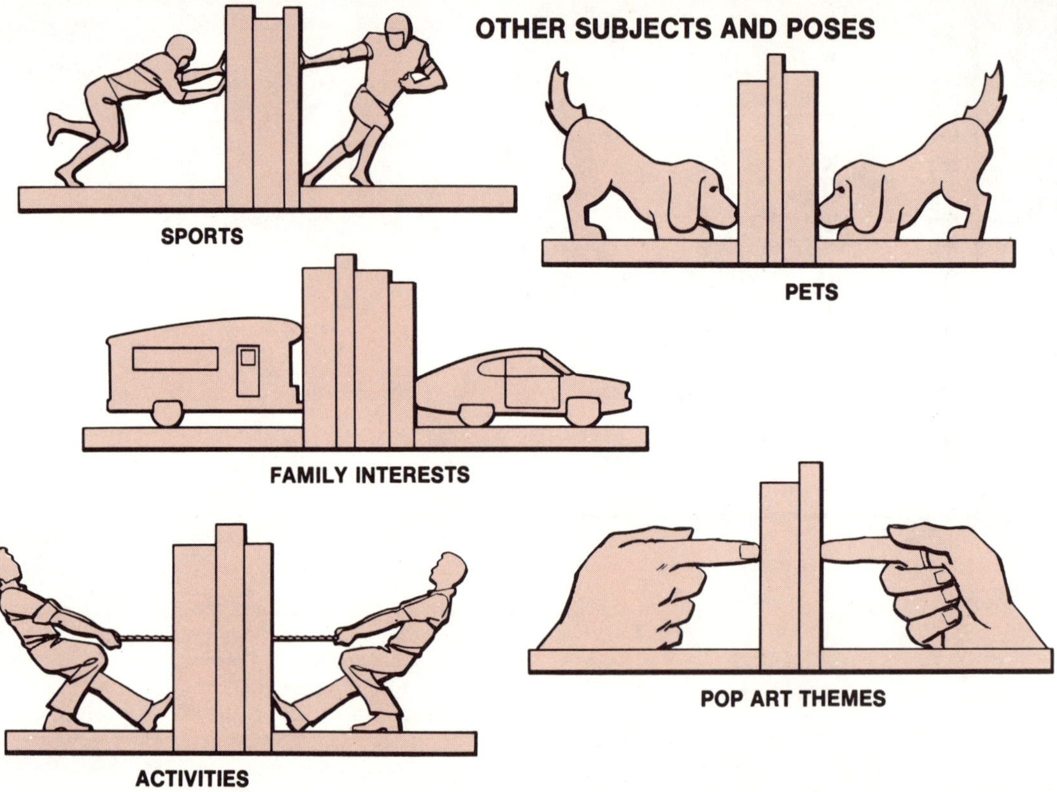

other than cardboard, but there is a special tissue which does. Called Fotoflat, it's made by Seal, Inc., Derby, Conn., and sold at photo and art supply houses. This low-temperature tissue adheres well to wood and requires no special equipment—only an ordinary electric iron.

Set the iron for 180° and pass it over the board and back of the print to preheat. Attach a tissue to the back of the print by spot-tacking it once or twice with the tip of the iron. Tacked spots should be no bigger than ½ in. If the tissue extends beyond the edge of the print, trim it flush. Place the tacked print on the board and cover it with a sheet of clean wrapping paper.

Now apply heat by making a few slow passes with the iron. A total heat time of 5 to 10 seconds for a given area should do. Since the tissue sets while cooling, place the mounting under a flat weight after heating.

If you don't own a power jigsaw, you can make the cutouts by hand with a coping saw. Either way, use a very fine-tooth blade. Before cutting, decide on a suitable design for ending the picture at the bottom and mark this outline on the picture with a ballpoint pen. Also, leave about ¼ in. below the usable part of the picture to serve as a mounting tab which sets into the wood base. (See details below.)

Size and shape of the base is optional but it must have a "tongue" long enough to reach under three or four books to hold properly. Thin galvanized (22-ga.) sheet metal with edges smoothed and felt cloth glued on the bottom serves nicely.

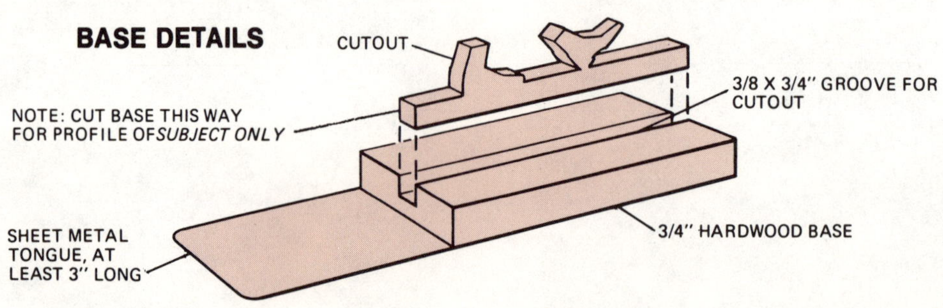

■ HERE'S A GIFT that is as personal as it can be—bookends of a friend's first and last initials. Letters C, O, U, J and V must be altered a bit to provide flat bottoms for attaching sheet-metal bases to the bookends. The project provides a good way to use up scrap wood and pieces of plastic laminate.

Formica's English Oak was used on the face of the letters shown here and the rest was painted. Cement the laminate to the wood and tape a paper pattern of the initial (enlarged from the drawing below) to the laminate before bandsawing.

Initial bookends

SANDING the bandsawed edges of the letters goes a lot faster with a band sander, of course, but it can be done by hand with the sandpaper wrapped around a dowel or block.

SEE ALSO
Bandsaws . . . Book shelves . . . Bookcases . . . Bookracks . . . Bookstands . . . Letter racks . . . Magazine holders . . . Sanding

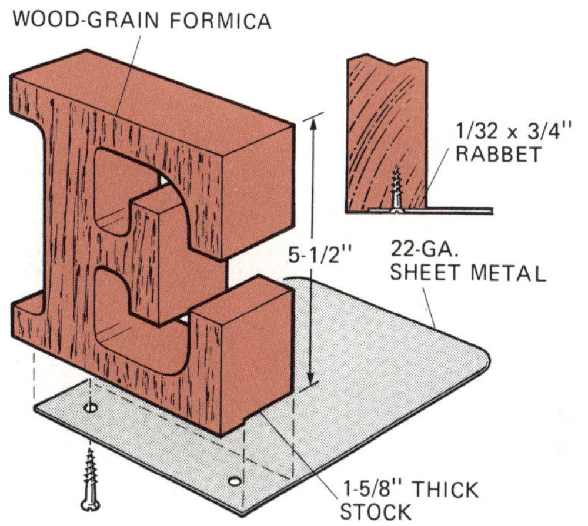

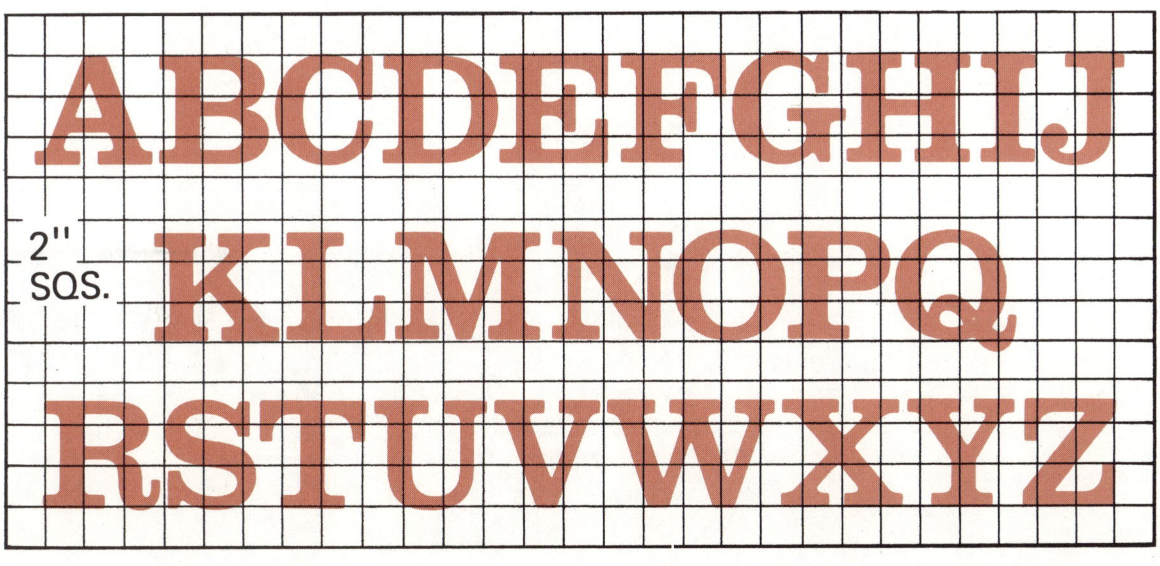

Colonial bookrack

Here's a weekend project to provide an attractive answer to the problem of where to put those extra books

By RICHARD SICKLER

■ A HANDSOME BUT SELDOM SEEN PIECE these days is the small bookrack that was set upon a chest or other piece of furniture. My version is a replica of those that were found in almost every American home a century or so ago.

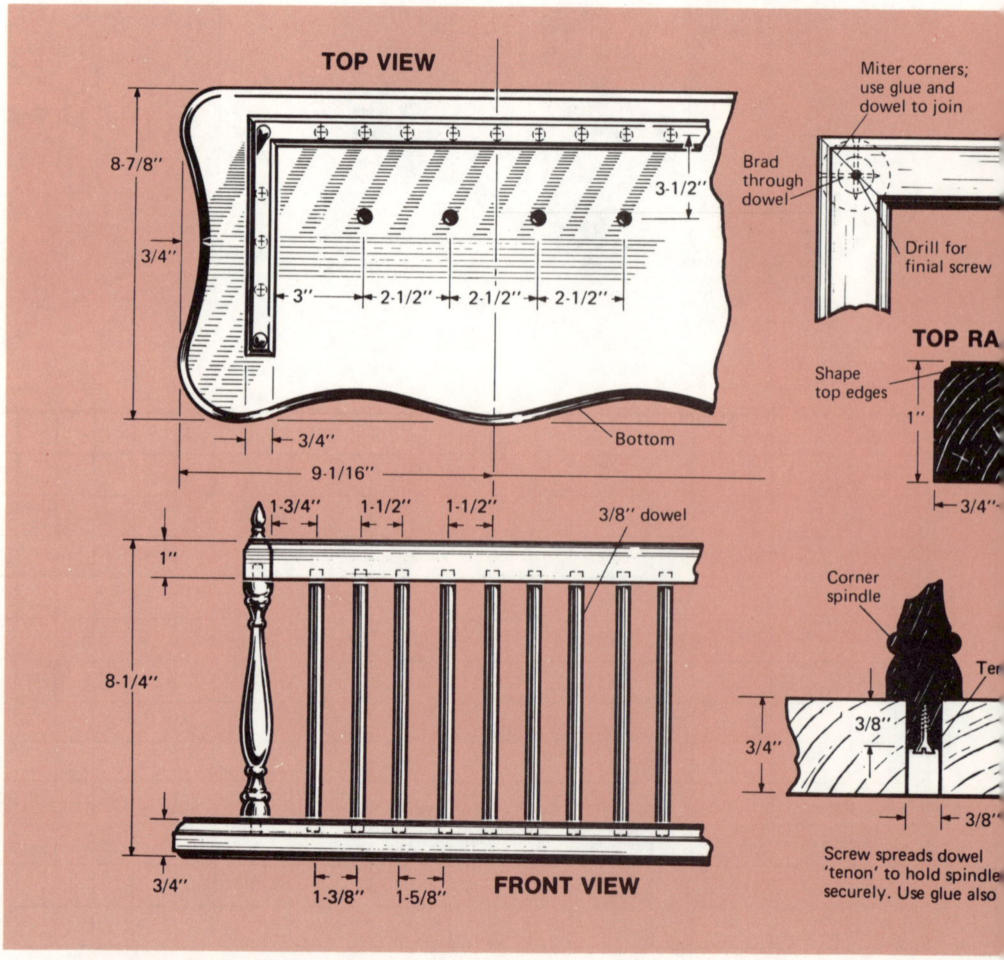

Except for the spindles and dowels, the entire piece can be made of pine. However, if you prefer, the rack can be cut from hardwood, such as walnut or cherry which have particularly attractive grain patterns.

Start by making a full-size pattern of the base and, after cutting and shaping, lay out the dowel and spindle locations. The dowels can be turned on your lathe, but if you prefer, the commercial hardwood dowels that are available at lumberyards will do the trick; if you use the latter you'll just have to spend a little more time staining to insure a good overall match.

Assembling the rack calls for a little planning. The nature of the project requires that a number of pieces be assembled simultaneously. First, assemble the top rails as one unit. Then saw kerfs in the lower ends of the dowels and assemble the dowels and corner spindles to the base and top rail. A small screw driven up into each kerfed dowel wedges them securely. A little glue will provide additional support and guarantee a sturdy bookrack.

SEE ALSO
Bookcases . . . Bookends . . . Bookstands . . .
Desk accessories . . . Desks . . .
Gifts, Christmas . . . Weekend projects

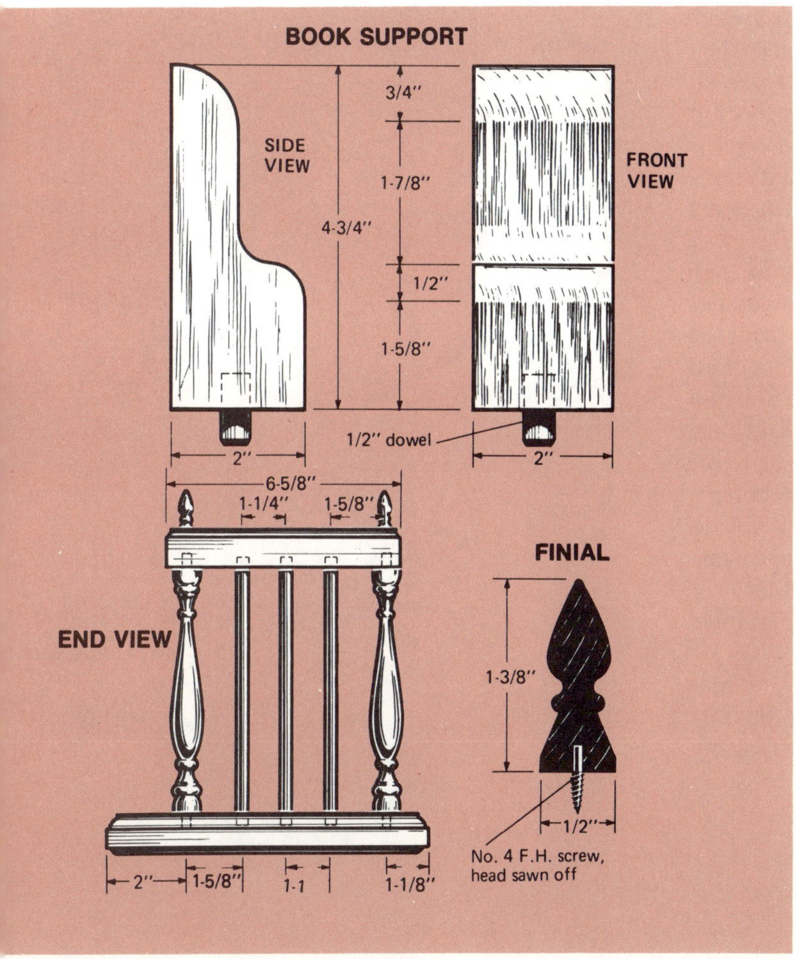

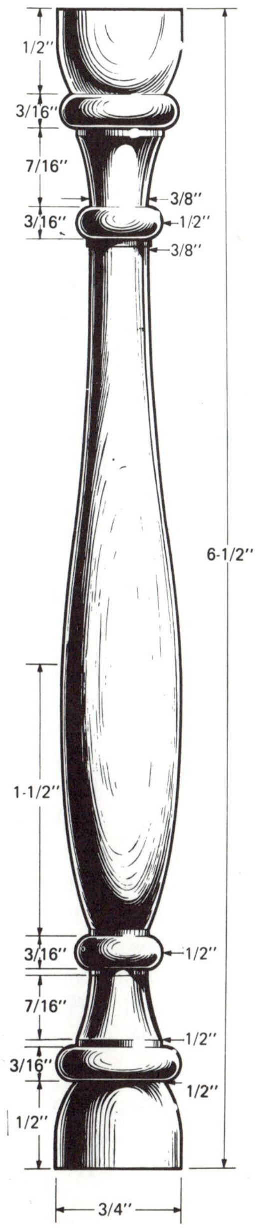

SPINDLE

Book-go-round for your desk

By ROSARIO CAPOTOSTO

HERE'S A DESK carousel for books that rotates with a flick of the finger for convenient access to any one of four compartments.

For good looks, cabinet-grade mahogany plywood is used. The unit is dimensioned so that all pieces can be cut from a standard ½-in. x 2-ft.-sq. sheet of plywood. (Use a scrap piece of plywood without a veneer for the 8-in-sq. base piece because it does not show; the leftover piece of mahogany-veneer plywood can then be saved for another project.)

First cut the two crosspieces with slots in each piece exactly as wide as the stock is thick so they will fit tightly without using glue. (Because ½-in. stock is specified, slots should be ½-in. wide, but sometimes the standard thickness dimension is not exact.) Cut four endpieces, mark and saw a curve on one corner of each as shown in drawing on the opposite page and sand.

Glue and nail one pair of endpieces to each crosspiece using two 1¼-in. finishing nails per joint. Set nailheads, fill with wood filler to match mahogany veneer and sand. Join notched crosspieces, turn upside down and glue and nail bottom piece in place. Drill 1-in-dia. hole in base piece, positioned as shown in drawing at right. Screw bearing to base piece and then to bottom piece by rotating base piece with 1-in-dia. hole to gain access to screw holes in upper plate of bearing as shown in photos at right. The 6-in. lazy Susan bearing used here is a product of Triangle Mfg. Co., Oshkosh, WI 54901.

Apply a clear finish on all surfaces. Edges should also be finished with paint or flexible wood tape that's stained to match the mahogany veneer.

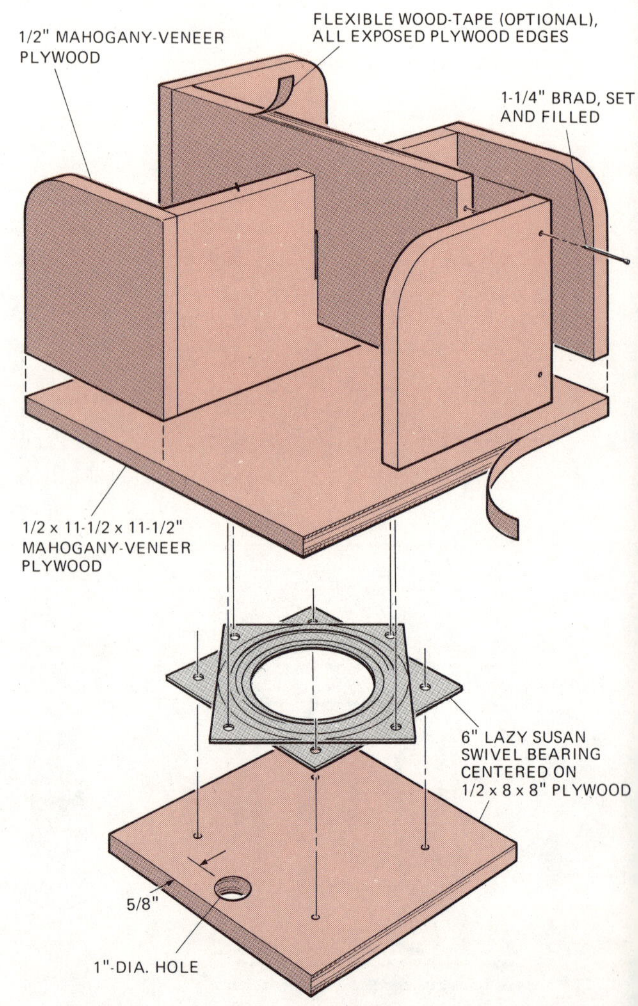

SEE ALSO

Bookcases . . . Bookends . . . Bookstands . . . Desk accessories . . . Lazy Susans . . . Racks, book . . . Storage ideas . . . Weekend projects

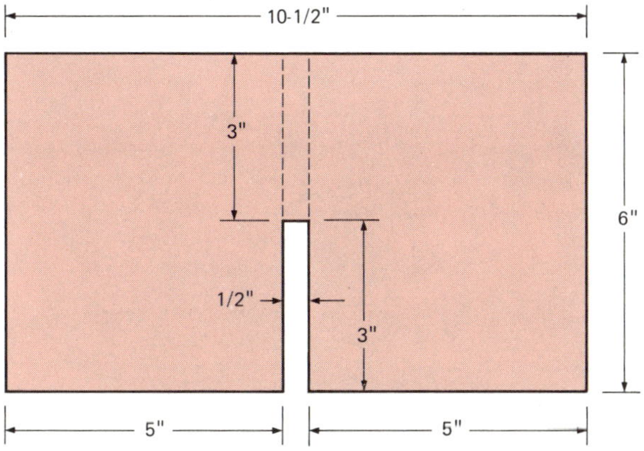

CROSSPIECE (2 reqd.)

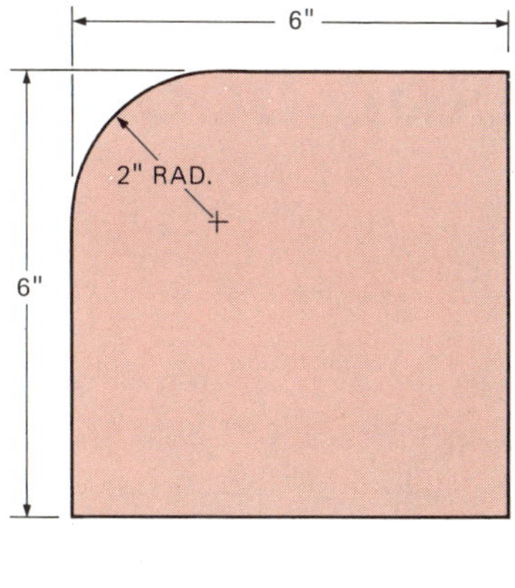

ENDPIECE (4 reqd.)

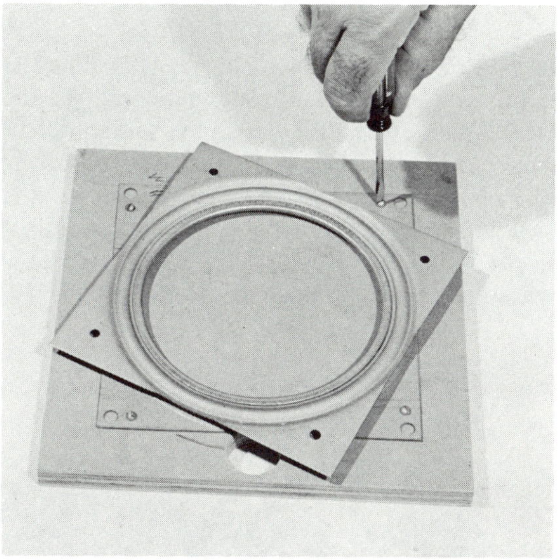

BOTTOM PLATE of 6-in.-sq. swivel bearing is centered and screwed to plywood base piece. Note access hole.

PIECES ARE TEST FIT, endpieces nailed to crosspieces, latter fitted together and the bottom attached.

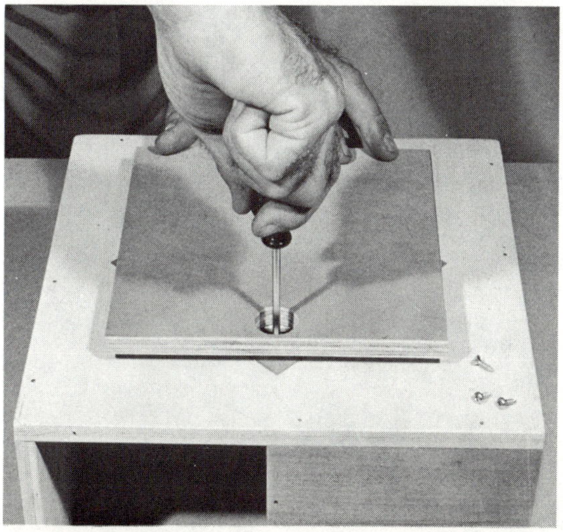

UPPER PLATE of bearing is attached to bottom piece of inverted bookrack through access hole in base.

MAHOGANY-VENEER plywood is treated with a clear finish, edges with paint or flexible wood tape.

Tabletop bookrack

By KENNETH WELLS

■ DESIGNED FOR PAPERBACKS, this smart-looking metal rack will hold 36 or more books. It's a bend-and-solder project and the photo below shows how the bending jig is used in a vise for making neat bends at each end of the brass-rod backrest. It's later attached to the ends of the steel base by peening the tenoned ends. Notice that the holes for the 3/16-in. rods in the end pieces are drilled clear through except for the middle ones.

The various parts are soldered by first applying flux to the feed holes provided, heating the metal with a torch and touching solder to the holes. Capillary action causes the solder to flow around the joint. The legs are bent after soldering by slipping a piece of pipe over the protruding rod, and then fitted with ball feet of wood or plastic. Paint the steel parts flat black, polish the brass and coat with clear lacquer.

SEE ALSO

Bookcases . . . Bookends . . . Bookstands . . . Metalworking . . . Racks, book . . . Storage ideas . . . Tubing, metal

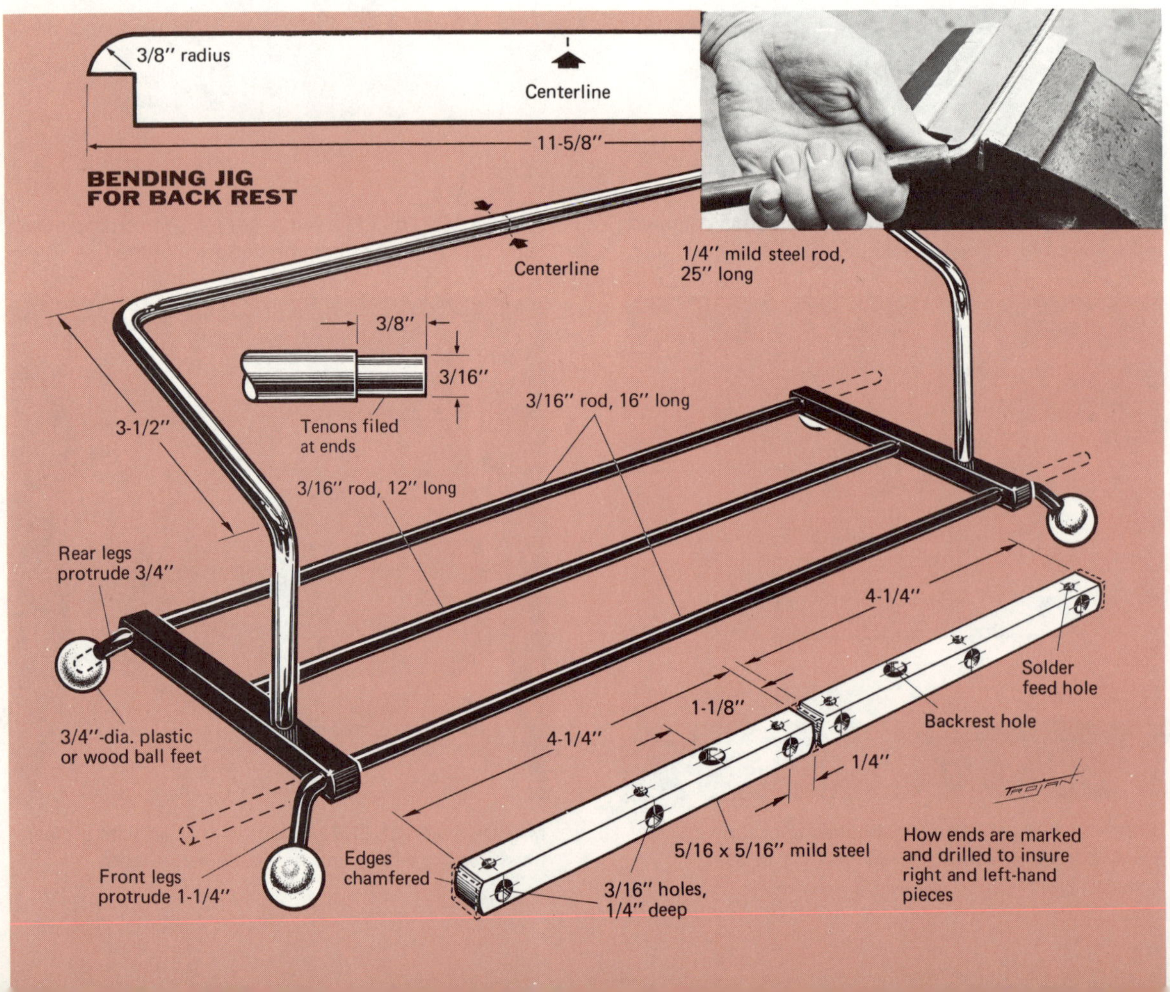

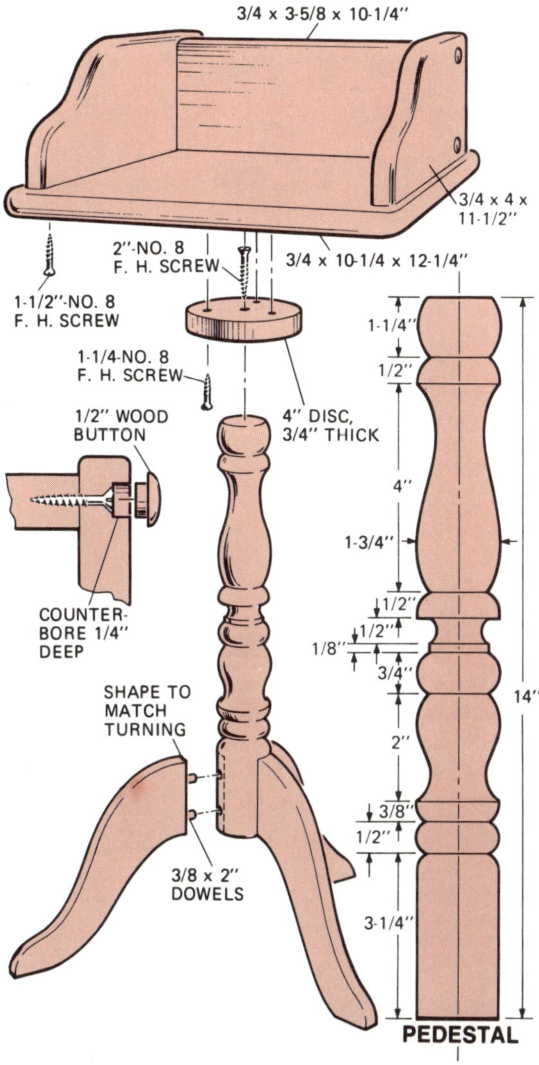

Colonial bookstand

By JOHN CAPOTOSTO

■ THIS QUAINT early American bookstand will cost less than $5 to make. If you own a lathe, you'll enjoy turning the centerpost; if not, you can buy it already turned.

To make it, cut the shaped shelf pieces and legs with a bandsaw, sabre saw or jigsaw, then round off the edges either by hand or with a router.

When drilling the dowel holes in the legs, be sure they are bored straight and true. Then shape the butting edges so they fit the post. This can be done by wrapping sandpaper around the post and using it as a form. Use dowel-locating centers to transfer the leg holes to the post. The center post is attached to the shelf by a 4-in. disc. Screws are used in counterbored holes to attach the sides of the shelf and the holes are capped with decorative wood buttons.

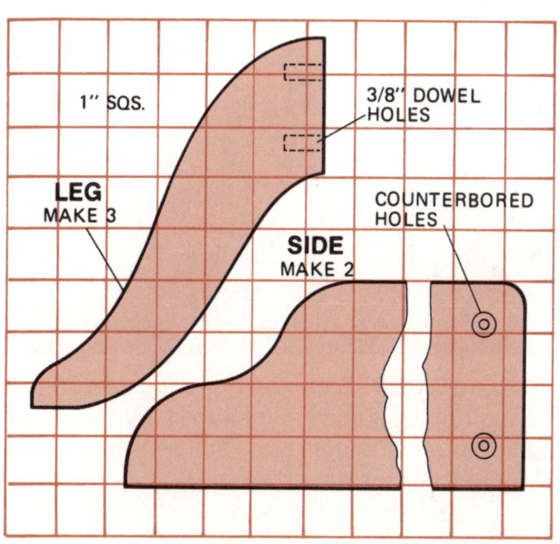

SEE ALSO

Bandsaws . . . Bookcases . . . Bookends . . . Bookracks . . . Desks . . . Finishes, wood . . . Gifts, Christmas . . . Joinery . . . Staining, wood

INEXPENSIVE PIPE CADDY can be fashioned from a coffee can that has a plastic lid. Cut square holes in the lid for pipe stems and decorate the can to suit your fancy.–*John N. Sisevich, Upper Lake, Ca.*

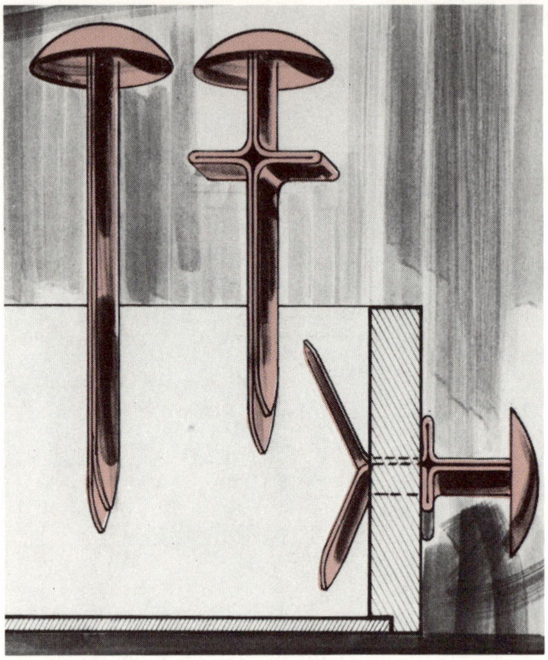

DRAWER PULLS for lightweight cardboard drawers can be created from standard 2-in. roundhead brass paper fasteners. Simply crimp them as shown, insert and bend the legs.–*A. J. Stephenson, Royal Oak, Mi.*

HANDSAWS can be stored on the inside of a closet door to protect the teeth. Drill a small hole near the ends, suspend from a brad and use pivoting strip to lock saws in.–*R. Hertzberg, N.Y.*

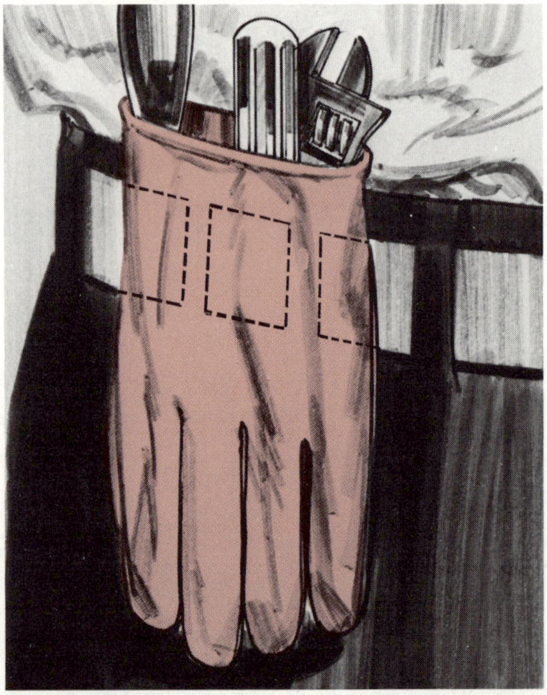

MATELESS GLOVE can be put back to work as a belt-toolholder if used as pictured. Make two slits for slipping the holder onto your belt, and use the holder to tote small hand tools.–*Frank Shore, N.Y.*

SELF-CLOSING GATE can be made—a la Williamsburg, Va.—with a ball and chain arrangement. Use a galvanized chain and, if a heavy ball isn't available, substitute a brick.–*Harry G. Remington, N.Y.*

CURTAIN RODS that are no longer needed for their intended purpose can still be put to work. Mounted inside a closet door, one will provide ample room to store belts and neckties.–*Frank Shore, N.Y.*

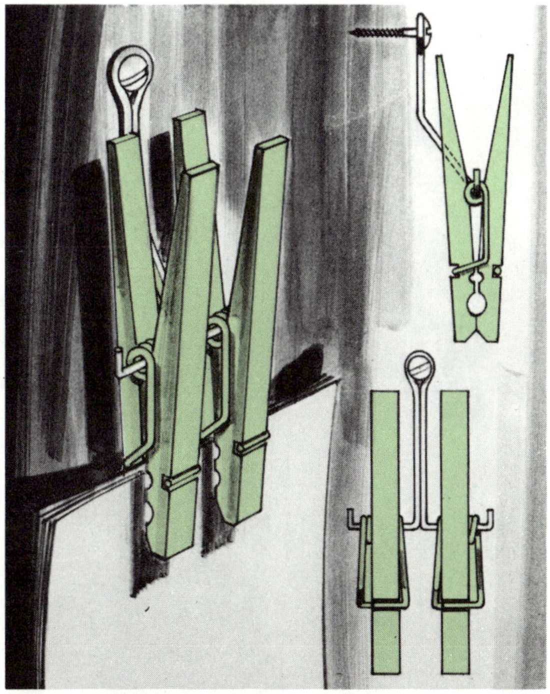

HANDY MEMO HOLDER can be rigged using a couple of spring-type clothespins and bent coathanger wire. The latter prevents pins from falling apart and provides loop for wall fastening.–*N. Murray, Ogdensburg, Wi.*

V-BELT can be stretched, if you need a bit more diameter, by using a bumper jack. Left stretched tightly in the hot sun for a couple of days, it will pick up about an inch.–*George Mayerchak, Minneapolis, Mn.*

From bottles to fancy glassware

There is no end to the things you can make from bottles with the new bottle and jug cutters

By WAYNE C. LECKEY

THERE IS SOMETHING UNIVERSAL in the appeal of an attractive, fancy bottle—its color, size and shape—and for years people have tried to make things from bottles. The big bugaboo was cutting them. Many makeshift and primitive methods were used, including the old trick of soaking a string in kerosene, tying it around the bottle, igniting the string and then plunging the bottle in water to fracture it at the string. There was no guarantee the method would work, and seldom did you wind up with a clean, even break.

new cutting equipment

The current bottle-cutting craze has changed all that. Now simple cutting equipment available in kits has taken all the guesswork out of cutting a bottle. It's so simple you can make a clean, even cut every time. Wine and beer bottles, even large glass jugs, which were normally thrown away, are being converted into all kinds of attractive and useful pieces of glassware such as you see displayed here. Tall wine bottles make graceful bud vases when the tops are cut off and cemented to shallow sections of the bottoms. A gallon jug cut near the top and then cemented to a base cut from a quart bottle becomes a pretty fruit bowl. The bottom part of the jug will serve as a candy dish when cut 2 in. deep. The lower half of a straight-sided liquor bottle makes a perfect hurricane lamp when fitted with a stubby candle. Ashtrays for the patio or porch can be made from the bottoms of bottles. The possibilities are practically endless.

Beer bottles make good practice bottles as they cut and polish easily. Wine bottles offer an interesting range of shapes, colors and sizes. The glass is of better quality than beer bottles and thicker. Burgundy, Bordeaux or champagne bottles, which have dimpled bottoms, make extra-attractive pieces.

Basically, there are two types of bottle-cutting kits on the market: One cuts the bottle vertically,

SEE ALSO

Candles . . . Christmas decorations . . . Gifts, Christmas . . . Internal carving . . . Jewelry . . . Lapidary . . . Marquetry . . . Stained glass . . . Wood sculpture

THE STYLECRAFT KIT includes a bottle cutter, candle, strips of coarse-grade and fine-grade silicone-carbide paper and a vial of carbide grits. The candle is used to heat the etch. The glass is then cracked with an ice cube. The paper and grit are used to grind and polish the cut edge.

the other, horizontally. The vertical cutter uses the top of the bottle as a guide to swing the glass cutter around the outside of the bottle. The horizontal cutter uses the bottom of the bottle as a guide, the glass cutter remains stationary and the scoring is done by rotating the bottle around the cutter.

Of the two methods, I found the horizontal one the easier. You don't have to go through a lot of adjusting and fussing to cut bottles of different diameters; you just cradle the bottle against a stop and turn it. Once the stop is set for height, you can't miss when making matched sets of glasses—all will be of uniform size. I also found there is less waste. If two sections don't break cleanly when you're using a horizontal cutter, you can continue to salvage the base of the bottle since you don't need the neck to recut it.

Ephren's Old Time Bottle Cutter Kit by Stylecraft (shown here) cuts the bottle in a horizontal position. It sells for about $10 at stationery stores or by mail from Stylecraft, 1800 Johnson St., Baltimore, Md. 21230.

• **Cutting.** The key to successful bottle cutting is the scoring. Only a *light etch should be made, and only one time around the bottle.* It is important that the adjustable cutting wheel always be at a right angle to the glass surface to assure a straight cut and a flat edge. It's also important to put a drop of oil on the cutter each time you cut a bottle.

To score a bottle, remove the label and place the bottle in the cradle on the rollers with the bottom against the backstop. Grip the bottle with both hands as shown and with a constant, even pressure, turn the bottle toward you without stopping. A jerky motion will cause the cutter to skip and make an uneven etch. A slight crunching sound will signal one time around the bottle and when you hear it, stop. Avoid retracing the original score as this will chip the glass and damage the cutter. To assure perfect alignment of the

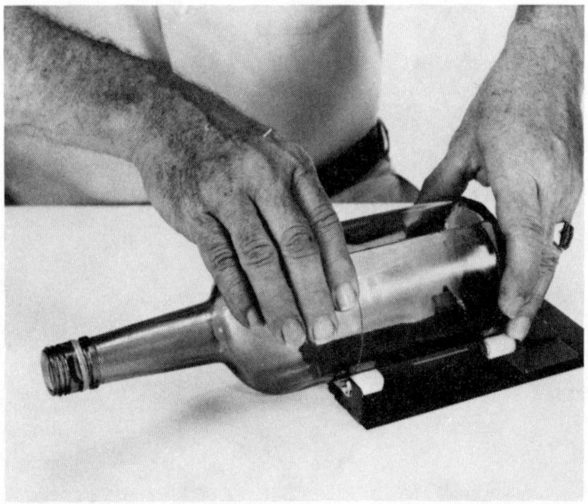

1. THE BOTTLE is cut by placing it on the cutter rollers and rotating it one turn to etch the glass lightly.

2. THE ETCHED LINE is heated by holding the bottle over the candle flame and rotating it two or three times.

3. THE GLASS is cracked neatly along the etched line by chilling the heated glass with an ice cube.

4. THE EDGE is polished by dipping it in water and rubbing on a flat surface sprinkled with carbide grit.

etch from beginning to end, it is important to keep the bottom of the bottle in contact with the backstop as you turn it.

• **Heating.** To separate the bottle at the etched line you first heat the line with a candle. Hold the bottle horizontally over the candle about ¼ in. away from the tip of the flame, and slowly rotate it three or four times in one direction. Then turn it three or four more times at a faster pace. The glass should feel hot to the touch, but not too hot to handle.

• **Cooling.** Now place the bottle in an upright position and, before the bottle cools, rub an ice cube around the etched line several times until the etch becomes a crack. If the etched line has been properly heated, a crack will start to form the instant the ice touches the glass and will

THESE ARE TYPICAL wine, beer and liquor bottles you can turn into handsome and useful pieces of glassware.

continue around the bottle as it is chilled by the ice, resulting in a comparatively smooth fracture. The smoothness of the edge is very important because the grinding of the edge is the hardest part of bottle-cutting.

If the two sections fail to part with a slight tug, don't force them; reheat the etch and try again. Sometimes it's necessary to repeat the heating and cooling steps several times depending on the thickness of the glass.

• **Polishing.** The final step is polishing the cut edge. This is done by first rubbing the inside and outside edges lightly with the coarse carborundum paper. Then carbide grit is sprinkled on a flat, hard surface such as a piece of window glass. The cut bottle is dipped in water and placed on the polishing surface. Start to grind in a circular motion. After a short time (10 to 15 minutes, depending on the thickness of the glass) the edge will become perfectly flat and take on a "frosted" appearance. While you're grinding, keep the rim of the glass wet at all times—the water will make the grinding action more effective. Sprinkle the carbide grit in a circle rather than concentrate it in one spot. Now you are ready to round the sharp edges with the fine-grit paper, dipping it in water as you rub.

• **Cementing.** Epoxy adhesive (I used Scotch Epoxy Adhesive, 3M Co.) is used to cement the top of one bottle to the bottom of another. Mix a small amount of the two-part cement and apply it sparingly. Support the work in an upright position and set aside overnight for the cement to harden. Finally, polish your finished piece with glass wax.

By VIRGINIA DEMOSS

Try bottling houses!

An art teacher and ship-in-a-bottle modeler turns his talents to building houses under glass. Here's how to try this surprising hobby yourself

■ MANY OF US HAVE a dream house we planned in detail. For nine years, Ron Rousch, an art teacher of San Pedro, CA, has been perfecting a system for building those dream houses in glass bottles—be they castle or cabin, mansion or Swiss chalet.

Rousch shares his building techniques here to help you become an architect in miniature:

■ Keep your first project simple. It takes practice to work in a confined space with minute material.

■ Avoid tinted bottles or those with surfaces that distort your view and cause eyestrain.

■ Plan the house before you begin so you won't run out of space at the top. A rough sketch with dimensions will help.

■ Prebuilding outside the bottle won't work. Unevenness of the bottle bottom causes a house made outside to be crooked when it is reassembled inside.

Among major tools you'll use are varying lengths of aluminum clothesline wire—some equipped with hat pins to lower wood into place and others bent into hooks for prying and lifting. Also needed are model-making knives, tweezers, small files, razor saw, clamps, sandpaper and fine paintbrushes.

Rousch uses a power saw to cut wood to workable size and a small hand saw to cut it exactly. Simulated lathe work is really small doweling rounded with a grinder and carved with a modeler's knife.

materials required

A bottle is the first necessity. It may be anything from a plain juice jar to a hand-blown decorator-type container.

Several types of wood comprise the house. Ice cream sticks are perfect for subflooring and roofing. Walnut or fir makes window frames, doors, joists and paneling. Shingles are of veneer. An open-grain wood like oak is used to fashion bricks. Balsa isn't used—it can't support material above.

SEE ALSO
**Airplane models . . . Carving, wood . . .
Hobby centers . . . Internal carving . . . Jewelry . . .
Lapidary . . . Marquetry . . . Modelmaking . . .
Ship models . . . Shops, modelmaking . . .
Tin-can crafts**

You'll need modeling clay for the base, plus rocks and pebbles for landscaping or embedding in a modeling-clay fireplace. Other materials are: plastic, glass, screening, cardboard and Styrofoam.

Epoxy glue cements the house foundation to the bottle. White glue is strong enough for construction. Other materials include wood stain and quick-drying tempera.

First, secure four ½-in. corner cubes inside the bottle to the bottom with epoxy. Then place crosspieces—ice cream sticks work well—to form a square. When glue holding the blocks has dried, press modeling clay around the foundation to the desired level. Lower landscaping rocks and pebbles on masking tape; press them in the clay.

A subflooring of ice cream sticks or other thin strips comes next, followed by the first-floor uprights. Rousch cuts one to approximate length from a master, lowers it into place with a needled wire, measures, pulls it out and cuts it to the exact length, measures again and modifies, if needed. Then he glues the piece, lowers it and twists the board free.

Once all first-floor uprights are placed, he adds horizontal pieces for window and door frames. Plastic or acrylic windows and prepainted siding finish the first floor.

Unlike building a real house, Rousch finishes one floor before he moves on to the next. Each additional floor is built just like the first one.

When he reaches the top, Rousch glues rafters in place and covers them with a subroofing of flat sticks. Then he cuts tiny rectangular veneer shingles, whittles them at one end to form a wedge shape so they rest in place and glues them to the roof.

Decorative touches will depend on the style of house. Once you've mastered the structural basics, there's no limit to what you can build.

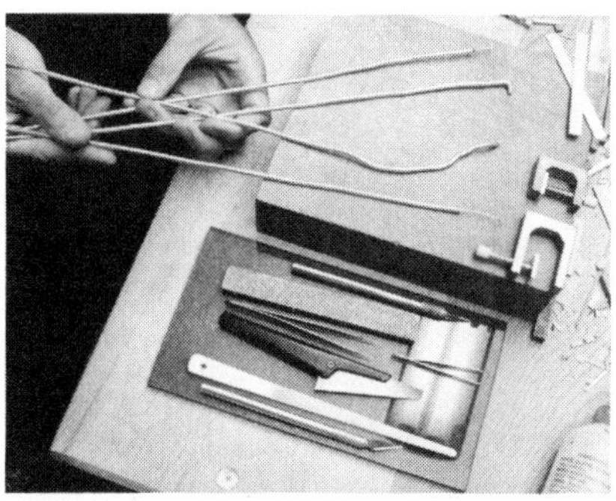

TOOLS THE ARTIST uses: Aluminum wire, model knives, file, tweezers, clamps, saw and sandpaper. Below, Rousch lowers wood into place.

SUBFLOORING and first floor uprights are in place and fireplace is complete (above). Same construction steps are used (below) on second floor.

RUSTIC HOUSES and cabins are Rousch's favorite subjects. These wood veneer shingles are individually carved.

Wine rack has a handy tray

■ FEATURING a lift-off tray, this wine rack makes serving wine extra convenient.

Use a fly cutter to cut the bottle notches. Break the hole edges with a corner-rounding router bit, sand with a 3-in. drum, then rip the boards.

First, preassemble two rail units (upper and lower) using glue and finishing nails to form two rectangles. Then attach them to the front posts with glue and one diagonally driven screw. Next, drill screw pilot holes through the backs of the three front rails, and glue and screw. Finally, glue on rear posts and attach the rails to the legs with screws driven from the backs.

By ROSARIO CAPOTOSTO

SET FLY CUTTER for 3½-in. hole. Clamp work to a scrap board and drill-press table (above). After cutting holes, rip the board to produce half-round notches (below). Or holes can be cut with sabre saw.

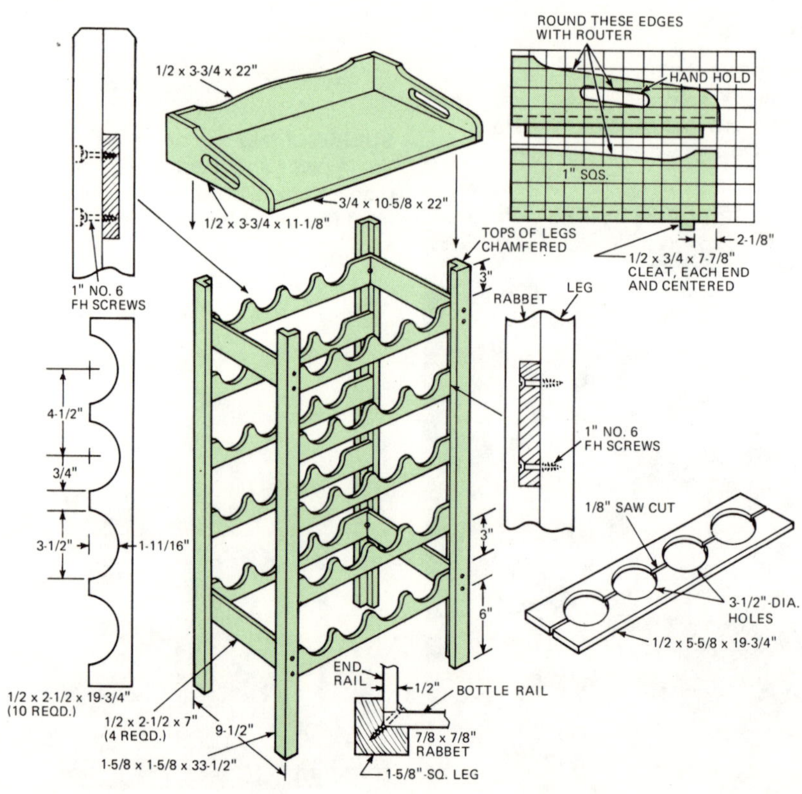

SEE ALSO

Bars . . . Butler's tables . . .
Laminating wood . . .
Patios . . . Plexiglass projects . . .
Veneering . . . Wine racks

Bounce light—the flash that flatters

It's always been good, and new automated bounce units make it easy. By bouncing light off the ceiling you can obtain a soft, sweet portrait rather than the mug-shot that usually comes from a dead-ahead flash

By DAVE SAGARIN

IT'S A FAR CRY from the soft, glowing quality of portraits made under an overcast sky to the harsh, pasty, wanted-poster quality of shots taken with a flashgun on your camera. It's always been possible—though difficult—to match portrait

SEE ALSO

**Camera accessories . . . Camera bags . . .
Camera care . . . Cameras . . . Close-up photos . . .
Copy photography . . . Darkrooms . . .
Lightboxes . . . Mountings, photo . . .
Photography . . . Slides, photo . . . Theaters, home**

quality by bouncing the flash's light off a ceiling or wall to diffuse it and to change its angle. Now a bunch of new, moderately priced electronic flash units are making it easy.

Lighting effects depend on the size of the light source, its angle to the subject and the amount of other light available to fill in shadows. The larger the source is in relation to the subject, the softer and more rounded the quality of lighting will be. That's why the sun—far enough away to be a pinpoint source of light—casts sharp shadows on a clear day, but soft ones when its light is diffused by a cloud layer—shadows cast by light from any point in the sky are filled and gentled by light from many other points.

The angle from which the light hits the subject makes a difference, too: Since we're used to light from above, a face lit from below looks unsettling and unnatural—that's why monsters in horror films are lighted that way. But on a subtler, more practical level, overhead light deepens eye sockets and cheek hollows; side light thins a face; front light broadens it.

differences are surprising

The pictures on page 425 show the difference light-angle and size make. In the bounce-flash shot at top, note how the broad spot of light the flash cast on the ceiling gives a softly modeled effect, while the light's direction gives more highlights to the hair, darkens the collar (making the face stand out more) and shadows the eyes. In the direct-flash shot, the light quality is harsh—note the edge shadow behind our model on the wall, the highlight on her pendant and the sharp modeling of her skin. Because the flash is right on the camera, we get the further disadvantages of hot-spot light reflections in our model's eyes, and the loss of such small, detail-enhancing shadows as those that separate her pendant from her sweater in the upper shot.

For shooting people—the subjects of most indoor flash shots—bounce flash usually gives more pleasant results, and professionals have used it for years. What's stopped amateurs has been the difficulty of getting correct exposure with bounce. It's not really that difficult if you know a few tricks and practice what you learn.

doing it the hard way

Before the advent of automatic-exposure flashguns, getting the right exposure for a straight bounce shot meant figuring the flash-to-subject distance (easy enough if your flash was on a rangefinder or reflex camera), dividing that distance into a guide number, then setting your lens to whatever f-stop that gave you (with a guide number of 110, for instance, a distance of 20 feet meant f/5.6).

For the bounce flash, though, you had to take into account the total distance from flash to ceiling to subject, figure the f-stop from the guide number, then open the lens a little more than that to compensate for light absorbed by the ceiling. Calculating the distance and how much to compensate for dark ceilings took experience and judgment.

Even the early auto-flashes didn't help with bounce. Point them at your subject and their electric eyes would measure the light bouncing back, cutting off the flash as soon as you had enough exposure. But point them at the ceiling and they measured how much light bounced back from there—not how much bounced onto your subject.

easy, automated bounce

But some of the units, like the Vivitar 283, Toshiba BS-7, and the Honeywell Auto-Strobonar 480-S, let you aim the light up or to one side while the electric eye cell still points straight ahead to measure the illumination of your subject. You tell these units the ASA rating of the film you're using, and about how far you think you'll be from your subject. Their calculator dials (which you can also use for non-automatic flash exposure) then tell you what f-stop to set, and whether you're likely to get enough light. When you flash, a green light signals if the subject got enough exposure.

Since we usually bounce flash off ceilings, all three flashes are designed to bounce light upward: The Toshiba's and Vivitar's flashheads tilt up, while a plastic dome snaps onto the Honeywell to direct some light upward while aiming some diffused light forward to fill shadows in eye sockets and elsewhere. You can also swivel the Toshiba sideways to bounce off a wall or for ceiling bounce shots when you hold your camera on its side. You can do that with Vivitar, too, by using accessories. What makes the Vivitar 283 unique is not so much the capabilities built into it but those you can add on. Included in the Vivitar system are a recharger, high voltage battery pack, filters, a clip-on card attachment for outdoor bounce, light-sensing cell and wide-angle and telephoto adapters.

points to remember

With any of these flash units, bounce flash is as

easy as straight, head-on flash. Just check the green light to be sure you're getting enough light to the subject, and don't bounce off colored ceilings or walls—they'll tint the picture as though you'd used a filter on your lens. If you find your eye-socket shadows get too deep, bounce light to fill them with a white card held below your subject (out of the lens's field of view, of course). Experiment with various combinations of direct, bounce and fill light and keep track of what you do in each shot—differences will be subtle, not startling.

SPIRATONE Spiralite Sr. BB (above), though not automatic, offers direct flash, bare-bulb flash or ring-light attachment for close-ups.

VIVITAR 283 tilts up to bounce flash off ceiling; when there's no ceiling, you snap on this adapter—card is replaced when it gets dirty.

SMALL light-source casts sharp, strong shadows (top). Broad light-source casts smaller, softer shadows and gives a more rounded look to subject.

TWO WAYS to bounce: Toshiba (below, left) tilts up to bounce off ceiling or swivels to bounce off nearby walls. Honeywell (below, right) converts to bounce when you snap on a strobodome, which diffuses forward flash and re-directs undiffused light toward ceiling. Domes of different intensity are available.

Easy-build box for chain-saw accessories

■ A CASE for your chain saw and accessories saves you the time normally spent gathering screwdrivers, wrenches and oil, and makes it less likely you'll forget to bring an item along.

Cut all pieces to size. Draw a line 3½ in. from the top of all pieces B and C. (The box will be separated into lid and case at this line after assembly.) Assemble pieces A, B and C with white glue and 1½-in. ringed (annular) nails. Start with pieces A and B to form an open-ended rectangular box. Then add endpieces, making sure marked line runs unbroken around box and no nails are within 1 in. of this separating line. Clamp and let dry for 24 hours.

Saw off box top along line to separate top and case. Place chain saw in case and mark along sides B for installation of divider later (make marks 1 in. from body of saw for clearance).

To make the tool rack, use a drill to bore holes for files, and a sabre saw and chisel to fashion the rectangular plier spaces. Draw around base of oil and lube cans on accessory rack (E). Cut out patterns with a sabre saw. Nail piece E to D.

Nail divider, then accessory rack with support to inside of box. Secure tool rack (G) with roundhead machine screws (K). Attach handles to endpieces (C), hinges to back of lid and base, and lid catch to front center. Prime and paint if desired.

SEE ALSO
Chain saws . . . Firewood . . . Log cutting . . . Miter joints . . . Power-tool maintenance . . . Trees . . . Workshops

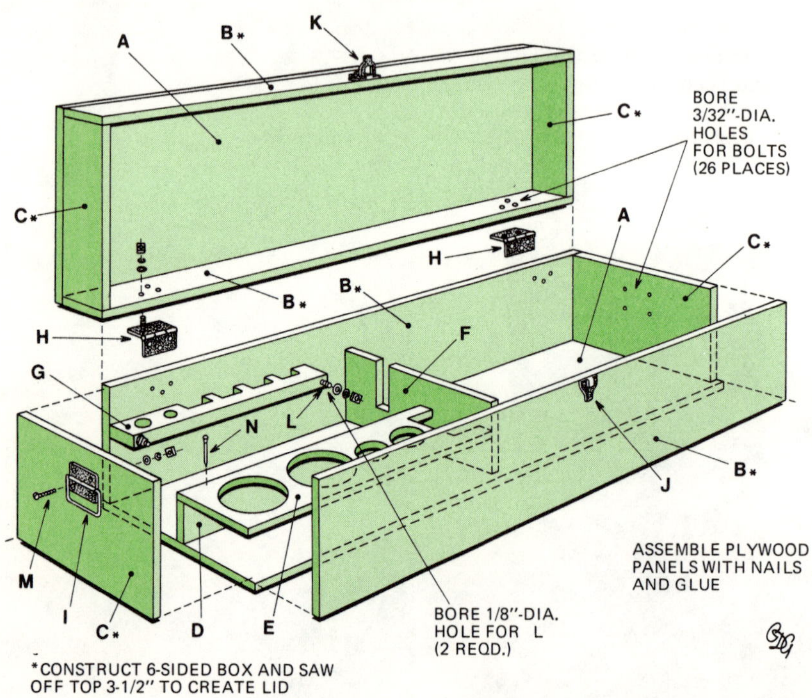

MATERIALS LIST—CHAIN-SAW BOX

Key	No.	Size and description (use)
A	2	½ × 12 × 39" plywood (top and bottom pieces)
B*	2	½ × 12 × 39" plywood (front and back pieces)
C*	2	½ × 11 × 12" plywood (sidepieces)
D	1	½ × 3 × 19" plywood (accessory-rack support)
E	1	½ × 6 × 19" plywood (accessory rack)
F	1	½ × 6 × 11" plywood (divider)
G	1	¾ × 1½ × 16" pine (tool rack)
H	2	3" cabinet hinges, Stanley No. 284
I	2	3½" chest handles
J	1	Lid catch (bottom) and screws
K	1	Lid catch (top) and screws
L	2	No. 4 × 2¼" rh machine screws, washers and nuts
M	20	⅛ × 1" bolts and nuts, or to suit

Misc.: White glue, 4d ringed nails as required.
*Overall dimension prior to cutting off lid.

Squaring steel posts

In my basement there are two steel posts supporting an I-beam. I know how to box in the beam but how do I provide the nailers necessary to enclose the round posts?—L.G., Mont.

You don't give the diameter of the posts but I assume it is 4 in., a common size. One way is to make semicircular, 2-in.-radius cuts at the centers of two short lengths of 2x6 stock. Then drill the two pieces edgewise so clamping bolts can be used (holes for the bolts should just clear the semicircular cuts). Counterbore these holes in both pieces so that the heads and nuts of the bolts will seat below the surface. Then clamp the nailers in place on the post and measure the overall width. Cut the 2x6s to length equal to the width. This will give you a nailer for a square wood box, or post.

Although two nailers per post might do, three would be better with one each near the top, the bottom and the center. After fitting the nailers it's a good idea to secure them with epoxy.

Mix a batch as directed and spread it on the semicircular surfaces and immediately clamp the nailers permanently in place. If the posts are painted, scrape away the paint before applying the epoxy. Be sure, of course, that the nailers are in line.

Improvised 'mud room'

We don't have a mud room in our house and our family of six has a problem with tracked-in dirt, snow and even wet mud. Continuous mopping keeps the floor near the doors fairly clean but mats of any kind are hopelessly soiled and dirty nearly all the time, and cleaning them would be a daily project. Isn't there some other effective way short of me enduring housemaid's knee?—M.L., Pa.

There is, if you can endure mats made from newspapers. These are relatively cheap and when they're wet and soiled you merely toss 'em in the garbage can. Open several newspaper sheets full out, stack them neatly to about 8 to 10 layers and staple the edges to form an absorptive mat. Make several such mats so you have a supply on hand. Instruct the juniors to brush snow and mud from their footwear before coming inside and the improvised mats will last for days of inclement weather.

Any other paper, of course, can be used for this purpose. With a bit of imagination you might make up mats of plain paper with fanciful edges, such as a modified sunburst pattern or perhaps a huge shape in the form of a foot track, as a reminder.

Attaching ornament to brick

How can I attach a fairly heavy cast-iron eagle ornament to the brick above my fireplace mantel?—J.M., Ga.

Perhaps the best way is to make a hole about 3 inches deep in a mortar joint with a star drill, then drive in a slightly oversize dowel. Drill the end of the dowel and turn in a roundhead screw to nearly full depth. Hang the eagle from the screw, centering it to hang level.

Mildew or dirt?

I've been told there is a simple method of determining whether what looks like mildew is actually that or something else. Can you outline the procedure? Painted wood siding on my home shows a spotty, dark brown casting in places, especially on the north exposure. Incidentally, are mildew-proof paints effective?—W.T., Miss.

One way is to apply a laundry bleach to the spotty coating. If it's mildew, the spots will lighten appreciably but won't come off entirely without a lot of rubbing—even then, some discoloration will remain. If the coating is ordinary dirt or the oily-black variety, such as that from an oil-burning heating unit, the bleach will remove it entirely, with no noticeable change in color.

I don't know that any manufacturers describe their paints containing inhibitors as "mildew-proof," rather than "mildew-resistant." Under average conditions these paints are effective in reducing mildew formation, if not in preventing it entirely.

Replace old wiring?

I've just purchased an old home which has what my electrician calls "knob-and-tube" electrical wiring. Although he says that the wiring is still in good condition, he strongly recommends that it be replaced. Is he right, or is he just promoting a job?—Roy Wilkins, Columbus, Ohio

Knob-and-tube wiring uses unshielded, rubber-covered wire threaded through porcelain tubes which are placed in holes bored through joists; porcelain knobs are used to secure the wire at outlets and taps. Your electrician is undoubtedly thinking of the hazard of overloading this old type of wiring with modern appliances, some of which have current requirements beyond its normal capacity, particularly on branch circuits. There is also the danger of accidental damage to exposed sections of wiring as they are not housed in conduit. I, too, would strongly recommend that you have new wiring installed in accordance with present-day electrical needs and codes.

PIRATE'S CHEST is a perfect place to stow away teddies and other booty.

ALPHABET BOX: A personalized trunk may give your child incentive to keep his room in top shape. It's a good way to show a toddler how to keep all his toys organized in one spot.

These toyboxes please everyone

From one basic plan you can choose which of these four different styles you want to create. All you need for each box is a single sheet of plywood, some pine to frame the box, glue, paint and some hardware

SEE ALSO
Children's furniture . . . Dump trucks, toy . . . Gifts, Christmas . . . Pull toys . . . Toys . . . Weekend projects . . . Wood finishes

STAGECOACH TRUNK: Here's a rugged-looking trunk that is handsome enough to grace your family room.

PENNSYLVANIA DUTCH blanket chest: A touch of decoration turns our basic box into a dainty storage place for fabric and yarn in the sewing room.

YOUR CHILD will learn that getting organized can be a pleasure with a handy toybox to help. By following this basic design, you can make a toybox or storage chest with one sheet of plywood; then finish it with one of four decorative touches. Choose a design to match the setting.

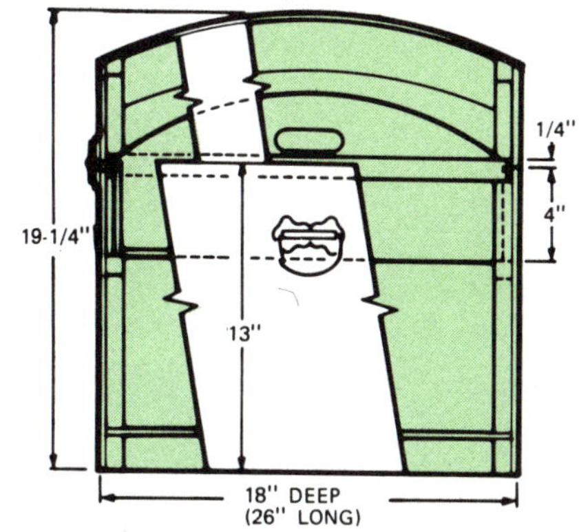

SECTION VIEW OF TYPICAL CHEST

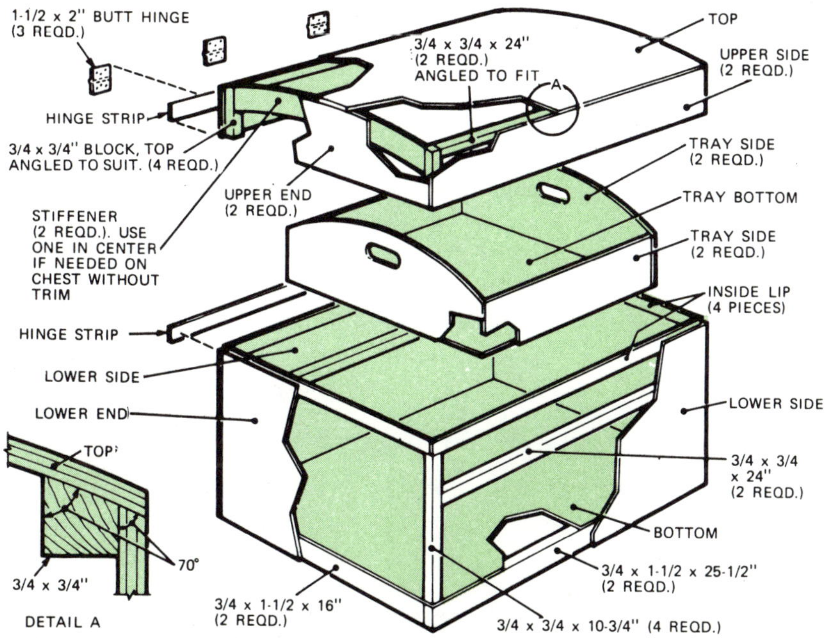

EXPLODED VIEW OF CHEST (TYPICAL OF PENNSYLVANIA DUTCH AND INITIAL CHESTS)

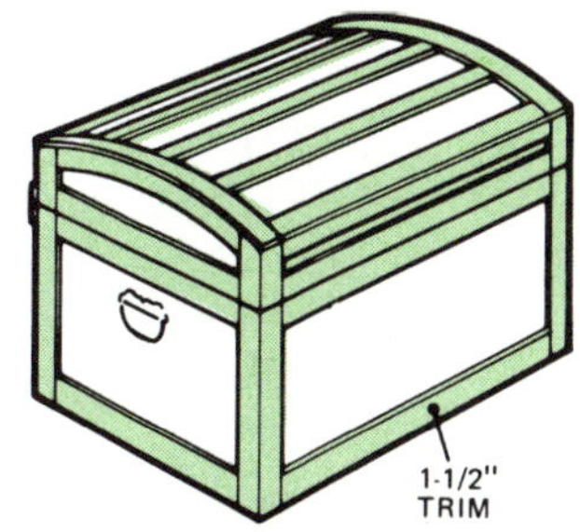

STAGECOACH CHEST

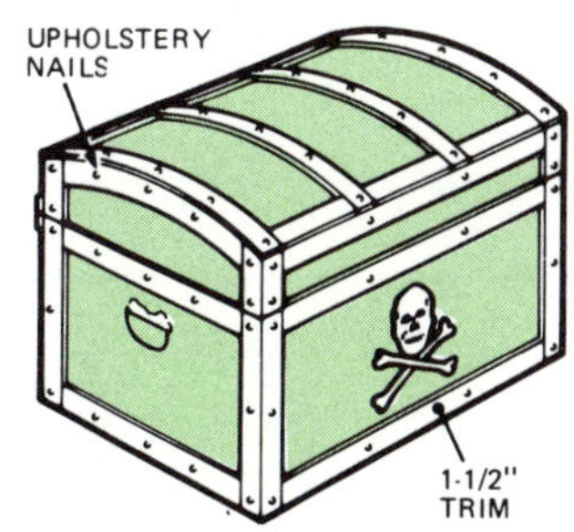

PIRATE'S CHEST

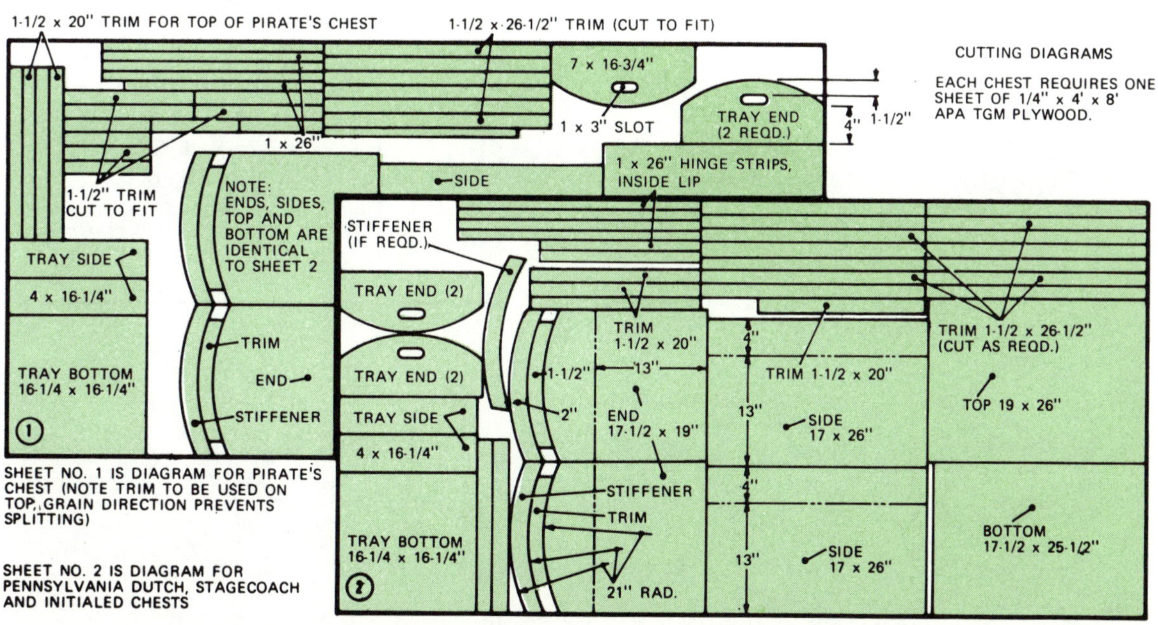

SHEET NO. 1 IS DIAGRAM FOR PIRATE'S CHEST (NOTE TRIM TO BE USED ON TOP, GRAIN DIRECTION PREVENTS SPLITTING)

SHEET NO. 2 IS DIAGRAM FOR PENNSYLVANIA DUTCH, STAGECOACH AND INITIALED CHESTS

CUTTING DIAGRAMS

EACH CHEST REQUIRES ONE SHEET OF 1/4" x 4' x 8' APA TGM PLYWOOD.

The toybox designs were created in conjunction with the American Plywood Assn. All versions can be built inexpensively. All you need for each chest is a single sheet of ¼-in. A-B plywood, some 1 x 1 and 1 x 2 pine to frame the box, carpenter's glue, paint and simple hardware.

The boxes have a 4-in.-deep, 16-in.-square tray with cut-out handles for lift-out storage of special small toys and supplies.

If you make the pirate's chest, you'll want to add gold-painted trim pieces cut from scrap plywood, brass upholstery tacks and a skull and crossbones. Use a wood-graining kit to give the stagecoach box an oldtime look. Then add trim and two handles to make heaving the trunk on the coach a little easier.

To make the Pennsylvania Dutch design, draw the pattern shown and cut a stencil on heavy paper. Or, trace the design on the box in soft pencil; then paint it freehand. The alphabet toybox is easy to paint by using masking tape to mask off the letters.

INITIALED CHEST

1'' SQS.

PIRATE'S CHEST

PENNSYLVANIA DUTCH CHEST

TWO EMPTY THREAD SPOOLS and a stovebolt of suitable length can be teamed up to serve as a useful clamp when the depth-of-reach is small. Though a nut can be used to tighten, a wingnut will be better.

DOWELS WILL FIT TIGHTER in their mating holes if the exposed ends are split with a small chisel and thin hardwood wedges are driven between the segments. The joints are snug, even without using glue.

SPRING-SUPPORTING BED SLATS will be prevented from falling out if you drive eyescrews into the ledger strips along the bed rails as shown. Then, simply fasten a hook to the ends of each slat to secure.

A MONKEY WRENCH can be quickly and easily set up to serve as an effective stop by clamping it at the desired spot on the saw fence. To prevent the handle from sagging, support it with small blocks of wood.

KEEP PAINT-CAN RIM free of paint slop that occurs whenever a brush is wiped across the rim by filling it with a bead of weatherstrip. When the strip is removed, the cover will again seat as it should.

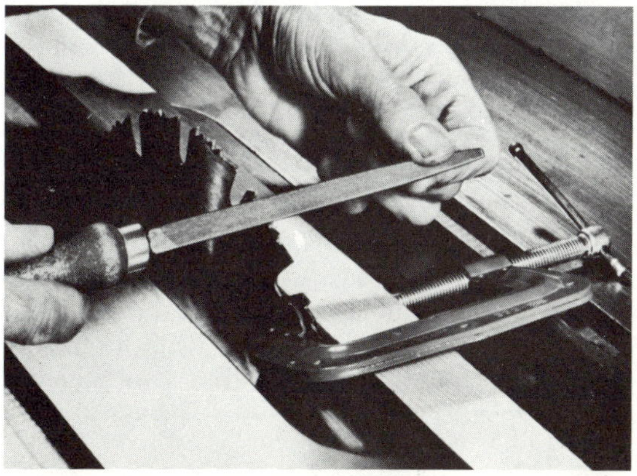

TABLE-SAW BLADE can be given a fast touchup (while still on the arbor) if you use a C-clamp and a strip of wood to hold it fast. To prevent an accident, make certain that the tool is disconnected from power.

Do a complete brake system check up

By MORT SCHULTZ

When you understand the system and its operation, you'll find a thorough diagnosis can be simple. Tests are made in your own driveway as well as on the road

BLEEDING THE BRAKES makes air in the hydraulic system bubble through the container of fluid. Close the bleed valve when the bubbles stop.

WE ALL WANT to be sure our car has ample "Go" for our needs. But any car is an unadulterated threat to its occupants and everyone else on the road if it doesn't boast at least as much "Stop." One of the most important things you can do for your car's braking system—and for yourself—is conduct a thorough brake inspection every 10,000 miles. That amounts to about once a year.

A proper inspection will let you catch and fix minor problems before they become major safety hazards. And it can save you money, since problems may well result from a relatively insignificant condition—one you can correct without resorting to costly professional help.

The full inspection has two general parts. Begin with tests you run while the car sits in the driveway. You'll follow this with a road test. In each case, you will learn precisely what steps to take, what results to watch for, and how to interpret them.

In many cases, problems you discover can have any of a number of causes. For example, there are four major reasons your brake pedal might feel spongy. They range from air in the hydraulic system, requiring that you bleed it (easy enough) to drums worn so thin they must be replaced (also easy—but costly).

Whatever problem you're faced with, begin with the easiest, least expensive of the procedures called for. Proceed by steps to the more difficult, more expensive operations—hoping that you will have cured the problem early.

The chart on page 437 shows eight different symptoms you may find, and matches each with a group of possible causes.

SEE ALSO

Autos, maintenance . . . Autos, ramps . . .
Cooling systems, auto . . . Gaskets, auto . . .
Lubrication, auto . . . Ramps, auto repair . . .
Steering and suspension, auto . . . Tune-up, auto

inspection in the driveway

Apply heavy foot pressure to the brake pedal (with the engine running at idle speed if you have a power brake system). The pedal should feel firm, not spongy or springy.

If it does feel spongy, however, check first to be sure the vent hole in the cover of the master cylinder isn't clogged. Remember that recent safety regulations require a dual master cylinder with one outlet feeding pressure to the front brakes, the other feeding the rear. (In some imports, the systems have been split diagonally—with the right-front and left-rear on one line. And there are even some in which one system feeds both rear brakes and one front-wheel brake while the other feeds the same rears and the other front.) Dual master cylinders have vent holes for each subsystem. There are two fluid reservoirs and two hydraulic pistons. They operate in tandem, controlled by a single push rod.

The usual cause of a spongy brake pedal is air trapped in the hydraulic system. Bleeding gets rid of this. Air can enter when the fluid level becomes low or a brake part is disconnected, then reinstalled.

A bleed screw is provided at each wheel cylinder. The order in which wheel cylinders are bled is of little importance, but be sure you hit all four of them.

Before you bleed a power brake system, purge the vacuum by depressing and releasing the brake pedal five or six times with the engine off.

brake bleeding procedure

Here are the steps to follow in bleeding a hydraulic brake system:

1. If necessary, fill the master-cylinder fluid reservoir (both reservoirs if a dual system) with new brake fluid. After bleeding each cylinder, recheck the reservoir and keep the level within ¼ to ½ inch of the top.

2. Attach the bleeder hose, about 18 inches of vacuum hose, to the wheel-cylinder bleed screw. Submerge the other end in a container partly filled with brake fluid. A transparent container is best; you'll be watching for bubbles.

3. While a helper puts steady pressure on the brake pedal, open the bleed screw about ¾ turn. Pressure must be maintained until the screw is closed. When the fluid from the end of the hose stops bubbling, close the screw. Repeat the procedure at the other wheels.

Discard the old fluid. After bleeding the brakes, make sure the master cylinder is full.

Another cause of a spongy pedal is a soft or weak brake hose that expands under pressure. Feel hoses; they should be firm. If not, replace 'em.

After checking for a spongy pedal, observe pedal reserve. If the pedal is low, brakes probably need adjusting.

checking self adjusters

Brakes in cars built since the early 1960s arc self-adjusting. Make several forward and reverse stops, coming to a complete stop every time. Pedal height should build up. If not, the linings are probably too badly worn to be adjusted or there is another problem. The self-adjusting mechanism may be in bad shape.

Now check for leaks in the hydraulic system by holding your foot lightly on the pedal for 15 seconds. There should be no pedal movement. The pedal should be just as firm when you try again, pressing down hard. If the car has power brakes, repeat the procedure with the engine

NEWER MASTER CYLINDERS have double reservoirs. Be sure the vent hole in each cover is clear to let atmospheric pressure keep brake lines full.

A PIECE OF VACUUM hose about 18 inches long helps in bleeding brakes. It's important that this hose fits snugly on the bleeder valves.

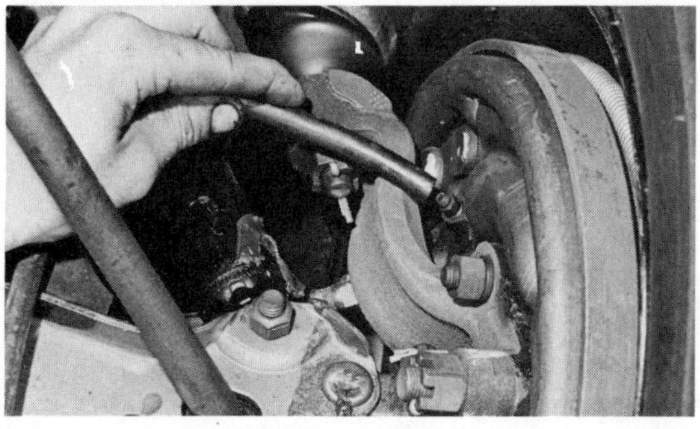

THE DIAPHRAGM covering the fluid reservoir of a dual master cylinder is marked "fluid side" and "cover side." Be sure the diaphragm is installed the right way.

BE SURE RUBBER brake-fluid hose lines are tight, firm, clean, without cuts, cracks, or obvious leaks. Keep them clear of the running gear's moving parts.

CHECK CONNECTIONS AT the master cylinder. All must be tight. Watch carefully for indications fluid has been leaking or that lines are vulnerable.

PEEL BACK BOTH boots when inspecting wheel cylinders. Leaks mean you lose fluid pressure and any fluid on the linings can destroy their braking effectiveness.

running.

If the brake pedal gives way, there's a leak somewhere. Inspect the master cylinder first. Look for fluid around connections and see that the connections are tight.

Check all brake lines to each wheel for leaks. Try to tighten leaky connections before replacing hose. Make sure hoses and lines are free of dents, cracks, and cuts.

Wheel cylinders can also leak. You'll have to pull the wheels to check them. Peel back both boots of each cylinder. If fluid leaks, the cylinder must be rebuilt.

the master cylinder

If hoses, lines and wheel cylinders show no leaks, the fading brake pedal is caused by damage inside the master cylinder. Fluid may be leaking from around a secondary cup into the boot where you can't see it, although you may be able to detect the odor inside the car.

It isn't economically practical or 100-per-cent safe to rebuild a master cylinder, especially the newer, dual type. Besides the work involved, the necessary kit runs close to the cost of a new cylinder. Wheel cylinders are something else. It pays to rebuild them yourself.

Continue your driveway inspection by putting the car on jackstands or a lift (if you can talk gas station operator out of the use of his). If you jack the car up, be sure to block the wheels still on the ground. Test the front wheels, then the rears. Release the parking brake and be sure each wheel spins freely without drag.

With light pressure on the pedal, all wheels should have similar drag as you spin them by hand.

If wheels don't revolve properly during this test, you probably have an inside problem with linings or cylinders. But if only the rear brakes drag, the parking brake may be hung up or adjusted too tightly. Release the lever. The cable should have some play. If not, adjustment or lubrication should cure the problem.

Finally, pull one of the front wheels and inspect brake linings. New linings are generally $^3/_{16}$ in. thick. Used linings should be no thinner than $^1/_{16}$ in. If you can't judge, use a gauge. If one set of linings is worn, replace them all.

now for road testing

Putting a brake through its paces on the road tells how it's working under actual operating conditions. Pick a dry, clean, reasonably smooth and level road. And make sure tires are properly inflated.

Be careful not to fade brakes by overusing them during tests. If they do fade, let them cool for 10 minutes before proceding.

The first test is at 10 to 15 mph. Make several stops, alternating between light and medium pedal applications. Come to a full stop each time.

Notice the effort required. Do brakes grab? Does the car pull? Is too much effort needed? If so, there's probably a problem with the linings, master or wheel cylinder(s), or drums.

Remember that conditions other than brakes can make the car pull. Loose or worn wheel bearings, loose steering, and maladjusted camber are all possibilities.

SOME SLACK is called for in the parking-brake cable. Otherwise that system may be constantly applied, making the brakes drag too much and wear too fast.

diagnosis by sound

Open the windows, turn off any accessories, and listen. Try to tell the wheel that's generating a squeal, click, or scraping sound. Driving beside a wall makes noises more audible.

Speed up to 60 mph and make a few light-pedal stops. Is there chatter or shudder? If so, check for worn or loose wheel bearings. If the bearings are okay, suspect out-of-round drums.

From 60 mph, make several hard-pedal stops—as hard as you can without skidding. Come to a complete stop each time and drive at least two miles between stops to avoid overheating and fading the brakes. Listen for any unusual sound and check for undue effort in stopping.

You can make sure your car's "Stop" is at least as good as its "Go."

BRAKE DIAGNOSIS CHART

CONDITION	CAUSE
Low pedal (excessive pedal travel needed to apply brakes)	D E G K
Spongy pedal (a springy sensation of the pedal upon application)	G I J K
Hard pedal (excessive pedal pressure needed to stop the car)	D E H J K L
Fading pedal (pedal falls away under foot pressure)	G I J K L
Grabbing or pulling	B C E F G H J L M
Noise (squeal, click, scrape)	D E F G H
Chatter or shudder	B E G H
Dragging brakes	A D E F H J K L

KEY:

A—Parking brake improperly adjusted or sticking.
B—Loose wheel bearings.
C—Front-end misalignment or uneven tire tread.
D—Brake shoes improperly adjusted; automatic adjuster out of commission.
E—Worn, contaminated or distorted brake linings.
F—Weak or broken shoe return spring.
G—Cracked, thin, scored or out-of-round drums.
H—Brake support plate rusted, loose or worn.
I—Air in hydraulic system fluid.
J—Hoses and lines soft or weak, kinked, collapsed, dented, clogged, loosely connected, or leaking.
K—Damaged master cylinders.
L—Damaged wheel cylinder.
M—Check tire pressure.

PULL EITHER FRONT wheel to check linings, since they do most of the braking. Both sides wear essentially the same; if one is going, replace both or—all four.

CHECK THE LININGS at their thinnest point; at least 1/16 inch is necessary. Using a gauge is more reliable than measuring the thickness by eyeballing it.

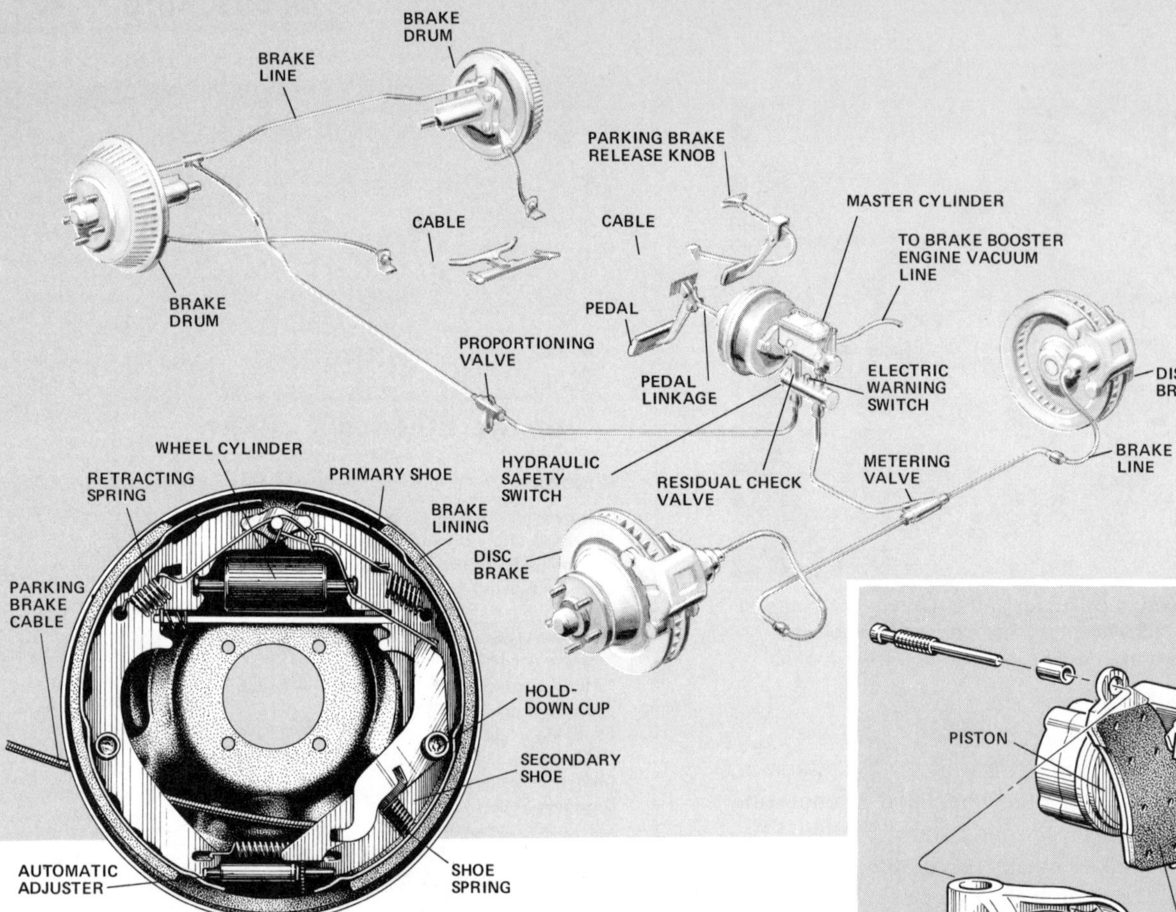

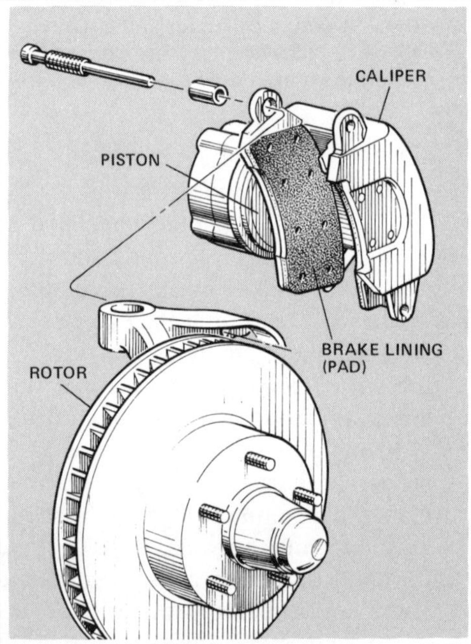

Troubleshooting guide for your brakes

Are your brakes pulling when you try to stop? Squealing? Slow to respond? This chart helps you match the symptom to the cause

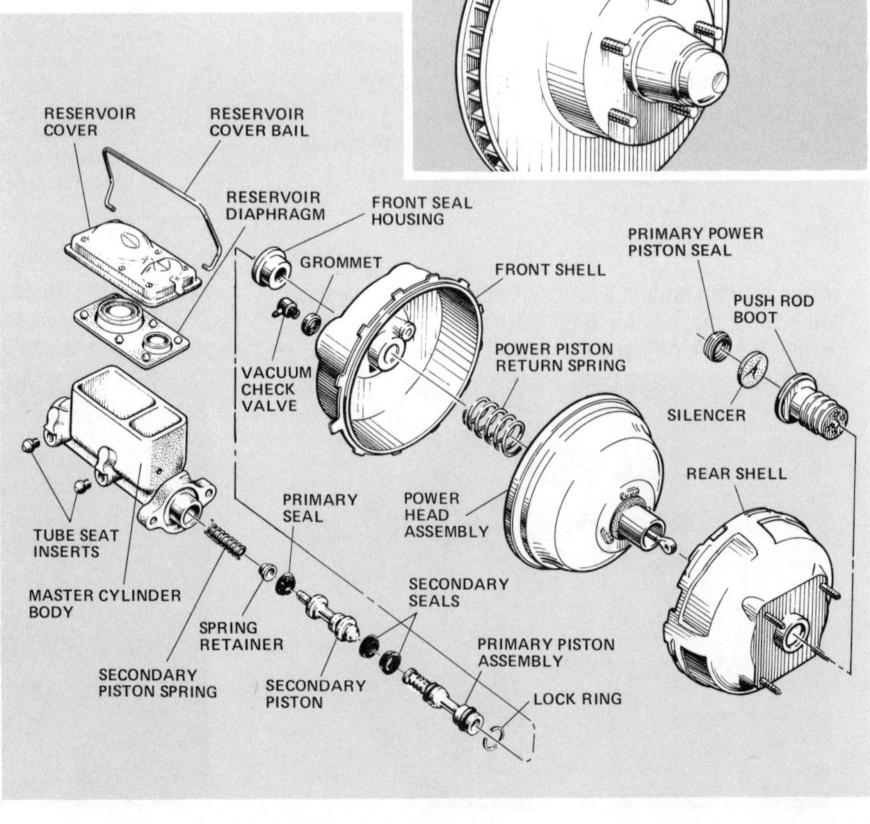

SEE ALSO

Autos, maintenance . . .
Autos, ramps . . .
Cooling systems, auto . . .
Gaskets, auto . . . Lubrication, auto . . .
Ramps, auto repair . . .
Steering and suspension, auto . . .
Tune-up, auto

TROUBLESHOOTING BRAKES

CAUSE / PROBLEM	Excessive pedal travel.	Pedal travel gradually increases.	Excessive pedal effort.	Brakes slow to respond.	Brakes slow to release.	Brakes drag.	Uneven (side to side pull) brake action.	Uneven (front to rear grab) brake action.	Scraping noise.	Brakes squeak when applied.	Brakes squeak during stop.	Brake chatter (roughness).	Brakes groan at end of stop.	Brake warning light glows during stop.
Leaking brake line or brake line connection.	*	**						*						**
Leaking wheel cylinder or master cylinder piston seal.	*	**					*							*
Leaking master cylinder.	*	**												*
Air trapped in brake system.	**							*						**
Contaminated or improper brake fluid.				*	*	*								*
Leaking brake booster vacuum system.			**		*									
Restricted air passage in brake booster power head.			*	**	*									
Damaged brake booster power head.			*	*	*	*								
Improperly assembled brake booster power head valving.			*	*	*	**								
Worn brake lining.			*				*	*	*	*	*		*	
Uneven brake lining wear.	*						*	*	*	*	**		*	*
Glazed brake lining.			**	*			*	*		*	*			
Incorrect lining.			*				*	*			*		*	
Contaminated brake lining.							**	**	*	*	*		*	
Too much brake lining dust.			*				**	**		*	**		*	
Scored drum(s) or rotor(s).							*	*		*	*	**	*	
Drums out of round.											*	**		
Rotors out of parallel.												**		
Excessive rotor run-out.												*		
Damaged automatic adjusters.	*					*	*	*						*
Incorrect wheel cylinder size.			*				*	*						
Weak or incorrect brake shoe springs.					*	**	*	*	**	*	**			
Missing or loose brake-assembly fasteners (cups).	*					*	*	*	*		*	*	*	
Brake-shoe guide insufficiently lubricated.					*	*	*	*	**	**				
Restricted brake fluid passage or sticking wheel cylinder piston		*	*	*	*	*	*	*						
Faulty metering valve.	*		*	*	*	*		*						*
Brake pedal linkage binding or being interfered with.			*	*	**	**								
Improperly adjusted parking brake.						*								
Tapered or threaded drums.									**					
Incorrect front end alignment.							**							
Incorrect tire pressure.							*	*						
Incorrect wheel bearing adjustment.	*								*			*		
Loose front suspension.							*		**			*	*	
Out-of-balance wheels.												**		
Driver rides brake pedal.	*	*	*			*		*					*	
Improperly adjusted master cylinder push rod.	*				*	**								*
Sticking wheel cylinder or caliper piston.			*		*	*	*	*						
Faulty proportioning valve.			*	*	*	*								

■ BRAKE PROBLEMS are one of the most common complaints heard from car owners. To help you identify the cause of malfunctions in your braking system, we have prepared the troubleshooting chart shown at the left. Use it to match brake problems with causes. It includes both disc and drum brakes.

Since some causes are more likely to create a problem than others, a double asterisk (**) indicates probable cause, while a single asterisk (*) signifies a less likely cause. Investigate the probable cause or causes first.

The illustration on the opposite page identifies parts mentioned in the chart and will make it easier for you to troubleshoot the brake system.

It is imperative for safety that the warning signs of a defective braking system are recognized and acted upon at once. A braking system seldom fails suddenly. Rather, it emits a warning for several hundred miles before the situation becomes dangerous.

The most common warning signs are:

■ Lighting of the dash brake warning light.

■ Harsh noise (a low-pitched squeal on brake application is usually normal).

■ Hard pedal.

■ Pulsating pedal.

■ A pedal that doesn't rise when the self-adjusting mechanism is activated (car moved in Reverse).

■ Severe pull when brakes are applied.

How to overhaul drum brake systems

By MORT SCHULTZ

THERE'S A BIG SAVING in doing your own brake work. However—you need several special tools you may not have, including:

- **Drum-to-brake shoe clearance gauge** **$9.80**
- **Brake-cylinder clamps (four)** **6.25**
- **Brake spring tools** **11.95**
- **Brake bleeder wrench** **3.70**
- **Adjusting tool** **4.10**

(Retail prices quoted above have been provided by a well-known tool company and were current when this was written.)

Another essential tool is a brake-drum micrometer that sells for about $75. You can avoid buying it by getting a brake shop to do your drum work. Shops charge about $3 per drum for milking and turning. More about this in a minute. You may also want to have a brake shop grind new brake linings to make full contact with drums, but this isn't always necessary since most high-quality linings are preground by the maker. More on this later, too.

Major tasks involved in brake overhaul are (1) servicing brake drums; (2) replacing shoes and linings; (3) servicing wheel cylinders. The master cylinder will also require overhaul or replacing if it's leaking. We'll assume it's not.

removing brake drums

■ **To remove rear brake drums,** release the parking brake and relieve tension on the parking-brake cable. On most cars this is done by loosening or removing the adjusting nut at the equalizer (Drawing 1).

It might also be necessary to back off the brake-shoe adjusting mechanism before drums, front and rear, can be removed. On some cars, there is a slot in the backing plate through which this is done.

■ **Remove the cover over the slot,** insert a brake-adjusting tool and engage the teeth of the adjusting wheel (called a star wheel). Back off the star wheel until drag disappears. Be sure to reinstall the access hole cover (Drawing 2).

On other cars, access to the star wheel is gained through a lanced area in the brake drum. Knock out the plug in the lanced area. Insert the tool and proceed to disengage star wheel tension as just described.

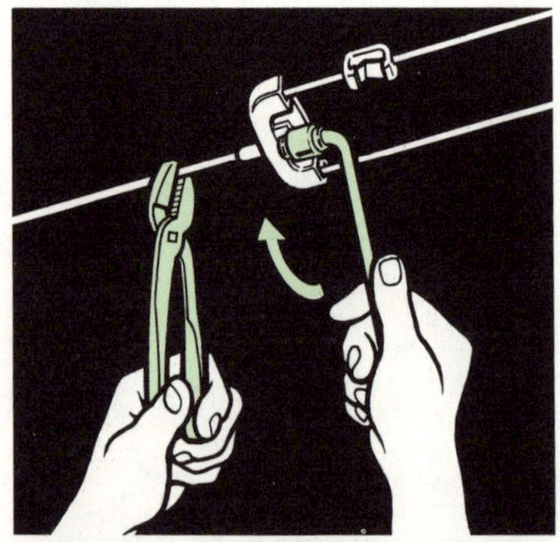

1. Parking-brake cable tension is released by loosening adjusting nut.

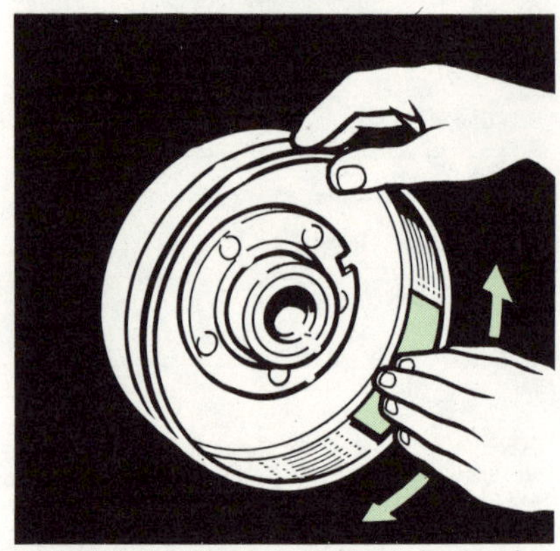

6. Lightly buff drums that are in good condition with emery cloth.

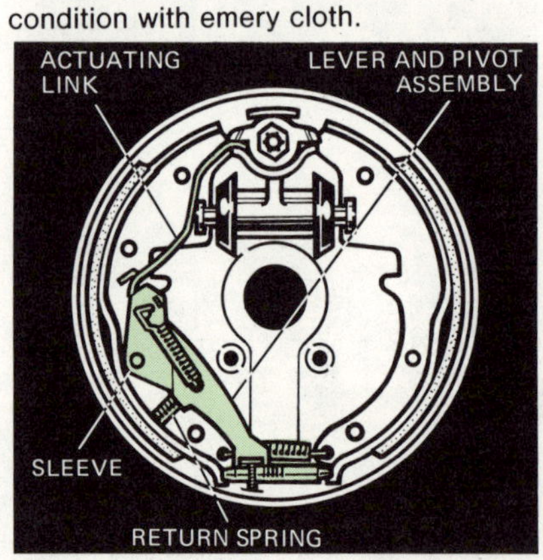

10. Self-adjusting mechanism for Delco-Moraine brakes is shown here.

SEE ALSO

Autos, ramps . . . Belts, auto . . . Chokes, auto . . . Emissions controls . . . Gaskets, auto . . . Lubrication, auto . . . Ramps, auto repair . . . Shock absorbers . . . Tune-up, auto

3. Typical front wheel bearing assembly is shown here. You'll have to disassemble the outer wheel bearing to remove drum. Take off grease cap, cotter pin, castellated nut (or plain nut and locknut), thrust washer and then outer wheel bearing.

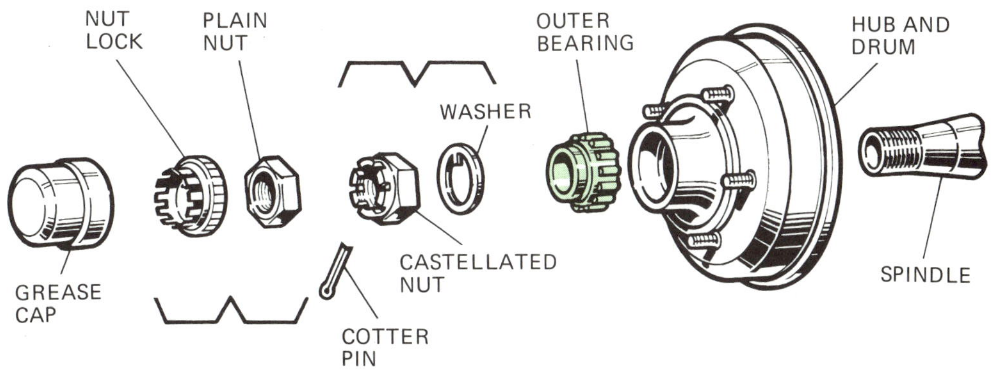

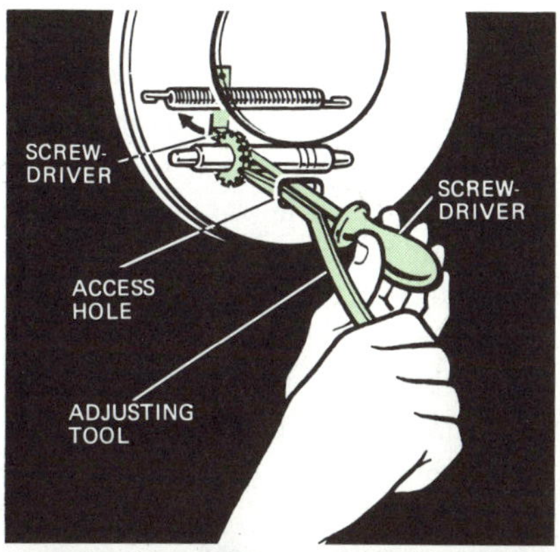

2. Adjusting tool is necessary to back off star wheel (except Wagner).

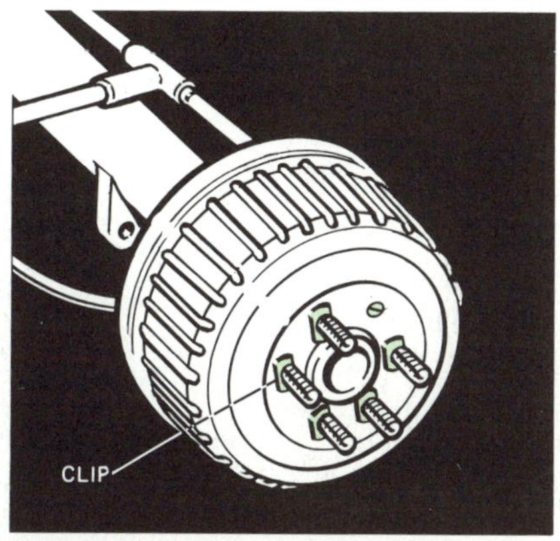

4. Rear-wheel drumclips (speed nuts) must be removed to remove drum.

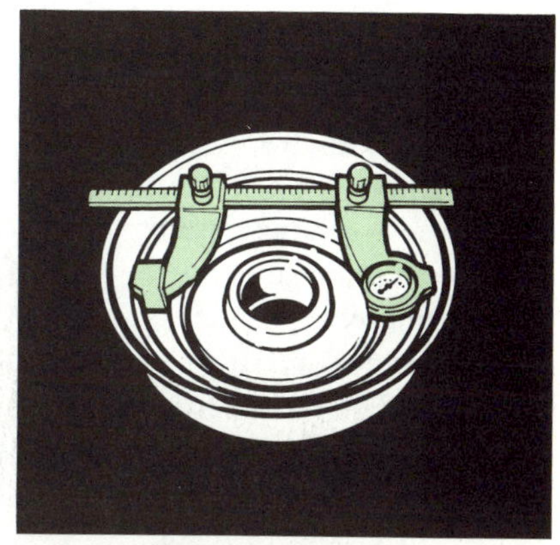

5. Brake drum is checked for wear, out-of-roundness and taper.

7. Use clamp to hold cylinder boots in place to prevent fluid leakage.

8. Remove anchor pins and take off the brake shoe return springs.

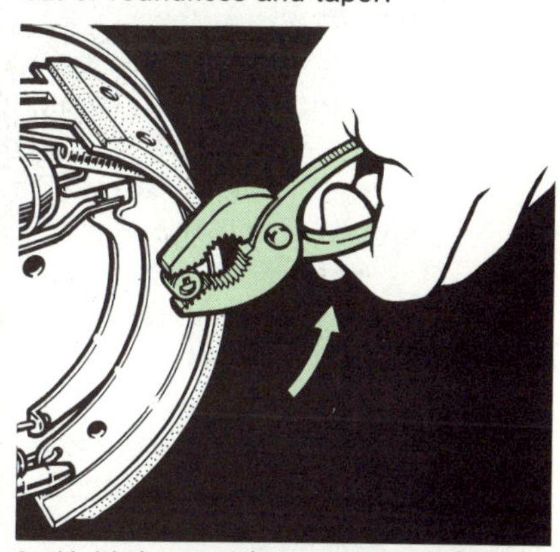

9. Hold-down springs are compressed and cups rotated to line up with pins.

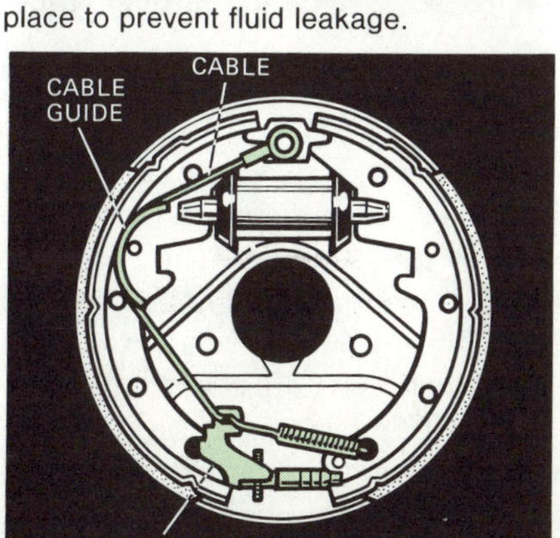

11. Self-adjusting mechanism for Bendix brakes is shown here.

12. Brake shoes, adjusting screw and spring are removed.

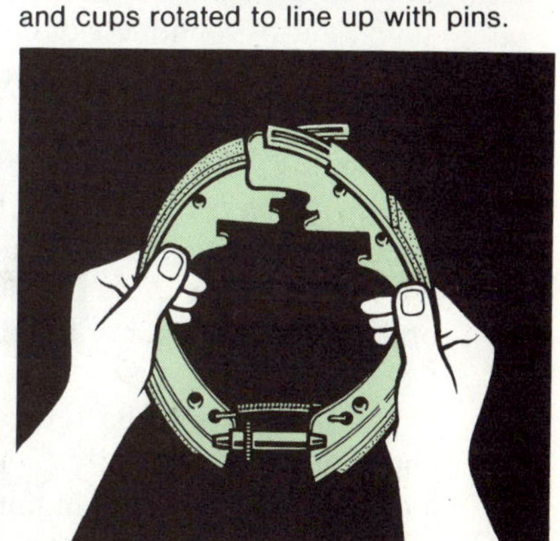

13. Separate shoes by relieving tension on the adjusting spring.

Remember: Before you finish the job, make sure you get new covers for lanced areas. Holes must be sealed to keep dirt and water from getting into the brake.

■ **If you are working on front wheel drum brakes,** in most cars you have to disassemble outer wheel bearings to remove drums. Take off the grease cap, cotter pin, castellated nut (or plain nut and locknut), thrust washer and outer wheel bearings (Drawing 3). Lay these parts on a clean surface.

■ **If you are overhauling rear wheel drum brakes,** take off the rear wheel and tire assembly. Metal clips (speed nuts) are probably holding the drum to the axle. Take off speed nuts and remove the drum (Drawing 4).

With drums off the vehicle, examine brake linings. Their condition can often tip you off to defective brake drums. Look for:

■ Linings serving one wheel that are worn down more than linings serving other wheels. The drum on that wheel is probably rough.

■ Uneven wear from side to side on any one set of linings. The drum is probably tapered.

■ Linings badly worn at toe or heel, indicating a drum out-of-round.

If compressed air is available, blow loose dirt from drums. If there is no compressed air, use a stiff bristle brush to remove dirt.

If drum has oil, grease or hardened dirt on it, wash it thoroughly with a nonoil-base cleaning solvent, such as carburetor cleaner or lacquer thinner. Check to see where oil or grease is coming from and make repairs before reinstalling drums. The leak likely is from a defective brake cylinder or front-wheel-hub grease seal.

Closely inspect each drum for cracks. A cracked brake drum should be replaced. Never attempt to weld it closed. This won't work and may lead to a serious accident.

■ **Even if drums look good,** with no indication of taper, out-of-roundness or damage, I suggest you still have them checked with a micrometer for excessive wear (Drawing 5).

Take measurements at open and closed edges of the friction surface, and at right angles to each other. If taper or out-of-roundness exceeds .006 inch (.004 inch for Chrysler Total Contact brakes), the drum is not fit for use and should be turned.

If drums have to be turned to get them even and smooth, remove only enough metal to obtain a true surface. But keep in mind that if one drum has to be machined, the other drum on the same axle should be turned to the *same* diameter—even if it does not need machining—to assure braking equalization. For the same reason, if one brake drum has to be discarded, replace the other one on the same axle.

Every brake drum made since Dec. 31, 1970, has been stamped with a discard dimension. This is the permissible *wear* dimension, not the allowable turning dimension. If the drum cannot be turned so .030 inch is left for wear, replace the drum.

■ **If drums are true and smooth,** needing no turning, use some fine emery cloth to polish out slight score marks (Drawing 6). If this won't remove them, the drum should be turned.

removing shoes and linings

The following step-by-step guide applies to drum brakes on most late-model cars. If your setup differs, the changes will be minor and you should be able to compensate using this outline:

1. Install brake-cylinder clamps to keep fluid from leaking (Drawing 7). Some brakes have brake-cylinder stops built into the backing plate, and need no clamps. In any event, don't press the brake pedal after shoe-return springs are removed.

2. Loosen the brake-spring anchor pin and remove the brake-shoe return springs (Drawing 8). Your set-up may not have springs attached directly to the anchor pin. They may be hooked to a plate that, in turn, is held by an anchor pin. Whatever, examine the arrangement closely before proceeding. Be sure the layout is firmly in mind (make notes and a sketch, if necessary) so springs may be reinstalled properly.

3. Remove shoe-retaining parts. There are differences from brake to brake. Some use a coil spring-cup-pin arrangement (Drawing 9). Others have pins with the outside end retained by a spring clip. Still others use tension hold-down springs, enlarged on one end and with a hook on the other that engages a retainer through the backing plate.

4. Remove self-adjusting parts. On Delco Moraine brakes, you must lift off actuating link, lever and pivot assembly, sleeve and return spring (Drawing 10). Discard damaged parts.

On Bendix brakes (Drawing 11), slip the adjusting cable off the anchor pin and unhook bottom end of the adjusting lever. Remove cable guide, but don't remove the adjusting lever yet. It's easier to get it off after shoes are removed.

On Wagner brakes, remove screw holding the adjusting crank, lift off crank and unhook adjusting links from the anchor pin and adjusting lever. Wait until you have taken off brake shoes to remove adjusting lever.

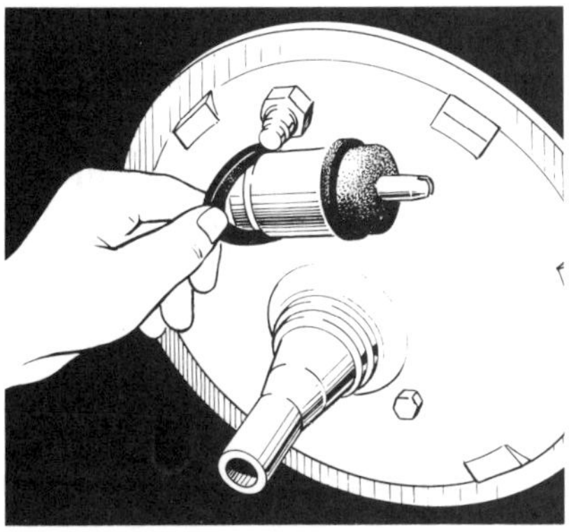

14. Brake cylinder at each wheel should be checked for leaks.

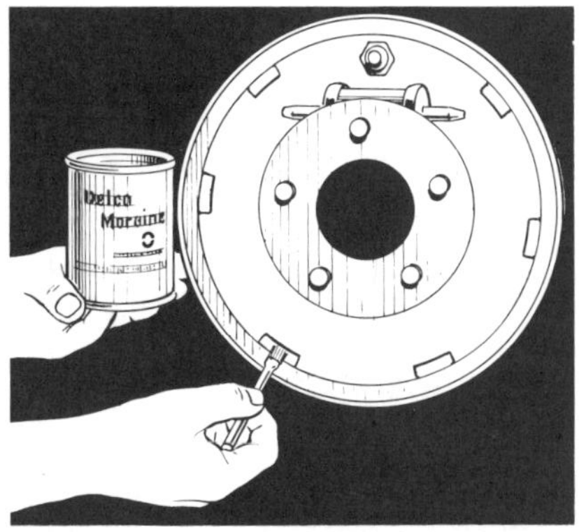

15. Pads on which shoes rest are lubricated to prevent noise and wear.

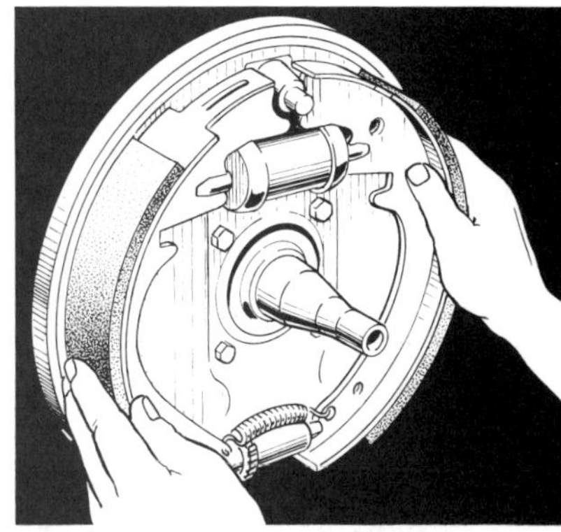

16. New shoes, with adjusting mechanism and spring, are installed.

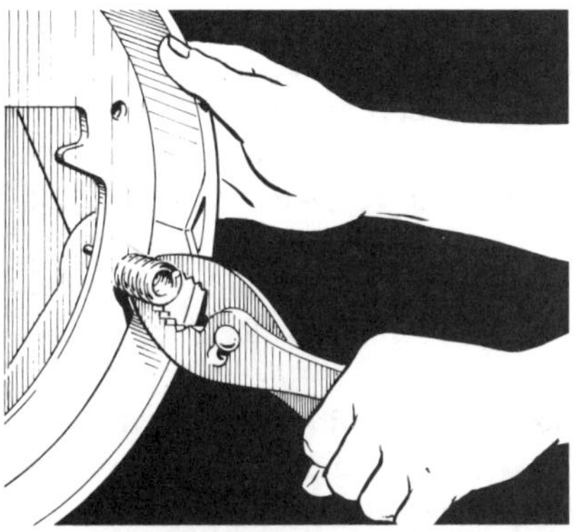

17. Hold-down pins that retain the brake shoe get a quarter turn.

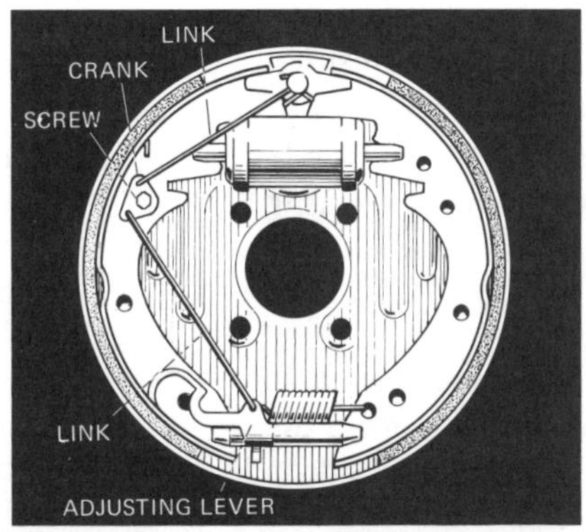

18. Delco-Moraine self-adjusting mechanism is shown here installed.

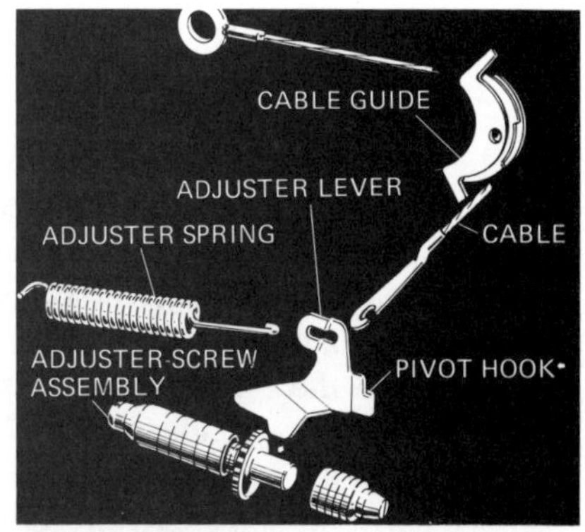

19. On Bendix unit, self-adjusting mechanism uses components shown.

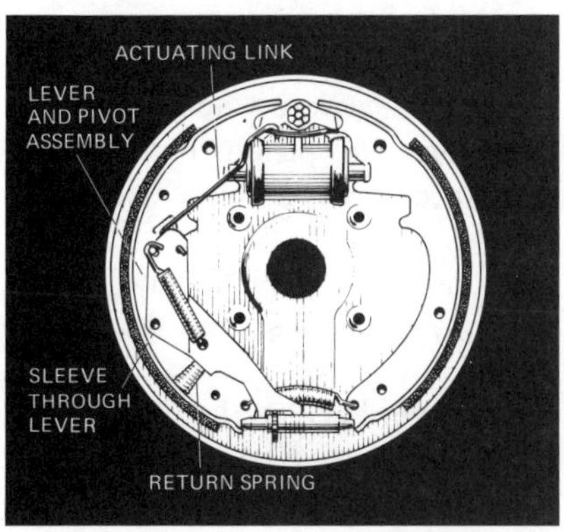

20. On Wagner unit, reassemble self-adjusting mechanism as shown above.

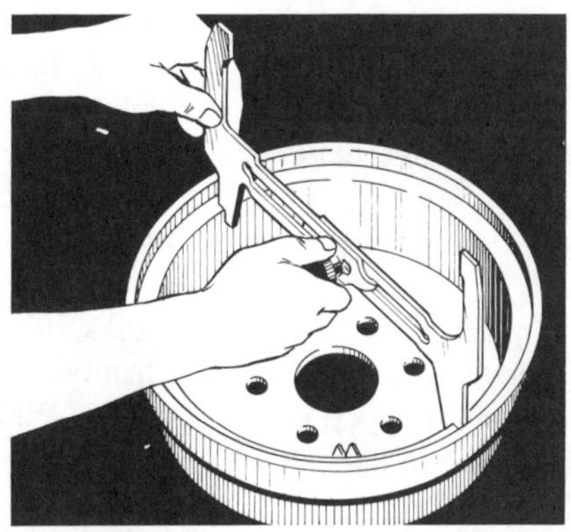

21. Drum-to-brake-shoe clearance gauge measures inside diameter.

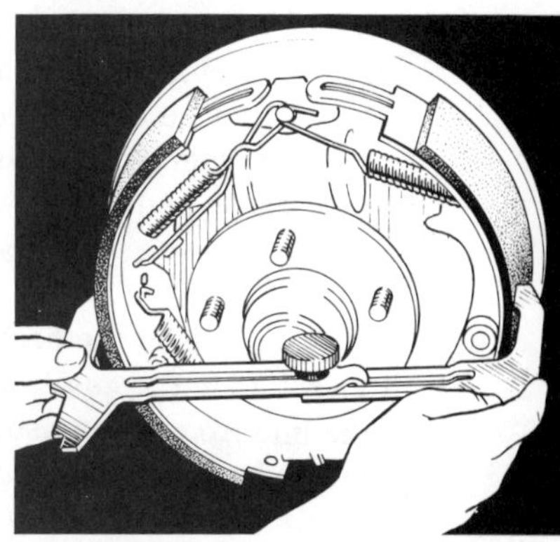

22. Gauge is turned over to fit over shoes. Expand linings to meet gauge.

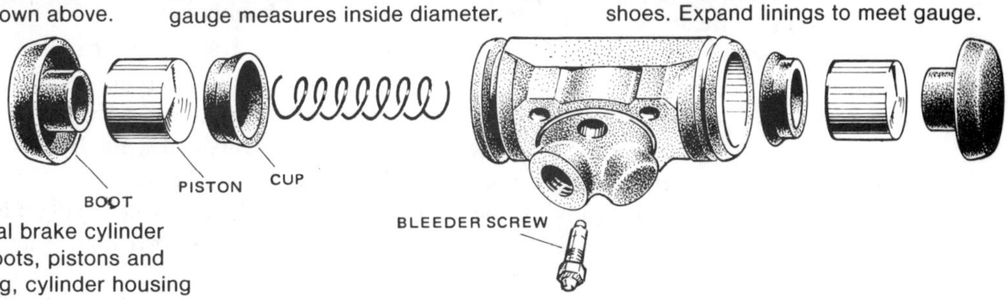

EXPLODED VIEW 1: Typical brake cylinder (wheel cylinder) has two boots, pistons and cups, plus a common spring, cylinder housing and bleeder screw.

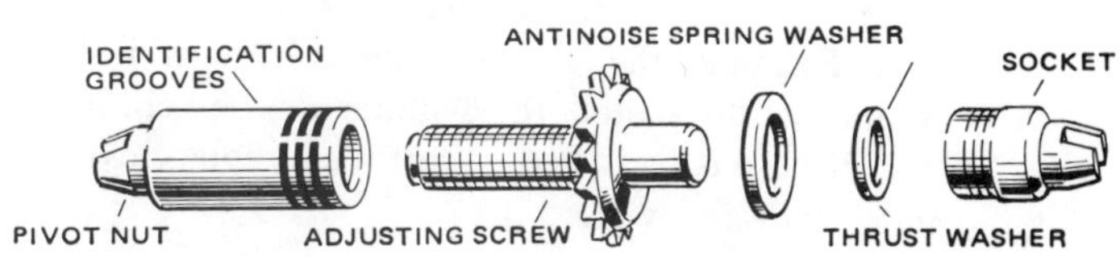

EXPLODED VIEW 2: Typical adjusting mechanism (less levers and cables) should be disassembled, cleaned and inspected; adjusting screw should be lubricated.

5. On rear brakes, remove the parking brake strut by spreading shoes apart slightly. Disconnect the parking brake lever, which may be held either by a retaining clip or bolt, or may be hooked in place.

6. If anchor plate is used, slip it off anchor pin; if plate is bolted on, leave it be.

7. Spread brake-shoe anchor ends and take shoes off brake-cylinder links. Remove shoes, and adjusting screw and spring as an assembly (Drawing 12). Some brakes don't have brake cylinder links. Shoes ride directly on brake cylinder pistons.

8. To separate shoes, relieve adjusting spring tension by overlapping anchor ends of shoes (Drawing 13). Unhook spring; remove adjusting screw. Parts are now separated.

Take a close look at your wheel cylinders while other brake parts are removed from the backing plate. Inspect boots for cuts, tears and cracks. Physical damage indicates a need for cylinder overhaul.

■ **If the cylinder has external (rubber) boots, as most do, carefully pull back the lower edge of the boot as shown in drawing 14.** If more than a drop of fluid spills out, the cylinder is damaged and should be overhauled or replaced. Each cylinder has two boots. Be sure to check both ends.

Some brake cylinders have metal caps. To check such cylinders for damage, you have to remove either the connecting link or cap on one end of the cylinder. If fluid runs out, overhaul or replace the cylinder.

Here's how to service brake cylinders that need repair:

1. From behind the backing plate, clean away dirt around the connection and disconnect the brake line from the cylinder. Tape the open end of line to keep fluid from leaking and to keep dirt out.

2. If links are used between cylinder and brake shoes, remove them. Now, pull off external (rubber) boots with pliers and discard them. Remove metal caps used instead of boots.

3. Remove pistons, cups and spring assembly as shown in exploded view 1. (Note how they come out, so that, later, you can replace them in the right way.) While removing the spring assembly, be careful not to scratch the bore of the cylinder. Also remove bleeder screw from the cylinder and make sure passages are clear.

4. Examine the cylinder bore. If it is just stained or discolored, the cylinder can be kept in use. If bore is scratched or corroded, replace cylinder with a new one.

Important: Don't confuse staining with corrosion. Pit marks or roughness in the bore indicate corrosion.

5. Remove stains and discoloration with crocus cloth wrapped around your finger. *Revolve the cylinder* on the crocus cloth. Do not slide the cloth lengthwise through the cylinder. You may scratch the bore.

6. Wash the cylinder in clean brake fluid, shake off excess, and allow the part to air dry. Do not use a rag to dry the cylinder. Lint can get on the bore surface.

7. A brake cylinder rebuild kit is needed at this point. All rubber parts are contained in such a kit. However, metal parts such as pistons may not be included in the kit. If not, clean used parts in clean brake fluid and let them dry before reuse. If pistons are damaged, and you can't get replacements, you will have to replace the whole cylinder.

8. Inspect the bleeder screw and bleeder screw inlet hole for stripped threads. Replace a damaged screw.

9. Lubricate the bore with clean brake fluid before putting parts in the cylinder (be sure your hands are clean). Insert the spring assembly and new cups. See that cups go in the right way. Recall how they came out. Usually, the flat surface goes to the outer end of the cylinder.

10. Insert pistons properly. They must go back in the same position they were when they came out of the bore. Normally, pistons are installed with their flat surfaces toward the center of the cylinder.

11. Press new boots into place and install links, if they are used. Boots must be seated firmly.

12. Place the cylinder back on the brake backing plate and tighten bolts. Hook up the brake line.

backing plate

■ **Turn your attention to the backing plate.** If you have compressed air available, blow off loose dirt. Use a wire brush to loosen caked-on deposits and scale. If there is no compressed air, use a wire brush only.

Check backing plate for minor surface defects, such as corrosion. Fine emery cloth will remove this.

Examine the backing plate. If it's cracked or bent, it must be replaced.

Apply a thin film of brake lubricant to the raised pads on the backing plate (drawing 15). On these pads the new shoes will rest.

self-adjust mechanism

Disassemble the adjusting mechanism at your workbench and clean the parts (see exploded view 2). Make sure the adjusting screw threads fully in the pivot nut without binding, and that no adjusting teeth are damaged. Discard bad parts.

Lubricate the adjusting screw and reassemble adjusting mechanism.

reassembly

At this point you can install new shoes and replace all other parts, but first there are a couple of points that needed emphasis:

Important: Depending on the final diameter of brake drums (if they have been turned), you may have to use oversize replacement brake shoes and linings. Generally, if a drum is turned from .060-inch oversize to maximum discard dimension, .030-inch oversize linings are used, but check your parts man to see what's recommended for your particular brake.

1. When you have drums miked and turned, have the brake shop match each new lining to its respective drum by grinding it to the drum's micrometer reading. This eliminates high spots and assures linings will make full contact with drums. However, high-quality brake linings are generally preground by the maker, so this may not be necessary.

2. In the case of Bendix brakes, hook the adjusting lever into the hole in the secondary shoe web. Wagner self-adjusting brakes should have the adjusting lever placed in the secondary shoe web with the slot in the lever engaging to the full depth with the slot in the shoe web.

3. Lay brake shoes on a clean surface in correct mounting position. Connect the lower spring between the shoes. On Bendix brakes, the spring is connected between the primary shoe and adjusting lever. Engage the adjusting mechanism.

4. Carry the assembly to the car and place it on the brake backing plate, engaging the brake cylinder (drawing 16). Position the shoes' webs on the anchoring unit.

5. On rear brakes, spread shoes slightly, reinstall parking-brake strut and springs and rejoin parking-brake lever to the secondary shoe.

6. On all brakes except Delco-Moraine, reinstall the shoe retaining parts. On Delco, do this after installing the rest of the self-adjusting mechanism.

On units with hold-down springs, push the hold-down pin through the backing plate and shoe, and hold pin in place. Grasp the hold-down spring and cup with pliers, place the spring on the pin, and give the pin a quarter turn to lock it in place (drawing 17). If spring clips are used, compress the clip and snap it in place on the pin.

If brake hold-down devices are tension-type retaining pins, fit the spring-retaining clip through the backing plate and use a small punch to extend the spring, hooking it on to the retaining clip.

7. Install the rest of the self-adjusting unit as follows:

On Delco-Moraine brakes (drawing 18), hook one end of the actuating link over the anchor pin or on the anchor plate if plate is bolted on. Hook the other end to the lever and pivot assembly. Position the lever on the secondary shoe, placing the lever return spring between the lever and shoe. Install the sleeve, then the hold-down parts.

On Bendix brakes (drawing 19), install the cable guide on the secondary shoe, hook one end of the cable on the actuating lever, run the cable around the guide, and slip the cable eye over the anchor pin.

On Wagner brakes (drawing 20), bolt the crank to the secondary shoe. Install offset ends of the links onto the crank holes. Hook upper link over the top groove in the anchor pin. Lift the adjusting lever slightly, and hook bottom link to the lever.

Important: Defer installation of the upper link until you install shoe return springs since it is installed on the anchor pin *over* the spring.

8. Install shoe return springs. Hook springs to shoes first and then attach them to the anchor assembly using a spring installation tool. Spring installation varies, so examine springs before removing them.

■ **To finish your brake job,** use a drum-to-brake shoe clearance gauge to check drum's inside diameter. Tighten the lock crew (drawing 21).

Turn the tool over and fit it over the brake shoes. You will probably have to expand the shoes manually by turning the star wheel to get the linings to extend to the gauge. The gauge should just slide over the linings. That's a proper fit (drawing 22).

Reinstall brake drums and tighten the parking-brake equalizer until there is tension on brake cables.

Before moving the car, check for ample brake pedal. Now drive the car forward about 200 feet, stop, then back up 200 feet. Do this a few times, coming to a complete halt each time.

How to replace disc brake pads

By MORT SCHULTZ

YOUR BIGGEST PROBLEM with disc brakes is worn pads. However, inspecting and replacing pads with those from a replacement kit isn't difficult when you know tricks the pros use. A brake-pad replacement kit generally consists of four pads—two for each of the two front wheels—and other necessary parts.

Frequent brake-pad inspection pays dividends. If you do it every time you're supposed to rotate tires, or every 15,000 miles, you should never have to resurface or replace rotors (discs). Remember that the main cause of rotor failure is the wearing down of pads, leaving metal shoe scraping against metal rotor. The shoe is the support for the pad.

pistons and pads

Disc brakes have one, two or four hydraulically driven pistons that force pads against revolving rotors. Except for some trucks, two-piston units are out of date.

Except for 1970 AMC models, 1970–72 Dodge Darts and Plymouth Valiants, Corvettes and early model Camaros with four-piston disc brakes at all four wheels, most cars with discs since 1970 use either Delco Moraine, Kelsey-Hayes or Bendix one-piston units.

Here we discuss typical Delco Moraine and Kelsey-Hayes one-piston units, which are used in nearly 98 percent of all cars with disc brakes built in the U.S. since 1969. The Bendix one-piston unit is used in the remainder of U.S.-built models, including Pinto, Mustang II, Maverick and Comet. If your car's disc-brake unit is other than Delco Moraine or Kelsey-Hayes, you still shouldn't have trouble changing its worn pads if you are guided by procedures outlined here.

Delco Moraine one-piston units

Generally, all General Motors cars and light trucks use this system—Buick, Cadillac, Chevrolet, GMC, Oldsmobile and Pontiac. To service a typical Delco Moraine one-piston disc brake, do the following:

SEE ALSO

Autos, ramps . . . Cooling systems, auto . . . Emissions controls . . . Lubrication, auto . . . Ramps, auto repair . . . Tune-up, auto

1. Jack up the front of the car and make secure. Remove the front wheel assemblies.
2. With a clean spoon, dip brake fluid from the master cylinder reservoir until it remains about one-third full. Discard fluid and replace the reservoir cover.

Don't unscrew the brake line to draw off fluid, and don't empty the master-cylinder reservoir of all its fluid. Doing so will make it necessary to bleed air from the hydraulic system.

3. Inspect outer pads: Look in each end of the left- and right-wheel calipers. Check inner pads by looking through the inspection hole in the top of both calipers.

If any pad is worn to the same or lesser thickness as the metal shoe to which it's riveted, replace both pads in the caliper *and* those in the caliper of the other wheel. Replacing less than all pads when one has to be replaced will result in unequal braking.

Steps in replacing the pads of a typical Delco Moraine single-piston unit are as follows:

- Put a seven-inch C-clamp on the caliper so the solid side of the clamp rests against the back of the caliper and the screw end rests against the metal side of the outer shoe.
- Tighten the C-clamp as much as you can to move the caliper out away from the car and to push the piston to the bottom of the bore. Brake fluid will transfer to the master cylinder reservoir.
- With the caliper moved out and the piston bottomed, remove the C-clamp.
- Unscrew the two mounting bolts which attach the caliper to the support bracket. Note that bolt heads are behind the caliper. Depending on the type of bolt head, use a socket-and-ratchet or a hex-Allen wrench.
- Lift the caliper off the disc. You needn't disconnect the brake hose, but be sure you don't

PAD INSPECTION can be done without having to remove the calipers on Delco Moraine assemblies and on most Kelsey-Hayes units as well.

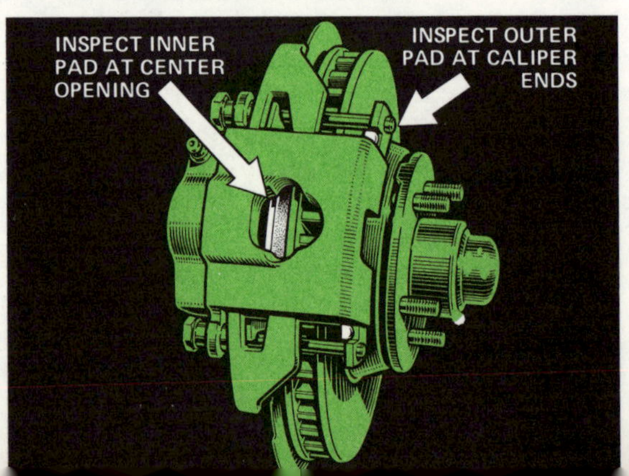

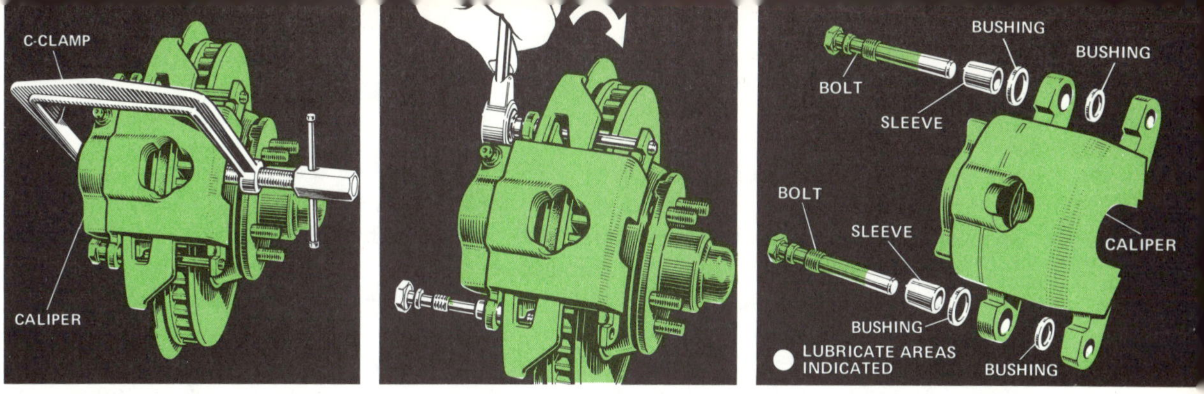

SEAT THE PISTON in the bore using a C-clamp as in the drawing on left (Delco Moraine single-piston unit). Release the caliper from the support bracket on the rotor by unscrewing the bolts using a socket-and-ratchet (center drawing) or hex-Allen wrench, whichever is needed. Lubricate new parts used when replacing pads as indicated in the right drawing.

drop the caliper or let it hang by the hose. Make up a hook from a wire hanger, connect it to the caliper and hang the caliper from a vehicle suspension member.

• You can now remove inner and outer pads. If either is stuck, pry it out carefully with a screwdriver, but be careful that the tool doesn't slip and damage the caliper.

• Remove the antirattle (shoe support) spring—it will be lying either in the piston cavity or on the inner shoe. Retain this spring.

• Turn to the two inner ears of the caliper. Push out and discard the sleeve from each. Then remove and discard the four rubber bushings from both the inner and outer caliper ears.

Some brake-pad replacement kits may not include new sleeves and rubber bushings, in which case these parts have to be purchased separately. Also buy silicone grease, if a tube isn't in the replacement kit, to lubricate new sleeves and rubber bushings before they are installed. HEI (High Energy Ignition) dielectric silicone grease, available from a GM dealer, is recommended.

• Clean holes and bushing grooves in the caliper ears with a dry rag and wipe dirt from mounting bolts. Do not use an abrasive cleaner or a brush. If bolts are corroded or bent, replace them. Clean inside the caliper with a dry rag. Do not use a solvent or compressed air.

• If there is fluid on the piston dust boot, the caliper should be overhauled. Otherwise, wipe the boot clean with a dry rag.

• Lubricate the entire surface of new sleeves, new rubber bushings, bushing grooves and tips of mounting bolts. Install rubber bushings in caliper ears.

• By hand, install sleeves, positioning them so the ends that face the pad assemblies—the inner ends, that is—are flush with the machined surfaces of the ears.

• Four variations of inboard pad assemblies are made for Delco Moraine units: no-notch, half-moon notch, flat notch with hole, and flat notch without hole. Your variation depends on your car. Examine the setup to identify the one you need and proceed with installation.

If pads have wear sensors, as most do, the brake rotor must rotate into the sensor for the sensor to work. Therefore, inner pads (the ones that possess the sensors) are left- and right-hand units; that is, the left-hand unit is for the caliper on the left wheel and the right-hand unit is for the caliper on the right wheel. Don't mix them.

• Place the spring-wire antirattle spring in the center of the piston so the spring's two tangs point up and toward the front of the caliper. Put the new inner-pad assembly in the caliper so the bottom edge of the shoe rests against the spring's tangs. Shift the spring, if necessary, so its tangs will fall in the center of the shoe.

FOUR TYPES of disc brake pads to meet the varying configurations of Delco Moraine calipers are shown in the far left drawing. Antirattle springs that hold shoes are shown in the next drawing: Top drawing is the spring-wire antirattle spring; clip-type antirattle spring is at bottom. In the third drawing the inner pad is installed using a spring-wire antirattle spring; note position of tangs. In the drawing on the far right, the inner pad is installed using a clip-type antirattle spring—note position of the single tang.

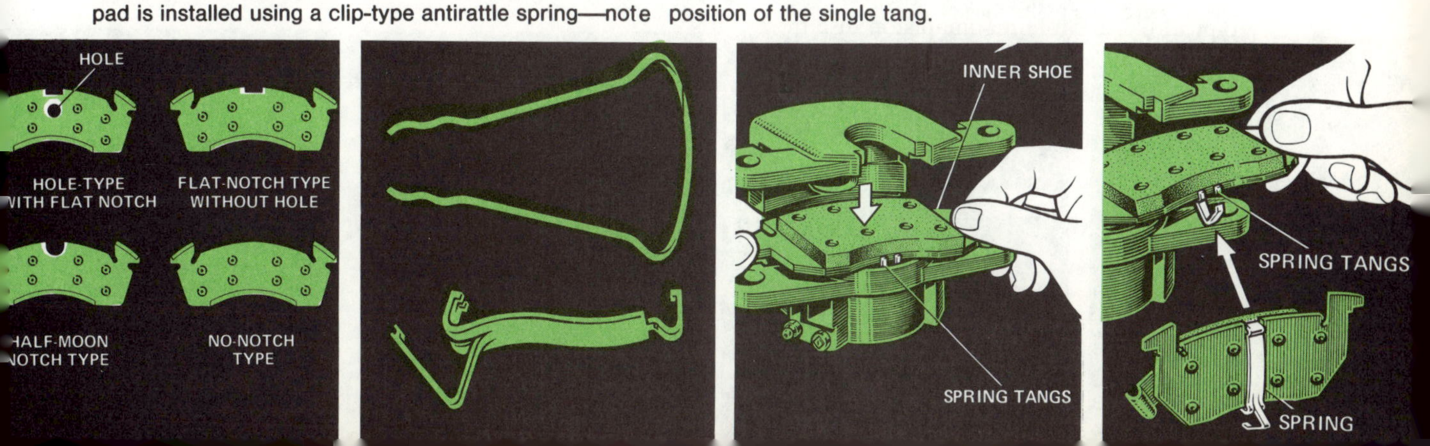

• If your setup uses a clip-type spring, place its top tang over the notch in the center of the inner shoe or into the hole from the rear of the shoe and press the spring on. It should fit the shoe securely at top and bottom.

• With the inner shoe in place, install the outer shoe by placing the large flange into its notch in the caliper housing. By hand, rotate the shoe's small tabs to fit them into their notches in the caliper housing. Test to see if the shoe is loose by trying to move it. If it is loose, remove the shoe and lightly tap the two small tabs until you think they'll fit securely. Install the shoe and test for looseness again. Shoe looseness is a major cause of brake noise.

• Place the caliper over the rotor, lining up the holes in the caliper ears with holes in the support bracket. Be sure the brake hose is straight.

• Insert mounting bolts through sleeves in the inboard caliper ears and push bolts through to engage bushings in the outboard ears, starting bolt threads into the support bracket carefully. Don't cross-thread. Tighten bolts with a torque wrench to 30–35 ft.-lb.

• After installing new pads on both wheels, put on wheel and tire assemblies and fill the master cylinder with Delco Supreme II brake fluid or fluid that meets Department of Transportation standard 3. Pump the brake pedal a few times to check for normal pedal travel and brake warning light function. Then, recheck fluid level. Add fluid if necessary to bring level within 1/16 inch of reservoir top.

Kelsey-Hayes single piston unit

Generally, Kelsey-Hayes single piston disc brake units are used on cars made by AMC, Chrysler Corp., Ford and Volkswagen. Inspection of pads is done the same way as for the Delco Moraine unit. If pads have to be replaced, proceed as follows (instructions apply to the unit used on 1978–82 Chrysler Omni and Horizon—others are similar):

1. Remove the caliper locating pins to separate the caliper and adapter.
2. Slowly move caliper out and away from the rotor.
3. Using a hook fashioned from a wire coat hanger, hang the caliper to a vehicle suspension member.
4. Remove the antirattle clip, followed by the inner and outer pad assemblies. Save the clip. Some Kelsey-Hayes units have two clips.
5. Use a drift to remove and discard bushings from caliper holes. Some Kelsey-Hayes calipers are also fitted with plastic sleeves. Discard them, too.
6. Be sure there is no fluid leak from the piston bore. If there is, overhaul the caliper.
7. Use a clean hand to push the piston back into the place if you can. If not, use a clean C-clamp.
8. Lubricate new bushings (also plastic sleeves, if used) from your pad replacement kit and install them.
9. Position the new inner-pad assembly in place in the piston bore. It must be seated fully.
10. Position the new outer-pad assembly into the caliper and slide the antirattle spring over the outer part of the caliper so it engages the outer shoe.
11. Hold the inner-pad assembly in place and carefully slide the caliper in position on the adapter and over the rotor. Align the locating-pin holes of the caliper with those of the adapter.
12. Install locating pins through the bushings and thread them in place. Take care not to cross-thread. Tighten pins to 30–35 ft.-lbs. Refill the master cylinder with brake fluid meeting Department of Transportation standard 3.

OUTER PAD ASSEMBLY is fitted and attached to the caliper so shoe ears engage notches outlined in yellow (far left drawing). If procedure outlined in text fails to provide a tighter outer shoe, use Vise-Grip or Channel-lock pliers to clinch the ears over their seats on the caliper (second drawing from left). Third drawing shows caliper being replaced on rotor; seen is a Kelsey-Hayes single-piston unit. The drawing on the far right shows how locating pins are installed through holes (called positioners) in the adapter and then into the caliper of a Kelsey-Hayes single-piston unit. Note that with this unit the locating pins are inserted from the inboard side of the caliper.

EGG CARTONS make excellent storage containers for Christmas tree bulbs. For breakage-free packing, simply punch an undersized hole in each well, then push the male end of the bulb in for a force-fit.

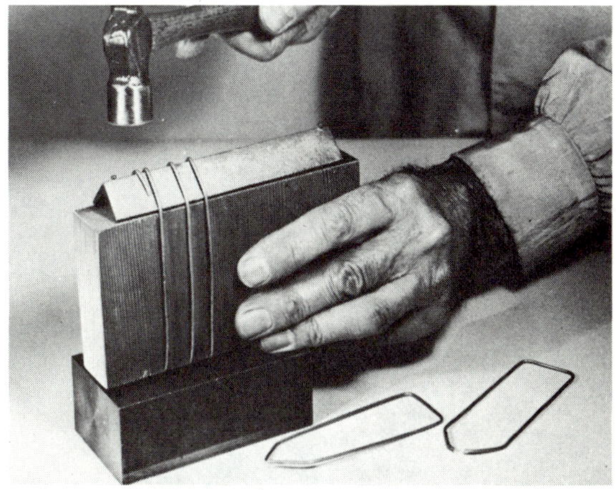

SHORT LENGTHS of tie-wire can be quickly cut to a uniform length by placing a piece of angle iron atop a block of wood (that produces the desired length). A sharp rap with a hammer does the actual "cutting."

A SANDPAPER "WASHER," if cut and installed on the knob-holding screw as shown, can be used to hold the loosest wood knob securely in place. When the knob is tightened, the abrasive grabs and holds it fast.

A WRECKING BAR can be used as the handle on your toolbox if you drill appropriate-size holes in the upright to receive it. Then the tool is conveniently at hand without using valuable toolbox space.

AN ADHESIVE-TAPE spool, along with its cover, makes an ideal "case" for carrying a plumb bob. Permanently tie the free end of the cord to the spool, wind up the remainder and snap the cover closed.

ORDINARY STORM-SASH hangers provide a quick, yet sturdy, method for hanging a window box. The box is then easily removable for painting and, if the hardware is galvanized, you'll have no rust stains.

Make any wall a brick wall

■ YOU DON'T HAVE to be a mason to turn a wall of your home into extremely realistic, but simulated, brick or stone. The job is done with individual molded "bricks" or "stones" only ¼-in. thick. Adhesive mortar (mastic) is applied to the wall and smeared thickly into the rear cavity of each molding just before it is pressed into place. Care must be taken to maintain uniform spacing around each piece. For details, write: Dacor Mfg. Co., 80 Gardner St., Worcester, MA 01610.

SEE ALSO

Basement remodeling . . . Family rooms . . . Home improvement . . . Insulation . . . Painting, interior . . . Paneling, wood . . . Shelves . . . Tile, wall . . . Wallpaper

ADHESIVE MORTAR (mastic) $^1/_{16}$-in. thick is applied to the wall to be bricked.

BRICKS can be applied around ranges and ovens but must be at least 6 in. from burners, 24 in. from any intense heat.

BACK CAVITY is filled with mortar just before the brick is applied to the wall.

FIRMLY PRESS the brick into position so that mortar squeezes out on all four sides.

Everything's ready when it's time for bridge

By ELMER E. SCOTT

■ IT'S TIME for bridge—do you know where your playing cards are? You will if you keep them in this attractive holder that stores two decks of cards, pencils and a score pad. If made of select hardwood and given a rich hand-rubbed finish, it makes a handsome desk or shelf accessory. It requires a lathe to turn its pedestal base and the lipped pencil well. However, if you lack a lathe, you can alter the shape of these parts and make them square for easy cutting on your table or radial saw.

Cut the top, bottom, ends and side pieces in pairs from ¼-in.-thick walnut or cherry. Jigsaw two card slots on the top and bore a 1-in. hole in the center; bore a ⅝-in. hole in the bottom; assemble the parts. Note that 1/16-in.-deep rabbets are cut along all four edges of top and bottom pieces. The side and end pieces fit flush in the recesses formed by these rabbets. The dividers forming the card wells must be in place before the rest of the parts are actually put together in the assembled form.

Turn the pedestal from a 3¼-in.-sq. block of solid stock and form a tenon ¼ x ⅝-in. at the top.

The pedestal can be finished while it is still spinning in the lathe. Since it would be difficult to finish the score-pad rack after it's attached to the holder, finish it before assembly. Then cover the bottom with felt held on with white glue, and you are ready to call your bridge group.

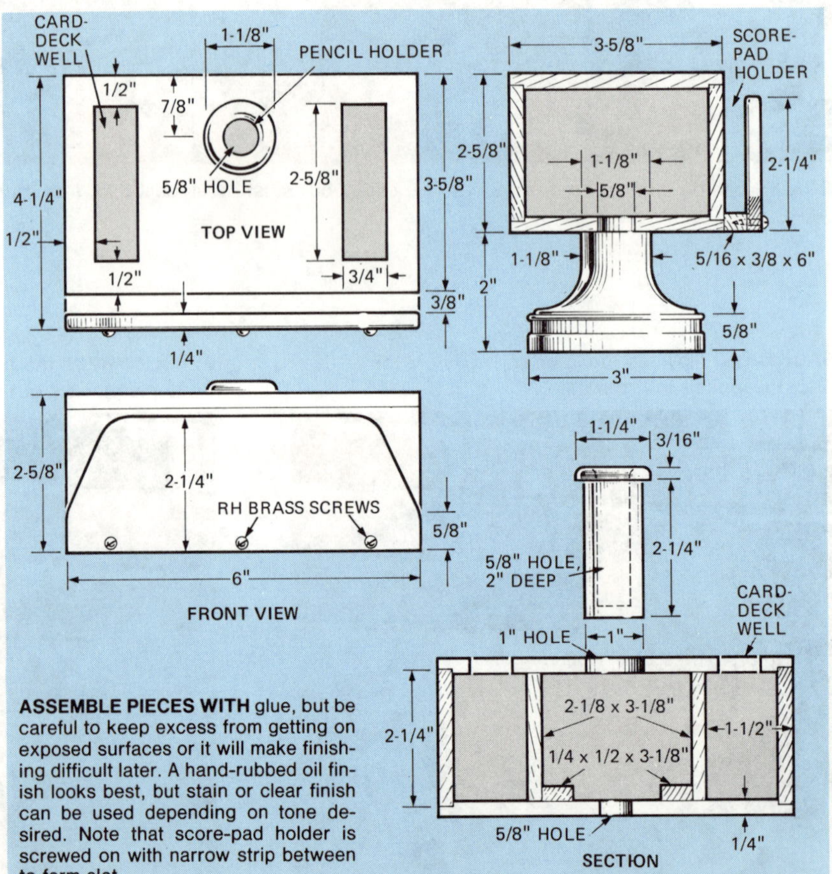

ASSEMBLE PIECES WITH glue, but be careful to keep excess from getting on exposed surfaces or it will make finishing difficult later. A hand-rubbed oil finish looks best, but stain or clear finish can be used depending on tone desired. Note that score-pad holder is screwed on with narrow strip between to form slot.

SEE ALSO
Backgammon tables . . . Bars . . .
Bridge tables . . . Chess sets . . .
Cribbage boards . . . Desks . . .
Family rooms . . . Game tables . . .
Lazy Susans . . . Letter racks . . .
Party tables . . . Pool tables . . .
Snack tables . . . Trays, folding

Build a parsons table

By WILLIAM SCHREMP

THE PARSONS TABLE has nothing to do with a parson, contrary to popular belief. Some say it was named after Albert Parsons, founder of the famous Parsons School of Design, and credit him with designing it. Others say it was designed by a Frenchman on the Parsons faculty.

Because of its overall flush design, the Parsons table has always presented a problem to the do-it-yourselfer when it comes to attaching the legs rigidly. I solved this by making the legs hollow and as an integral part of the whole table. The result is a table with incredibly rigid legs. After I covered all of the exposed surfaces with a white Micarta (decorative laminate), the table appeared to be molded of plastic.

SEE ALSO

Butcher block furniture . . . Butcher blocks . . .
Coffee tables . . . Dining tables . . . Game tables . . .
Hutch tables . . . Laminates, plastic . . .
Nesting tables . . . Occasional tables . . .
Party tables

The cutting diagram shows how you can economically lay out all 13 parts of the 30x30x30-in. table on a sheet of 4x8 plywood ¾-in. thick with a minimum of waste. The four U-shape sides are cut alike as are the pieces for the built-up hollow legs. Each side member laps the edge of the adjacent one, which accounts for one leg of each side being 3 in. wide and the other 2¼ in. All the joints are butted, glued and nailed (or screwed); the top is applied last.

The laminate is applied to the legs first, then to the U-shape sides and finally to the top.

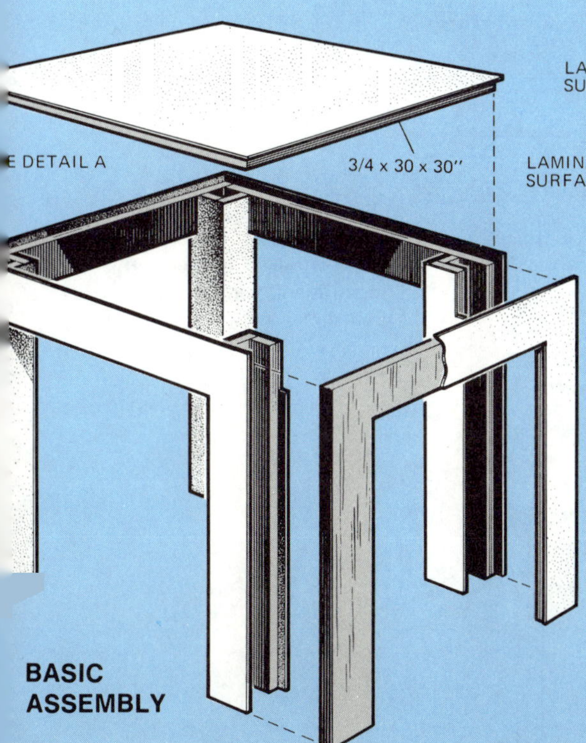

BASIC ASSEMBLY

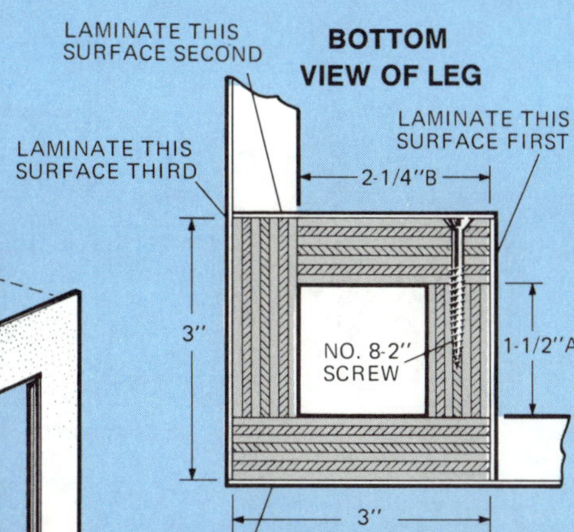

BOTTOM VIEW OF LEG

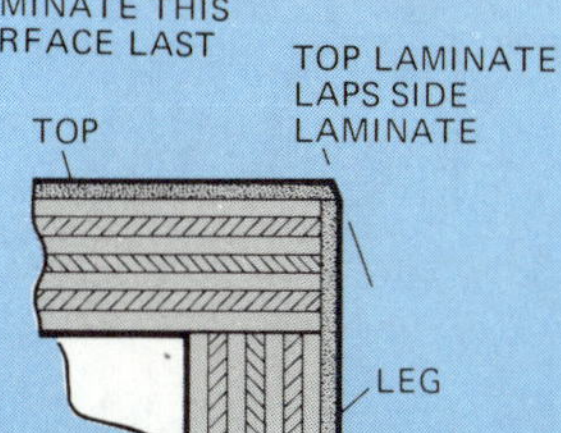

DETAIL A

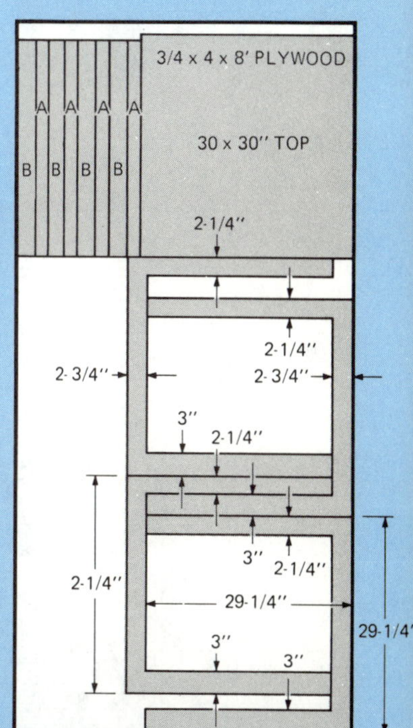

CUTTING DIAGRAM

Built-ins for kitchen and laundry

WIRE clothes-sorting baskets ride in grooved runners. Wash baskets also rest on sliding shelves.

ROLL-OUT appliance cart (left) poses as cabinet door when parked. Slide-out dish shelves are accessible from sides. Dishwasher (right), installed at counter level, requires no stooping to load and unload.

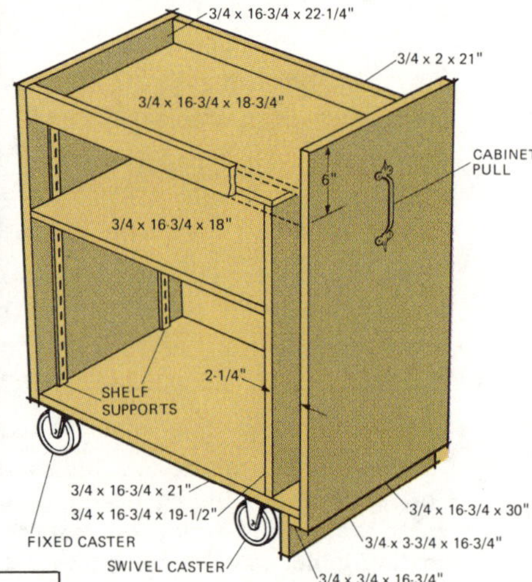

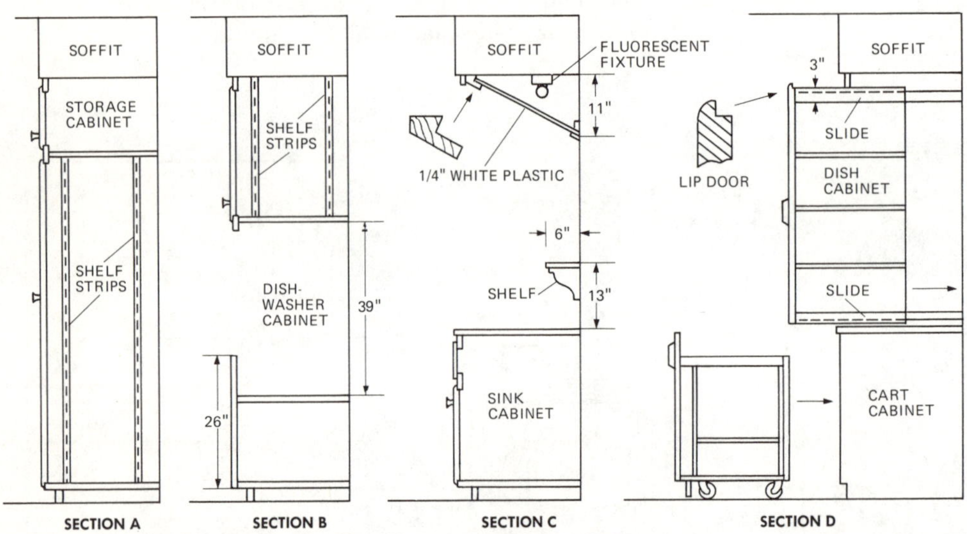

ELEVATION and section drawings at left show how one-wall kitchen is built. Plywood forms compartments; edges are faced with 1 x 2s.

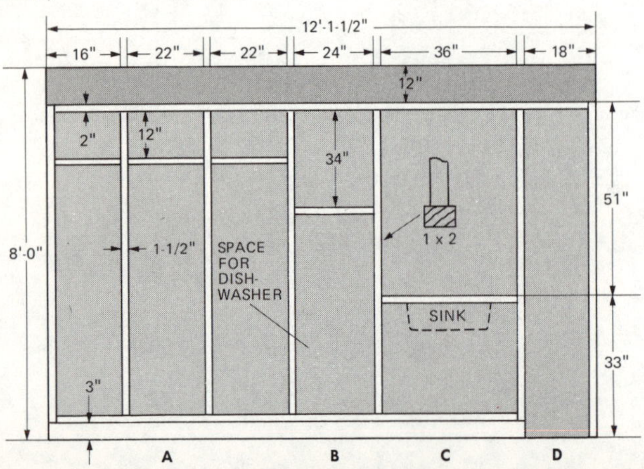

FRONT ELEVATION

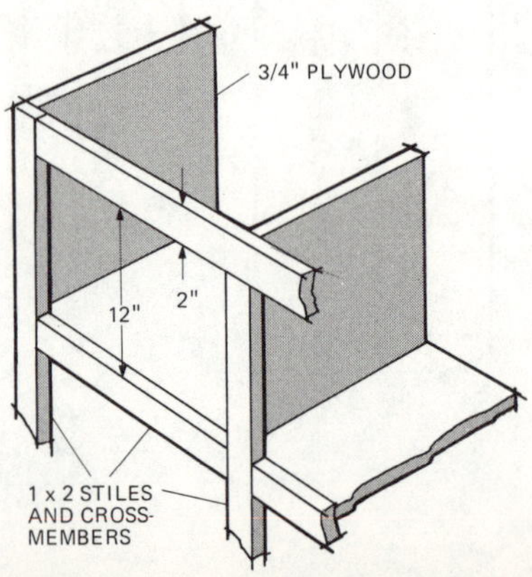

STORAGE IS NEARLY as important as good equipment in creating an efficient laundry area. In Maytag's laundry center, left, cabinets to the left of the washer are fitted with pull-out wire-basket drawers to store soiled clothes according to wash loads. With four such drawers, it's easy to sort whites, colored, wash-and-wears and delicates. The cabinets to the right of the dryer provide cedar-lined storage for off-season clothes. Upper cabinets are used to safely store laundry aids out of reach of children.

Unusual aspects of the custom-designed kitchen, far left, include a no-stoop dishwasher that's 18 in. off the floor, and a roll-around appliance cart that pulls out of the cabinet convenient to a dinette table. It has a warming tray on top and adjustable shelves to keep small appliances extra handy.

Dish storage is made convenient in a pull-out cabinet above the appliance cart, and the sink located between washer and storage is made bright as day by an overhead fluorescent "skylight."

SINK IS CONVENIENT to dishwasher and open-sided pull-out dish cabinet. Shelf over sink is for accessories; white plastic "skylight" conceals fluorescent fixture. Sink above is lined with matching room paneling. Appliance cart parks in compartment below dish storage, looks like matching cabinet door.

OVERHEAD shelf 12 in. from ceiling simplifies wiring of hanging lights and offers useful storage space.

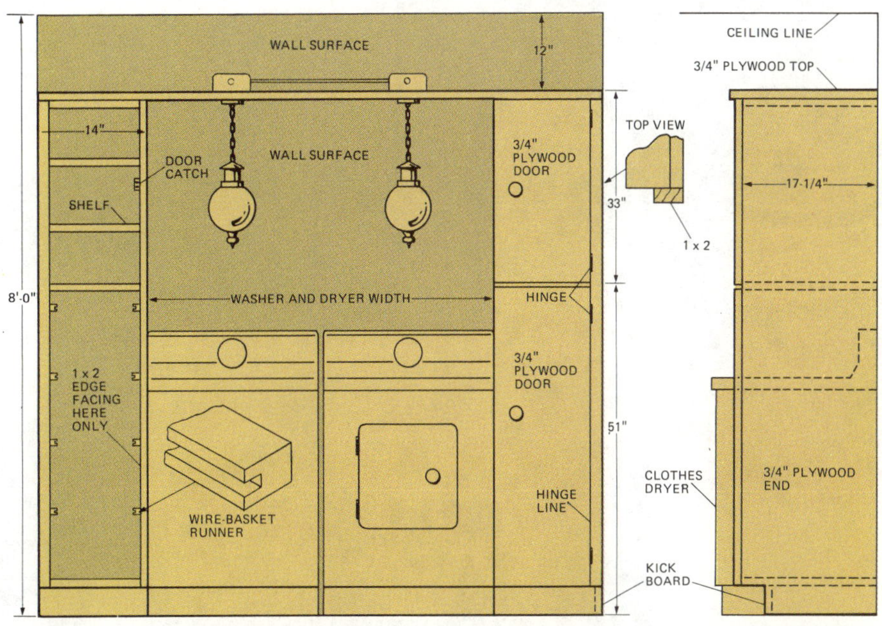

Build a safe inside a colonial cabinet

By HARRY WICKS

LOOK CAREFULLY around your home, and you will quickly realize that you have many items worth protecting. Electronic equipment, cameras, TV sets and other large items need protection from burglars. But, be aware that you have other possessions that need protection from an even more insidious enemy—fire. By filing valuable papers, deeds, insurance policies and the like in a safe with a fire rating label, you will be assured of having those documents on hand should fire strike your home.

SEE ALSO

Antique reproductions . . . Clocks . . . Comb boxes . . . Finishes, wood . . . Security, home . . . Staining, wood

To make a safe acceptable in any room, we created this colonial cabinet with its handsome raised panel door.

Our cabinet is sized to suit Sentry Standard safe model S-3, manufactured by John D. Brush

MATERIALS LIST—COLONIAL CABINET

Key	Pcs	Size and Description
A	1	1⅛ x 20-9/16 x 21⅞" pine (top)
B	1	⅜ x ½ x 18⅝" pine (cleat)
C	1	¼ x 19½ x 24" plywood (back)
D	2	¾ x 19 x 24" (side)
E	2	¾ x 1-15/16 x 24" (stile)
F	1	½ x 1⅞ x 20¾" (stop)
G	2	¾ x 2 x 21" (door stile)
H	2	¾ x 2⅛ x 16¼" (door rail)
I	1	¾ x 13 x 17½" (door panel)
J	2	¼ x ½ x 18" (door batten)
K	2	¼ x ½ x 13½" (door batten)

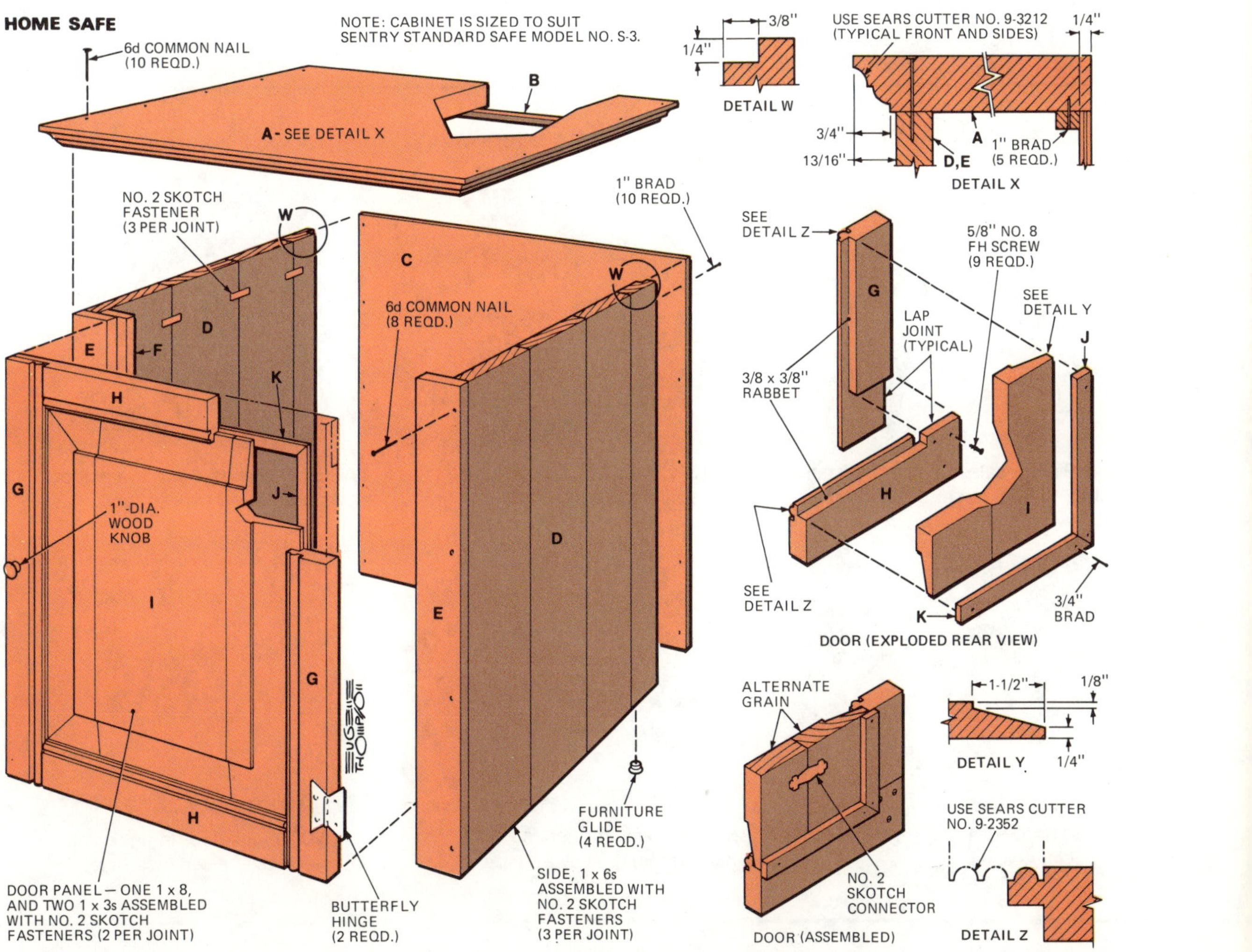

& Co. Inc., 900 Linden Ave., Rochester, NY 14625. It is available at department stores, home centers and the like. Since the materials for the cabinet should not be too expensive (if you use No. 1 common pine as we did), your total investment for great peace of mind will be reasonable.

Start by cutting the boards to length for sides, top and door panel. Mark the pieces with the letter code (i.e., A, D, I) to avoid mixing the parts. Edges to be butt-joined must be perfectly square, so run the boards through a combination blade on your table saw if they're not. Lay out boards for each section to get the most pleasing grain appearance. Then, flop the boards so they are inside surface up. Apply a light coat of carpenter's aliphatic resin (yellow) glue to mating board edges. Let glue air dry for a few moments, then press board edges together. Permanently fasten boards, using No. 2 Skotch Connectors as shown. Clamp the boards tightly before driving the connectors home. When all boards are joined, there may be a tendency for the section to curl. If so, flop the workpiece, wipe excess glue from joints with a water-dampened cloth and set heavy weights on boards overnight.

The decorative edge on the top's front and side edges is made with a molding cutterhead on the table saw. Push the top through to cut the end grain edges first and finish with the pass for the front edge. The back edge is not shaped. Sand the top smooth, dust and set aside. Next, finish the sides. Check length and width measurements and make sure both sides are identical. Using the table saw, cut the edge rabbets along the back edge of each side to receive the back panel. Cut the front stiles to size and attach to the sides using glue and 6d common nails. Use a stout nailset to set nailheads below the surface. *Do not* fill the nailheads; leave them rough set for an attractive primitive colonial look. Then install part F.

Trim the door insert panel to 13 x 17½ in. and set up your table saw to make the diagonal raised panel cut. Draw the shape (shown in Detail Y) on a piece of scrap lumber and use the scrap to set up your saw fence, blade height and blade angle. Make a test cut on the scrap and, when you're satisfied, set scrap aside. On the door panel make the two endgrain cuts and then the two cuts running with the grain. Next, return blade to 0° setting, and use that test piece of scrap to adjust blade height and fence to make the shoulder cutoff. Run scrap through the saw to be sure settings

FLOOR SAFE WITH CONCRETE JACKET CAN'T BE CARRIED AWAY

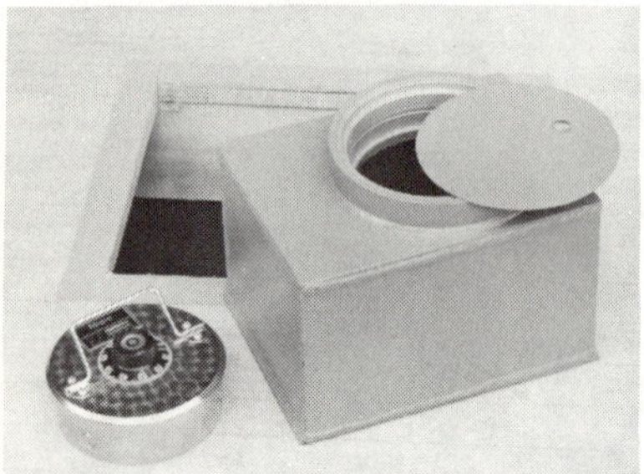

TO INSTALL safe, cut hole between joists 2 to 3 in. larger on all sides.

FASTEN metal lath basket to joists with roofing nails.

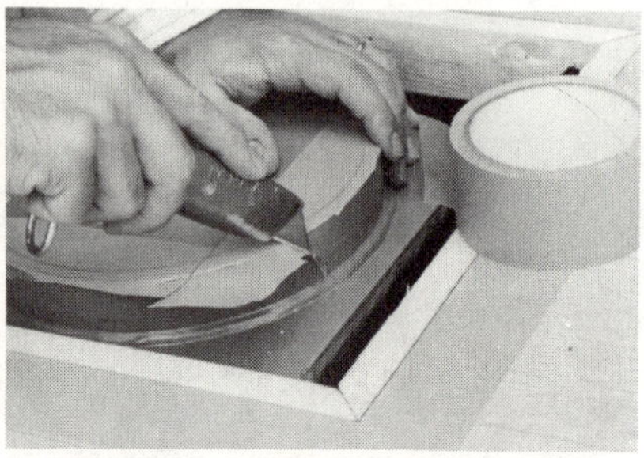

TAPE LID upside-down to neck of safe and trim off excess tape.

USE STRAIGHT 1 x 3 to screed topping cement level.

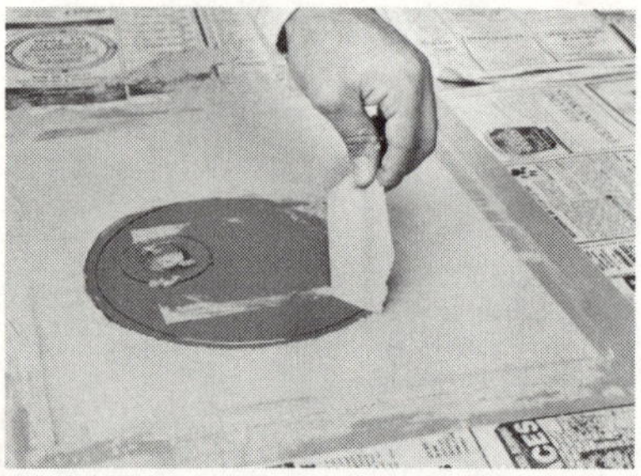

BEFORE cement dries, soak up moisture then pull away tape.

DO NOT place door in neck until concrete sets. Keep lock dry.

are correct. When they are, make the cuts on the panel itself. Once again, first do the end-grain passes, then cut with the grain.

Rip the door stiles and rails to width, then, using either router and rabbet cutter, or table saw and two passes, cut the edge rabbet in each member to receive the panel. Next, mount the molding cutterhead (Sears No. 9.2352) on your table saw and shape the inside edges. Finally, after double-checking the panel measurements, cut the lap joints at both ends of stiles and rails. Join the frame members, using glue and ⅝-in. No. 5 fh screws. Install the panel before driving screws home to assure the door remaining square. Hold panel in rabbet with a couple of brads, then lightly apply glue over the joint and conceal it with the ¼-in. batten (J & K) pieces.

Temporarily assemble the cabinet, using scrap strips tacked across the bottom to maintain correct distance between the sides. Tack the top in place and install hinges on the door. Mount the door to the stile and install the knob. (Note: The door on the prototype was created to be a press fit; there is no need for a friction or magnetic catch.) With cabinet assembled, carefully place it over your safe. It should fit with the safe door closed. Double check the cabinet for square and measure for the plywood back. Also measure for the cleat, part B.

Cut the back and disassemble the cabinet. Reassemble the cabinet without the door, using nails and glue. Tack a temporary strip between sides at the cabinet front (nailed to bottoms of sides) to keep the cabinet square while glue sets.

Dust off all wood parts and wipe with a tack rag. On the prototype, we used Beverlee's walnut stain, thinned a bit with turpentine, and tinted slightly with yellow ochre from an art supply dealer. Apply stain, allow it to set at least five minutes, then wipe with a clean, lintfree cloth. Let the cabinet stand for 24 hours.

The next step is to apply a wash coat of 3-lb.-cut white shellac thinned 50 percent with denatured alcohol. Allow shellac to dry at least four hours, then sand it lightly with 180-grit paper. Dust and wipe with a tack rag. Apply one coat of satin-finish varnish. Let it dry at least 48 hours, then rub lightly with 220-grit paper and remove all dust with a tack rag. Add a final coat of satin-finish varnish. When it's dry, mount hinges on the door and door on the cabinet. Install the doorknob.

Before laying out the hole for a floor safe, check to be certain that no cables or pipes under the floor will interfere with your installation.

Make the cuts with a heavy-duty sabre saw, using a tacked-down straightedge as a guide. Next, nail a metal-lath basket to joists and line its inside with 15-lb. felt. Add 1 x 3 frame inside opening, if desired.

Proceed to partially fill the basket with concrete and install the safe with the lid taped on. Level the top of the neck to the existing floor, then fill in around the safe with concrete to ½ in. below the neck top and allow it to set. Finish with topping cement, smooth and level.

The rectangular safe used in our installation weighs 67 lbs. The clear door opening is 6⅝ in. For your nearest distributor, write to Major Safe Co. Inc., 3600 East Olympic Blvd., Los Angeles, CA 90023.

BURGLARY PREVENTION THAT DOESN'T COST A CENT

There is a house break-in about every 12 seconds in the United States. By observing a few rules, however, you can lower the odds of your house being the next victim:

- Before leaving your home, make sure all doors are completely secured.
- Check seldom-used entrances, such as basement and porch doors regularly.
- Check locks on other possible access ways, such as basement vents, skylights and accessible windows.
- Close your garage door when you leave your home.
- Keep plantings near windows trimmed so they won't screen intruders.
- Leave a couple of lights on when you go out in the evening—but not in an obvious spot like the front window.
- Don't put identifying name tags or addresses on your key sets. They may be picked up by a burglar.
- When leaving a key for a friend or family member, don't hide it in an obvious spot, like under the doormat or in the mailbox. You should leave it with a trusted neighbor, if possible.
- Leave only your car ignition key at parking lots and auto repair shops. Lock your glove compartment.
- Store tools and ladders under lock and key to prevent burglars from using them.
- Have a locksmith change keys on all locks when you move into a new home.

Going on vacation?

- Only tell those people who *have* to know about it.
- Do carloading out of sight of passersby—in the garage or behind the house.
- Stop all deliveries and have a friend pick up your mail.
- Ask a neighbor to keep an eye on things.
- Tell the police; ask them to check your property occasionally.
- Don't leave your house looking empty or deserted. Draw open all the curtains and blinds slightly.
- Don't hide valuables in your bedroom, where many burglars look first.

Low-cost ways to burglarproof your house

By ROSARIO CAPOTOSTO

■ IT MAKES NO SENSE to spend a couple hundred dollars to install the latest in key cylinder technology in your door locks when all a burglar has to do is kick in an airconditioner and climb in through your side window. Little things, like the security tricks that follow, can often make the difference between a successful break-in and a foiled attempt. Although they won't make your house absolutely burglarproof, they will beef up your protection. The tighter your security, the more likely an intruder is to be deterred. As unneighborly as it sounds, most of us would much prefer to have a thief turn away from our own home to look for easier pickings down the street.

The simple steps shown in this article can be taken right now to eliminate, or at least strengthen, weak links in the perimeter defense of your home. Many will cost you almost nothing and most of the required materials for these projects can be found in the typical home workshop.

The projects fall into three basic categories: simple locking devices, lock reinforcement and improvement, and acrylic plastic shields. We've also included a rudimentary alarm that may make a thief think twice before ripping you off. Many of the principles involved can be modified to meet the requirements of your situation. The hints may also give rise to solutions that you can develop on your own.

One caution to keep in mind: Never install a device that will in any way hamper your exit during a fire or other emergency.

NO MATTER how good the lock, it's only as strong as the grip of the screws holding it in place. Most doors and jambs are constructed of softwood, which has poor screw-holding ability. To provide a better anchor for screws, counterbore the screw holes and insert hardwood dowels. Use ⅜-in.-dia. spiral-grooved dowels and resorcinol glue. Note that the door shown in the photo has a plywood veneer, but the interior consists of soft ponderosa pine. This is typical of many doors—and one reason a large number of homeowners have decided to replace wooden doors and jambs with steel units.

GARAGE DOOR LOCKS are easy to pick because builders usually use the cheapest-quality locks money can buy. It does a thief no good to pick your garage door lock, however, if you prevent him from raising your overhead door with this foolproof method: Drill a hole in the track slightly above one of the rollers and inset a ¼-in.-dia. steel rod to act as a stop. For a double door, drill the hole in both tracks and use a longer rod. A slight downward bend at each end will keep the rod in place.

Caution: Do not use this method with automatic-lifting doors; it can damage the lifting mechanism.

ONE OF THE easiest entries for a burglar is to push back a spring-latch lock when the doorjamb is the nonrabbeted type. To do it he slips a thin piece of plastic such as a credit card beneath stop and past door edge (arrow). To prevent such entries, drive four or five 6d finishing nails through the stop in front of the strike plate hole. Now a card can't be slid under stop. Use pilot holes to avoid splitting the stop and set nailheads below surface and fill with plastic wood filler to conceal nails. If greater strength is desired, substitute 1¼ in. No. 8 fh screws for the nails and insert them in counterbored holes.

THIS SUPPLEMENTARY, heavy-duty strike is sized to fit under the standard strike for a key-in-knob lock. The off-center holes permit the use of heavy, 3-in.-long screws which penetrate well into the stud behind the jamb. A second pair of holes (partly obscured) allows the original strike to be reinstalled with the original screws. Deepen the mortise with a chisel to accommodate the extra thickness.

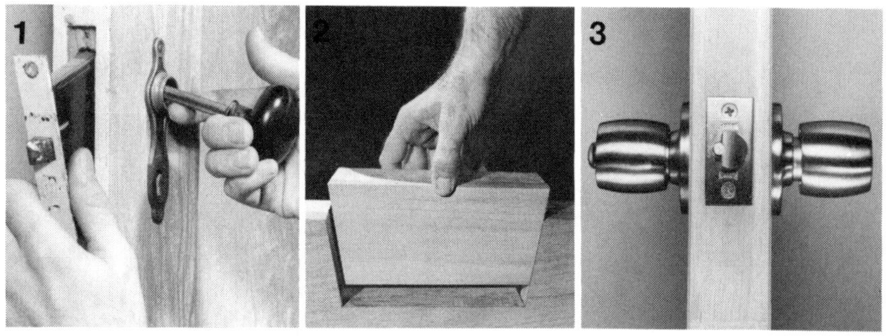

OLD FASHIONED, easy-to-pick lever-tumbler locks (photo 1) can be replaced with modern cylinder type or latch-and-deadbolt locks by cutting out the mortised section and replacing it with a block of solid wood called a Dutchman (photo 2). Taper the cutout and mating block slightly as shown.

Glue the block in place with resorcinol glue, applying pressure with a bar clamp between the strike and hinge edges. The keystone shape transmits clamp pressure to all three sides—which would be impossible with a square insert. No nails or screws are necessary, but if you use them, be sure to set or counterbore so heads are below the wood surface.

The surface of the door can be left as it is or faced with panels (photo 3), depending upon the original thickness of the door into which the new lock is fitted.

BASEMENT WINDOWS are frequently left open during the day for ventilation. Burglars know this and often gain entrance here. Install a Plexiglas shield/vent over the window to increase your security. Form the shield from a single ¼-in. sheet. Make the necessary bends with a strip heater. A homemade strip heater can be made with a Rohm and Haas heating element available at some hardware and most plastic supply outlets. Plans for the heater are provided with the heating element. To install, bore pilot holes for one-way screws in the window frame.

THE STANDARD lock strike is usually light-gauge metal "secured" to a softwood jamb with a pair of ½ to ¾-in.-long screws. Installation of a maximum-security strike like this one prevents easy entry.

To install, temporarily remove the doorstop molding to permit routing or chiseling the necessary recess. The doorstop will conceal the long portion of the strike when it's reinstalled. A large hole at the center of the oversize strike allows you to drive a nail through the stop into the jamb to prevent an intruder from using a plastic card to retract a spring-latch type of lock, a favorite technique with burglars.

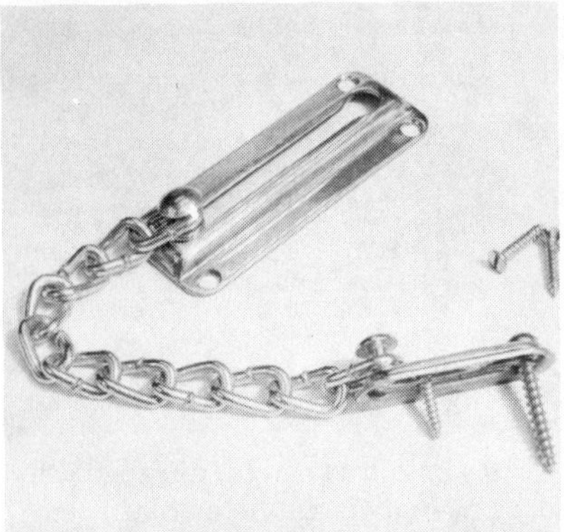

DOOR CHAINS are of limited value when installed with the small screws often supplied with these devices. Note how much larger a screw can be used without reboring the original holes in the hardware. Caution: Chains are secondary locking devices meant only to let you interview a stranger without unlocking door completely.

SLIDING ALUMINUM windows can be opened if a burglar pries apart the typically flimsy framing which usually houses equally-flimsy locks. Drill a hole through the track and window frame to allow insertion of a steel pop rivet. The pop rivet pin locks the sliding panels in a closed-position. Use two rivets at the bottom of each panel. An additional hole in the track will let you leave the window locked but slightly open for ventilation. If window ledge is deep, use a drill bit extension or a flexible shaft to permit drilling close to the edge. Heads of rivets are easy to grip and can be quickly removed from the inside in case of fire or other emergency that requires quick exit.

A PAIR of sturdy screw eyes installed on both sides of a door frame will allow the insertion of a ½-in. steel rod or pipe across the door. This is a simple, positive method of keeping out a lock-picking burglar.

Important: be certain that the bar is easy to remove and allows quick exit in emergency situations. Use at least 3-in.-long screw eyes anchored securely to 2 x 4 door frame members. You should find studs to fasten into between 2 and 5 in. from the edge of the door.

NONRETRACTABLE, one-way screws are often hard to find or not available in the size you require. You can easily make your own screws by filing or grinding two slants as shown above. Rubber or wood pads in the vise will protect screw threads.

Use this type of screw to attach any hardware or ornamentation exposed on the outside of the house, but keep in mind that removal of the hardware will be practically impossible without drilling out the screw or grinding off the screw head.

ENTRANCE DOORS that open to the outside and have removable hinge pins are a welcome sight to burglars. To prevent one from removing the pins and lifting out the door, drill a hole in one hinge leaf and insert a ¼-in.-dia. steel pin. Allow it to protrude about ½ in. Then drill a mating hole through the opposite leaf to receive the protruding pin. The hole should be slightly elongated to provide clearance for the pin as it swings. Add pins to all three of the hinges that hold a typical exterior door.

POLICE STATISTICS indicate that many burglars push in first-floor window airconditioners to gain entry to houses. A ⅛ x ¾-in. steel bar (you can also use ¼ x 1-in. aluminum stock), secured across the top and bottom of the airconditioner with lagscrews, will prevent such break-ins. Windows are rough-framed with double or triple studs, so you can use two 5/16 x 3-in. lagscrews at each end of the brace for a solid grip.

If the design of the airconditioner permits, it's also a good idea to drive screws into the housing to prevent removal to the outside as well.

Easy-to-build butcher block furniture

By MIKE McCLINTOCK

■ YOU CAN BRING butcher block out of the kitchen and show off its beautiful wood grain in your living room with this sofa, chair and coffee table. They're designed for rapid construction, rugged use and contemporary style.

The same methods are used to build the chair and sofa shown in the photo. We'll detail the chair, and if you make the sofa, just substitute the dimensions on the exploded drawing.

Cut a 2-in. thick, 30 x 72-in. butcher block slab into two 35⅞ x 29⅞-in. pieces. Orient the sides to hide or minimize blemishes. For shadow skids (a visual detail that makes the furniture "float"), rip 2 in. off the bottom of each side and trim skids to dimensions shown to give a ¼-in. reveal around the edges that meet the butcher block sides.

For the fascias, rip two 32½-in. lengths 6¼-in.

WELL-OILED, 2-in.-thick maple tabletop shows off elegant grain that used to be featured only in the kitchen.

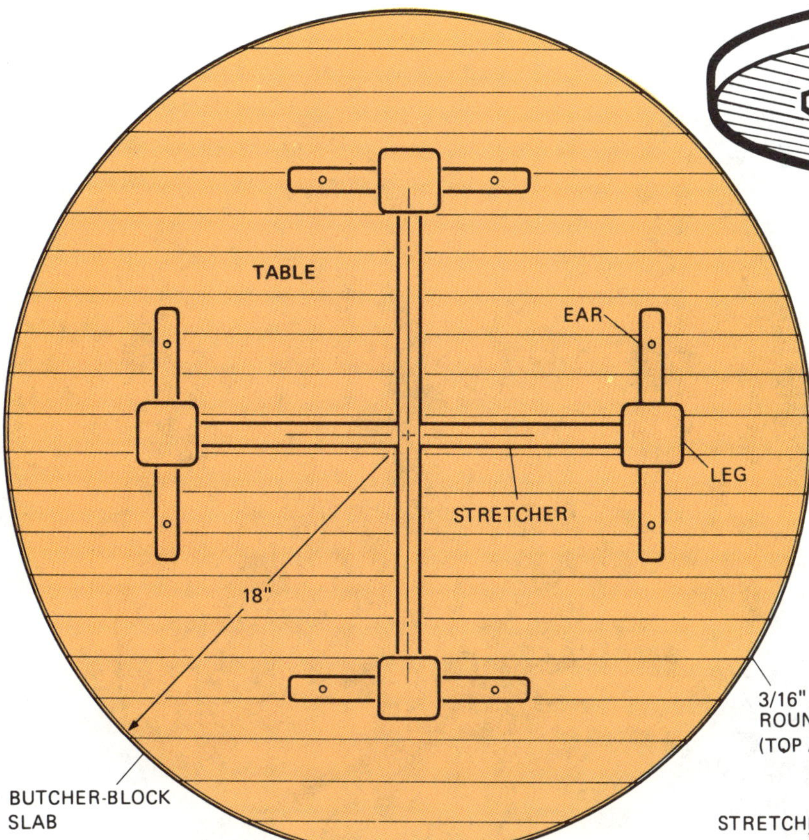

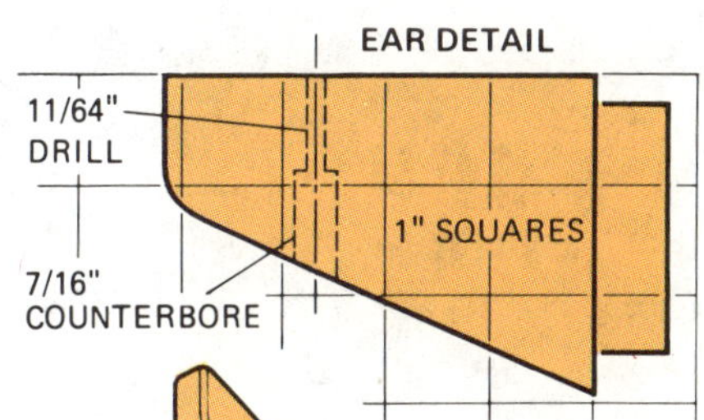

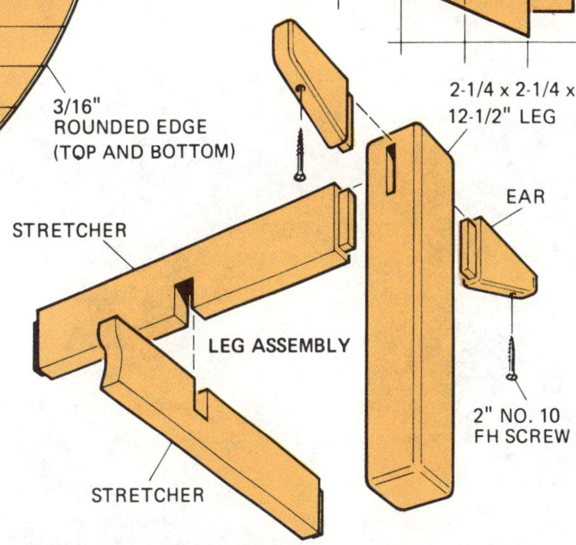

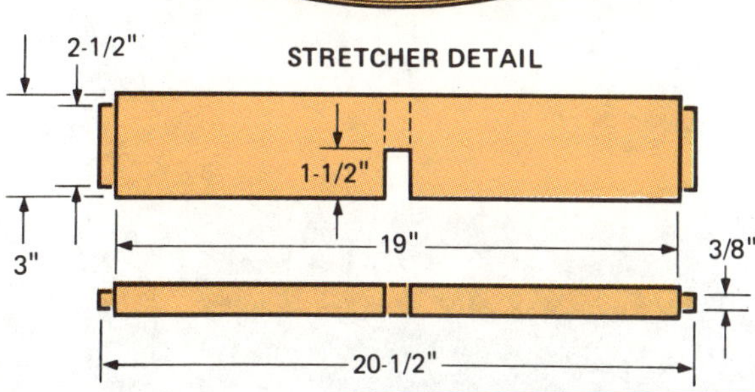

SEE ALSO

Butcher blocks . . . Cabinet furniture . . . Children's furniture . . . Legs, furniture . . . Mobile furniture . . . Modular furniture . . . Painting, furniture . . . Staining, wood . . .

wide from 4/4 maple. Sand down all butcher block and 4/4 maple pieces, finishing with No. 220 grit. Then, with a 3/16-in. self-guided rounding-over bit, kill all the hard edges except along the base of the large side panels.

Stain the skids ebony for contrast and, when they're dry, apply Watco teak oil to the surfaces. Attach the skids to the side pieces with 5/16 x 3-in. lagbolts and washers only, with 7/8-in. dia. counterbores for wrench clearance.

poplar framing and cleats

■ Base framing: Cut all base members and cleats from 5/4 poplar and assemble with glue and 2-in. No. 10 FH screws. Drop the cleats 5/8 in. down from the top edge of the base frame.

■ Back frame: Rip enough 5/4 poplar to frame the back and fasten the ends with glue and 2-in. No. 10 FH screws. Finish by adding the two 3/8-in. plywood panels with glue and 4d box nails.

■ Upholstery: Seating dimensions are a key part of a comfortable couch. If you're pretty tall (or short), you might want to adjust the proportions of the furniture. The back and the seat have to be soft but firm. One-inch foam is enough on the back, but the seat cushions need more flexible support. On this plan, the seat is supported by a weave of 2-in.-wide rubber webbing, with 3/4-in. spacing between rows.

Start each strip by nailing one edge to the cleat with two No. 14 tacks. Then fold the webbing over, hiding the first two tacks, and drive home two more tacks through the doubled webbing.

With one end tacked and the other end stretched across the frame, put a 2½-lb. weight at the half-way point. Adjust the webbing tension until the weight forces the webbing ½ in. down and drive two tacks into the second cleat. Fold over the flap, drive in two more tacks through the doubled webbing and cut away the surplus.

To complete the seat, use the same fastening procedure on the remaining sides and weave the webbing over and under, alternating rows as you go.

Install 1-in.-thick foam in the recess formed by the sides and rails and edge-staple the foam to the cleats. Then stretch No. 40, heavy-duty muslin over the foam and staple it to the rails and sides at the edges. You don't need single, large sheets of foam to do the job. Smaller widths can be butt-jointed into larger sheets with contact-type rubber cement.

Start with a piece of 1-in.-thick foam large enough to cover the front, rear and top surfaces of the back, and spray these surfaces with contact cement. Spray the entire inside surface of the foam and, when dry, roll the foam smoothly around the three surfaces of the back. You can trim the edges flush with a utility knife.

This layer should also be covered with muslin and stapled on the sides and bottom where it won't show.

stretching fabric

To keep fabric wrinkle-free as you stretch it over a surface, drive a tack (or staple) at the midpoint of one edge. Then stretch the material toward the corners, drive a fastener at each end and tack down the space in between. Repeat this procedure on the remaining three sides, removing any scalloping as you go along with additional fasteners. If your fabric has a nap (smooth when stroked in one direction and rough in the other), place it so the smooth stroke goes toward the *front* on the base and *down* the front face of the back.

If you use a patterned fabric, you'll have to check the pattern alignment from back to base.

Fabric usually comes in 45 or 54-in.-wide bolts. This will have no effect on the chair, but center seams will be required for the sofa.

Align the fabric on the base, stretch it out, and fasten it to the front rail face and the blocking piece with staples or tacks. Stretch the fabric crosswise and drive all fasteners into the side faces where they won't be seen.

On the back, make sure that fasteners are driven into the bottom and sides. Some tucking or slitting may be necessary at the top outside edges of the back.

For now, leave a 6-in.-long "tail" of fabric at the lower rear edge of the back.

assembling the pieces

Attach the back to the base with 5/16 x 2½-in. lagbolts and washers. They are screwed in from the bottom surface of the blocking piece—the space between the intermediate (C) and the rear (B) rails. Align the back so that the fabric-covered foam protrudes about 3/4 in. beyond the face of the rear rail in the base.

This is the time to make sure the base and back form a 90° angle. If they don't, loosen the lags and add shims to make up the difference.

Now stretch the "tail" down and fasten it to the face of the rear rail. Run the fabric ends around corners and fasten them at sides. This completes your back-base assembly.

Drill four evenly spaced 5/16-in.-dia. holes along the horizontal centerline of the poplar base sides

THE COMFORTABLE seat is supported by rubber webbing. Use a tack hammer to drive the No. 14 tacks.

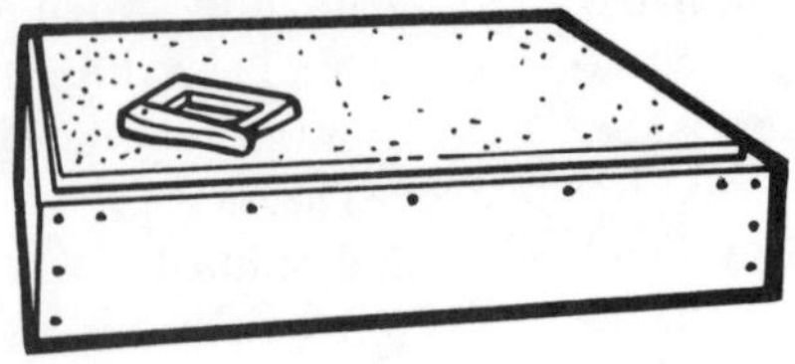

WEBBING is recessed into frame to provide room for 1-in. foam. Staple to cleats and cover with muslin.

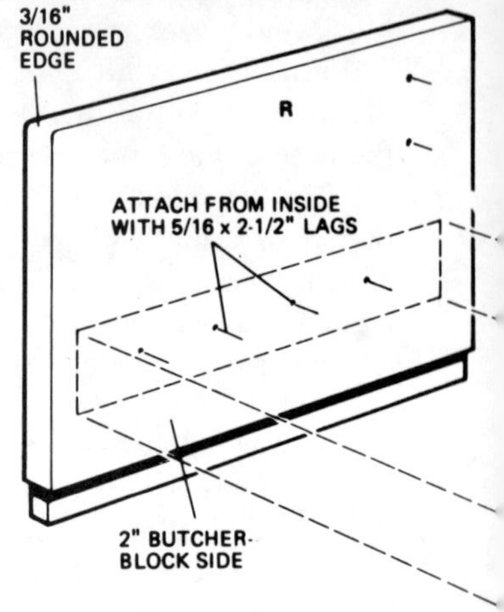

BUTCHER-BLOCK COUCH

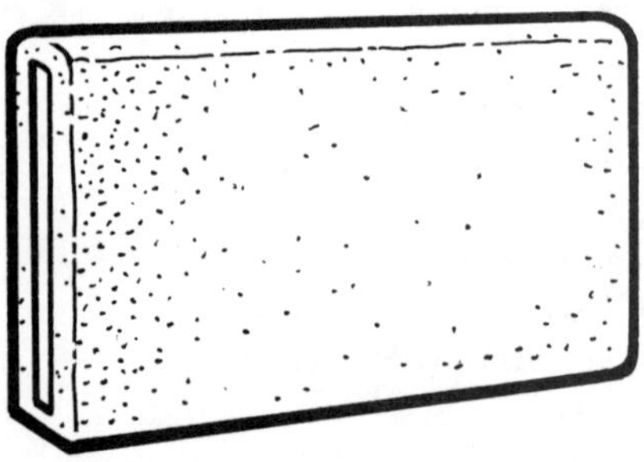

FOAM IS applied to back frame with contact cement; then edges are turned and stapled at bottom and sides.

AFTER ATTACHING back to base, staple 6-in. "tail" of fabric from the back onto the rear seat rail.

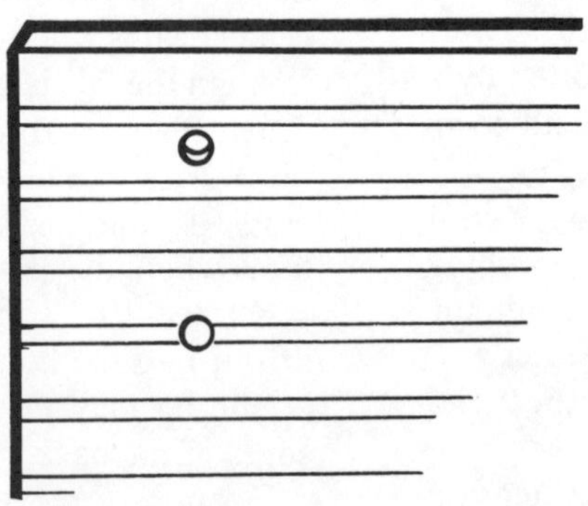

LAGBOLTING IS DONE through the space between the two back rails (top). In the side panels, legs are recessed and covered with maple plugs. To keep the fabric wrinkle-free, make "hospital" corners all around. Electric stapler is timesaver.

and punch-mark the inside of the butcher block sides through these holes for alignment.Using a ¼-in. bit, drill the punch marks 1½-in. deep to accept the lagbolts.

From the outside of the butcher-block side panels, drill and counterbore the two holes to install the 5/16 x 2½-in. lags and washers.

Complete the chair by trimming the ends of the fascias to the exact length between the butcher block sides. Fasten them to the rails from the inside with 1½-in. No. 10 FH screws.

making the table

You can make coffee-table legs out of almost anything from clay flue tile to cast-iron pipe. If you stick to maple, rip enough 4/4 maple to laminate four legs (three pieces in each) 2¼ x 12½ in. long. Machine a ⅜ x 2¼ x ¾-in. mortise on three sides of the legs, starting ⅜ in. from the top.

Rip two stretchers and eight "ears" from 4/4 maple (check dimensions shown). Machine the tenons on ends of the "ears" and notch each stretcher at its midpoint to lock the assembly.

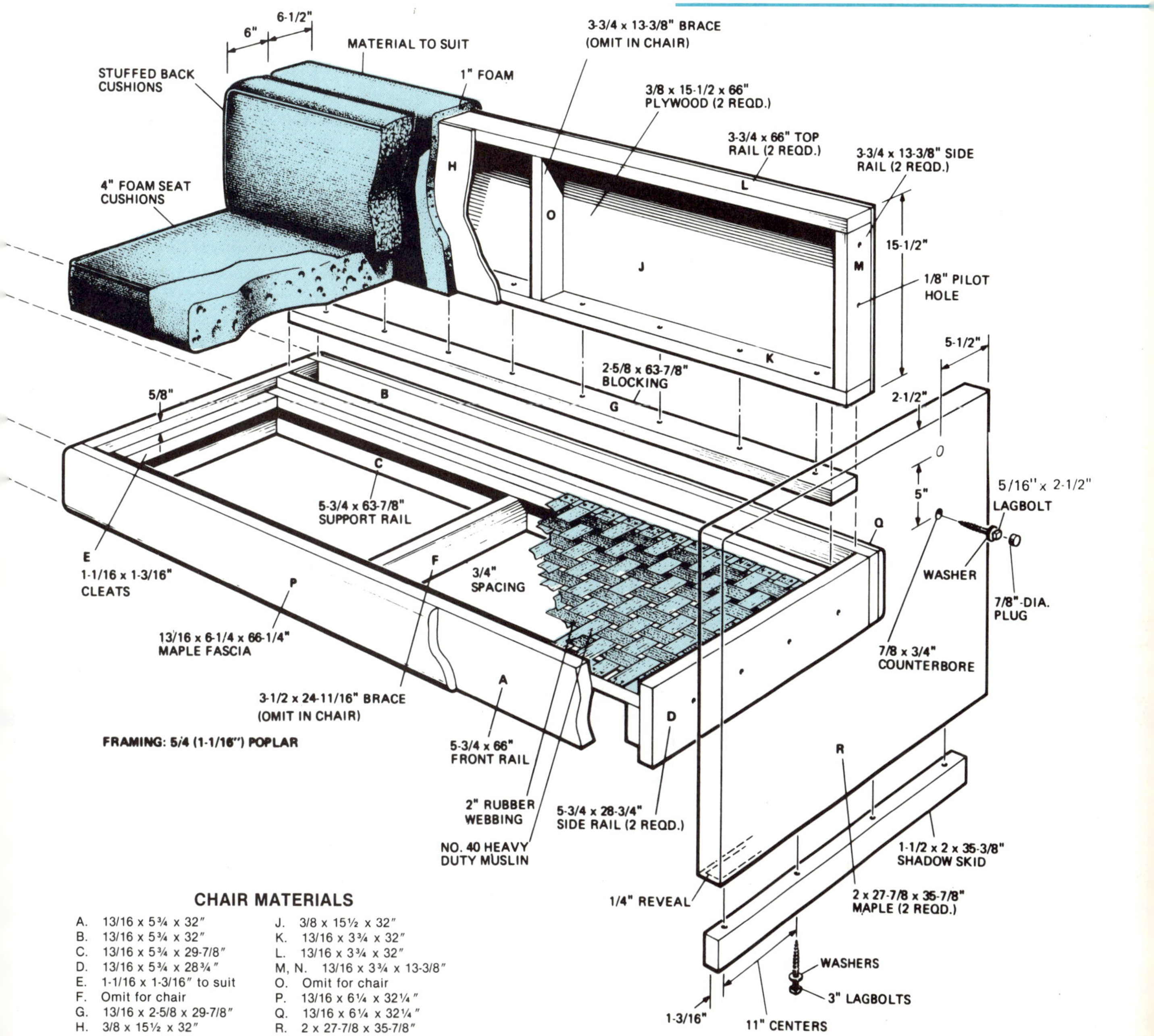

CHAIR MATERIALS

A.	13/16 x 5¾ x 32″	J.	3/8 x 15½ x 32″
B.	13/16 x 5¾ x 32″	K.	13/16 x 3¾ x 32″
C.	13/16 x 5¾ x 29-7/8″	L.	13/16 x 3¾ x 32″
D.	13/16 x 5¾ x 28¾″	M, N.	13/16 x 3¾ x 13-3/8″
E.	1-1/16 x 1-3/16″ to suit	O.	Omit for chair
F.	Omit for chair	P.	13/16 x 6¼ x 32¼″
G.	13/16 x 2-5/8 x 29-7/8″	Q.	13/16 x 6¼ x 32¼″
H.	3/8 x 15½ x 32″	R.	2 x 27-7/8 x 35-7/8″

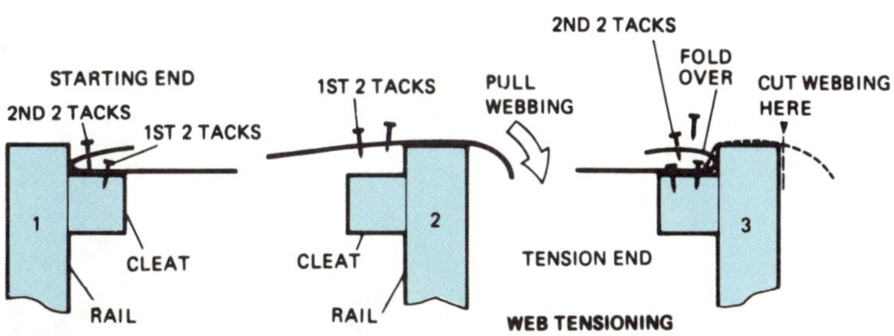

WEB TENSIONING

Clamp and glue these pieces as a single unit on a flat surface to assure complete contact with the bottom of the 36-in.-dia. tabletop.

To complete the table, place the top (good surface down) on a rug with the leg assembly centered. Drill and counterbore each "ear" for 2-in. No. 10 FH screws. Mark the tabletop through these holes, drill the pilots and assemble.

For a really pleasing finish, rub oiled surfaces (when dry) with 000 steel wool. Apply another thin coat of oil, rub wet surfaces with 0000 wool and remove the excess with a lintfree cloth.

Build a handy butcher block

The old-time chopping block is making a comeback and finding great popularity in the modern kitchen. You can save up to $100 by making your own with these plans

SEE ALSO
Adhesives . . . Bridge tables . . . Dining tables . . . Finishes, wood . . . Game tables . . . Hutch tables . . . Kitchen accessories . . . Kitchens . . . Occasional tables

REGULAR BUTCHER BLOCKS are true heavyweights with solid maple tops from 12 to 18 in. thick. Those sold for home use average about 10 in. thick. Some have solid tops; many are simply thin shells as little as 1¼ in. thick. I made mine 2⅝ in. thick and used poplar throughout instead of the traditional maple in the interest of economy and ease of fabrication. While poplar is considered a soft hardwood, it is nonetheless sufficiently hard in end grain.

Start by selecting kiln-dry lumber which is sound and absolutely warp-free. You'll need 50 ft. of $^{8}/_{4}$ by 4 in. for the top and 18 ft. of $^{10}/_{4}$ x 4¼ in. for gluing up the turning blocks for the legs. The dressed $^{8}/_{4}$ stock will normally measure $1^{13}/_{16}$ in. thick so that's the reason for the odd dimension of the blocks. The $^{10}/_{4}$ stock is necessary for the legs in order to permit dressing to a full 4-in. square after gluing. The lumber should

ASSEMBLY SEQUENCE

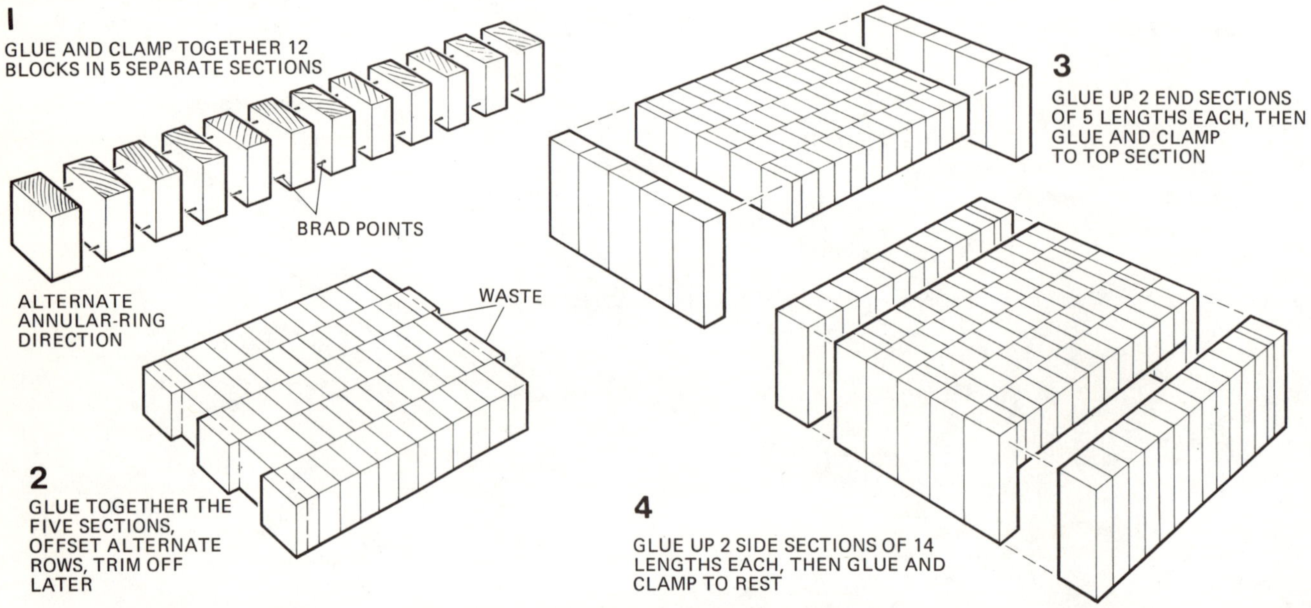

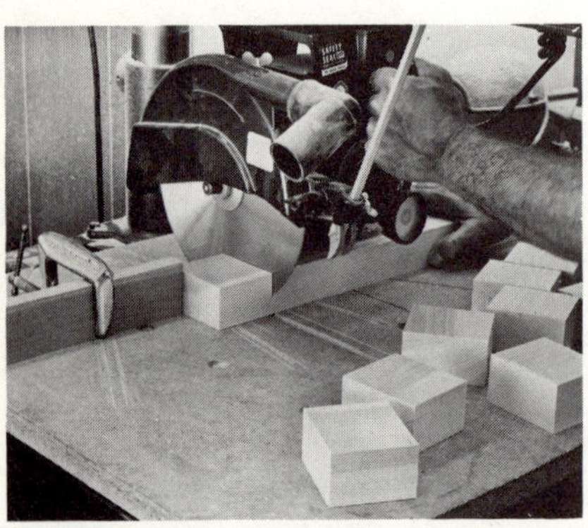

STOP BLOCK clamped to saw's fence, plus smooth-cutting blade, gives uniform blocks with nonsplintered edges.

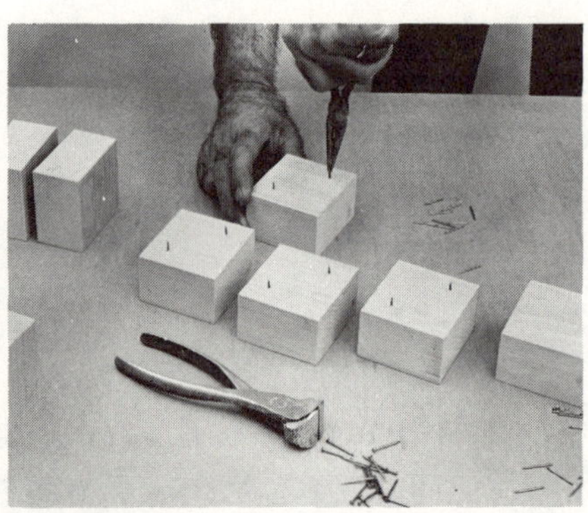

ALTERNATE annular rings of blocks, number blocks and insert headless brads in one side to prevent shifting when gluing.

SAW TABLE and rip fence, plus board, make alignment setup for imbedding brads with bar clamp. No glue is used here.

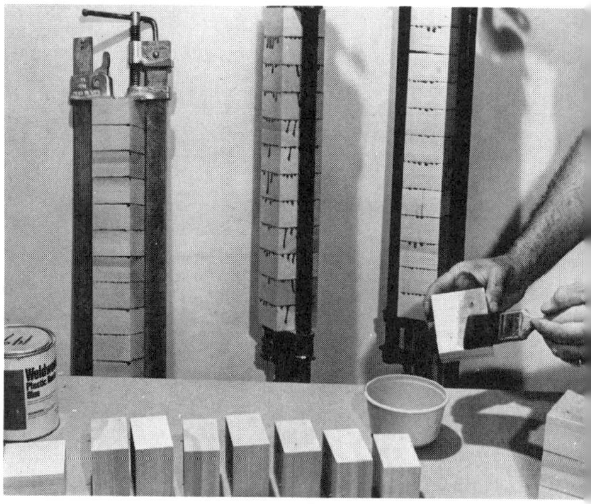

WORK FAST when gluing. Coat both surfaces thoroughly, stack blocks vertically, and use two bar clamps on each stack.

LINE UP five glued-up stacks so joints are offset, then mark the projections for cutting off the waste at alternate ends.

USE POWER block plane for fast surfacing of top, hand plane otherwise. Follow planing with belt and finishing sanders.

cost between $45 and $50. With $10 more for glue, abrasive paper, lagscrews and finish, you have a total of $60. A store-bought table of equal size and quality will run somewhere between $140 and $185.

make 60 blocks for the top

You'll find it best to work with easy-to-handle short lengths of about two feet. Rip and joint each piece exactly alike, then make the cross cuts to come up with 60 small blocks 3 in. long.

ROUGH-ROUND leg blanks with gouge and run lathe at medium speed. Parting-tool depth cuts simplify turning four duplicate legs.

CLAMP THE LEGS in place for drilling the pilot holes for ⅜x4½-in. lagscrews. Tighten the lagscrews before you remove the holding clamp.

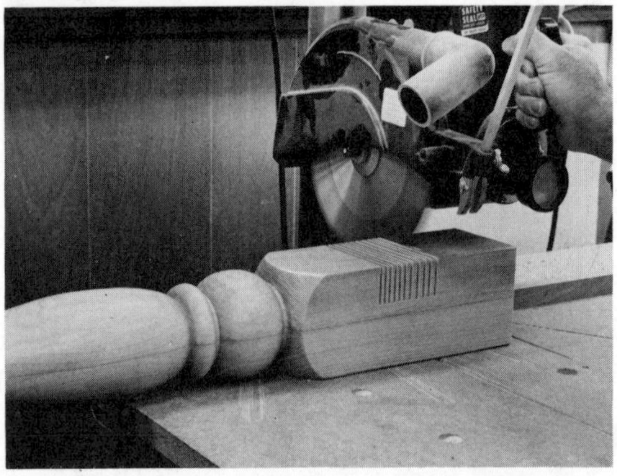

RUN A SERIES of kerf cuts to form a notch at the top of each leg. Hold the work securely against the fence with your hand (not shown in photo for clarity).

APPLY ONE coat of special wood-bowl finish; it produces excellent hard topping. Wood-glo was used to finish legs while each was still in the lathe.

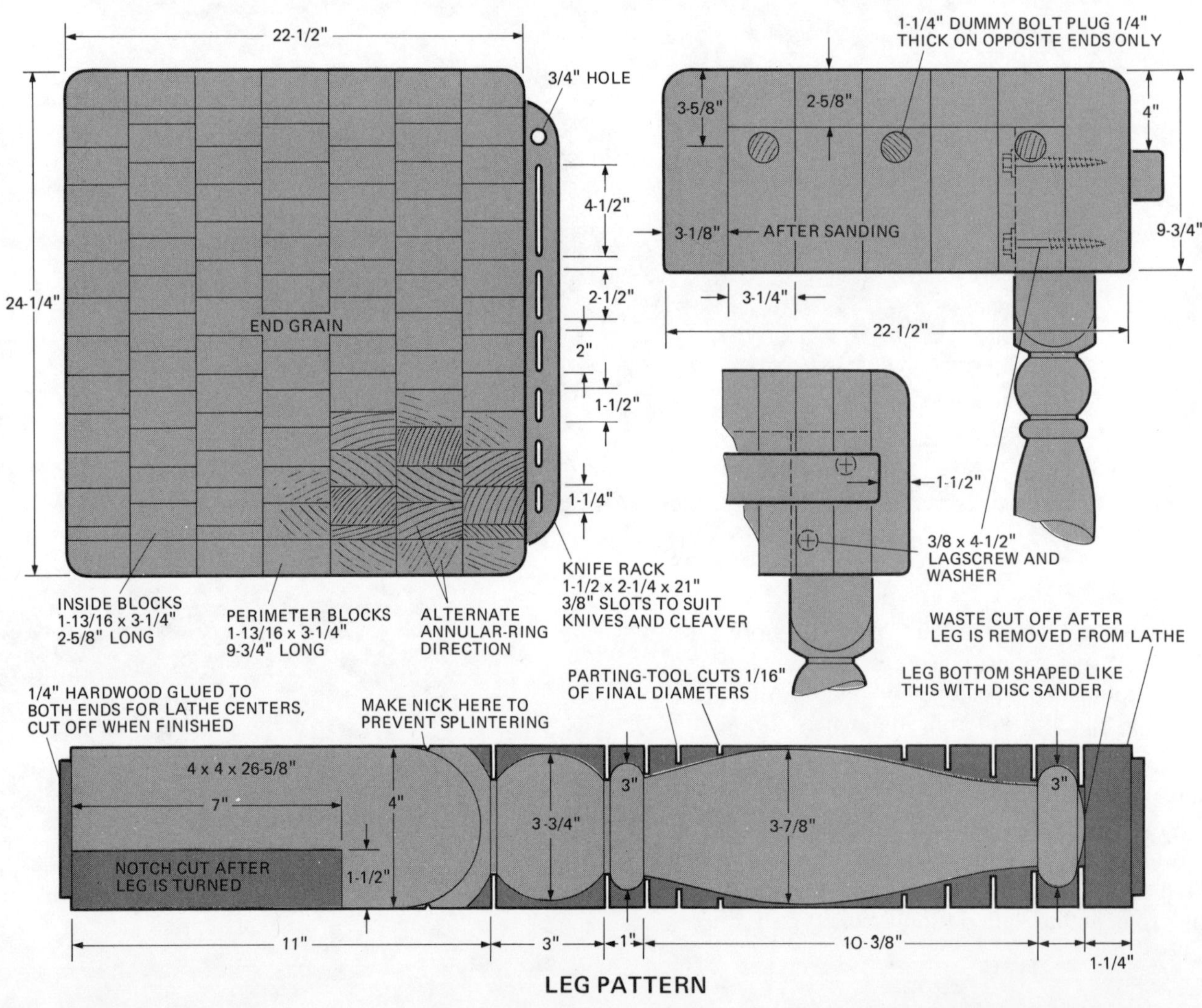

LEG PATTERN

All rip and jointing cuts must be perfectly square.

Gluing the block is done in stages. Five rows of 12 blocks each are made up to start the top. Pairs of headless nails are used in all phases of gluing line-up to insure the necessary accuracy. Use 1-in. No. 17-ga. nails with the heads clipped off. Drill pilot holes in all alternate faces to a depth that will allow about ¼ in. of the points to protrude. Line up a dozen of the short blocks on the saw table and up against the rip fence, then clamp a straight piece of wood onto the table and up against the blocks to keep them in perfect alignment. Apply a bar clamp over the stack, then slowly tighten it to drive the nail points into each mating piece. Number the blocks, then separate them for gluing.

Use water-resistant, plastic resin glue and a postage scale for accurate proportioning of powder and water. This is important: If too thin, a mix will be weak: too heavy, it may begin to set before you get all the pieces together. Work with vertical stacks; brush a coat of glue on both surfaces, then insert the nailpoints into the holes of the stacked pieces. Apply pressure to the stack with two bar clamps. If you wait about an hour before scraping off the excess glue, it will come off much easier and with less mess. When the glue has dried, joint the surfaces of each block slightly to remove all traces of excess glue before proceeding to the next gluing step.

Line up the five stacks so an offset joint pattern results. This will necessitate cutting off a bit of waste on alternate ends. The offset pattern does two things: It makes a stronger top and adds visual interest. Follow the same procedure with a pair of headless nail-positioning pins to align the five stacks for gluing. When the basic top is glued, it will measure approximately 3 x 16 x 20¾ in. Joint the four sides, then put the piece aside while you work on the end blocks. The drawing shows the top thickness as 2⅝ in.; this reflects the removal of stock in the final planing and sanding.

Make up two ends consisting of five 10-in. pieces glued edge to edge and two side pieces composed of 14 lengths glued face to face. Note that one block of half-thickness is required in each of the two side assemblies. Use temporary clamped-on cleats during the gluing to insure that the surfaces glue up perfectly true. Kitchen wax paper will prevent the cleats from sticking to the work.

Dummy bolt plugs are used for effect on the end blocks. Drill shallow holes, about ¼ in. deep by 1½ in. in diameter, then plug them with slices of thick dowel of the same size which you turn on the lathe. Position them so the grain runs clockwise.

If you have a power block plane, you can surface the top with little effort. Otherwise you'll need a jack plane and muscle power. Round off all corners with a plane, then sand all surfaces with a belt sander followed with a finishing sander. Apply a coat of sealer only to the inside surfaces to protect the wood against dampness. A special nontoxic salad bowl sealer, used for top and side surfaces, is available from A. Constantine & Son, 2050 Eastchester Rd., Bronx, N.Y. Apply one coat of the salad-bowl seal using a full brush and letting it soak in.

glue up blocks for the legs

The lathe work is next. Glue up the stock for the turning blocks and joint them to 4 in. square. Glue a scrap of extra-hard wood, such as maple or oak, to each end to provide durable temporary centers which will not readily wear during the rough turning. Use the gouge to rough-round the cylindrical section, but first make a shallow nick cut at the shoulder using the heel of the skew held vertically. This will prevent accidental splintering of square corners. After rounding carefully, make parting cuts to the required depths as indicated on the drawing. Shape contours with skew and diamond-point chisels, working to limits set by parting-tool grooves. Sand smooth.

To obtain a top-rate finish, apply several coats of Wood-glo or other finish of your liking while the work is still in the lathe. If you plan to use the salad-bowl finish for the entire job, it will take a full pint. When the finish coats are dry, saw off the waste. If you sand a slight convex curve on the bottoms of the legs, you'll be able to get by without casters, which would somewhat spoil the appearance. Shallow rounded ends will permit easy sliding on practically any floor.

Most dado cutters haven't the capacity to make the deep cuts required for notching the legs so a series of kerf cuts is made to clear out waste. You can use a table saw or radial saw, but the latter is preferred since repeated pushing of the leg on a table saw may mar the finish. The legs are secured with a pair of ⅜ x 4½-in. hex-head lagscrews. Glue is optional.

Finally the knife rack. Make it by boring a series of ⅜-in. holes, then clear out the waste with a chisel to form slots. Glue the rack in place before applying the finish.

Build a butler's table

Make this butler's table with a lift-off top, and you'll always be ready to serve coffee or tea to guests. With the top on the base, it's a handsome coffee table

By ROSARIO CAPOTOSTO

YOU'LL HAVE BOTH a coffee table and a serving tray when you make this attractive butler's table. When you have guests, its top lifts off for serving, then fits back firmly on the leg assembly when you use it as a table. As you can see, it is a beautiful table when you do careful work, and it is a handsome addition to any home.

The trick in making this project is to use friction hinges. These hinges let you position its four leaves at any angle from horizontal to vertical to convert it to a tray with built-in handles. The

SEE ALSO
Bed tables . . . Bridge tables . . . Coffee tables . . . Dining tables . . . Joinery . . . Legs, furniture . . . Occasional tables . . . Party tables . . . Trays, folding

TILT THE DRILL-PRESS table so a pencil line on the leg and drill bit are vertical, then clamp.

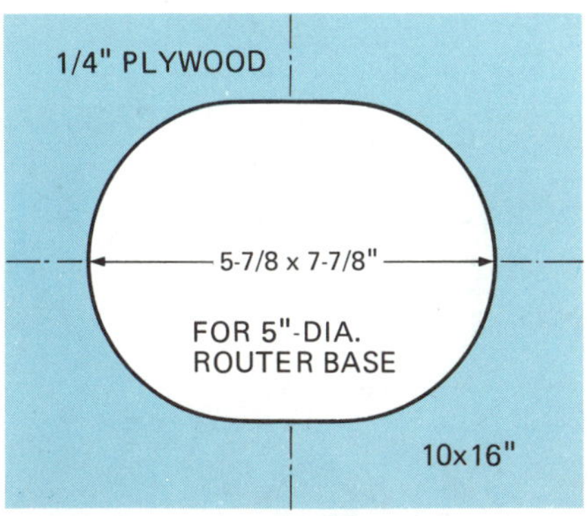

A TEMPLATE forms mortises for both leaves of hinges in one quick router operation to save time.

USE A PLYWOOD TEMPLATE to guide the router base for cutting semicircular hinge mortises.

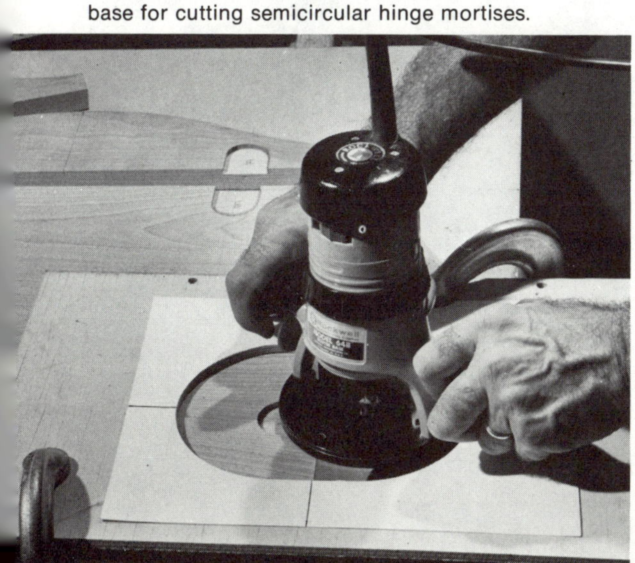

SHIM THE HINGE mortises in the table leaves to make up for the single-thickness hinge leaf.

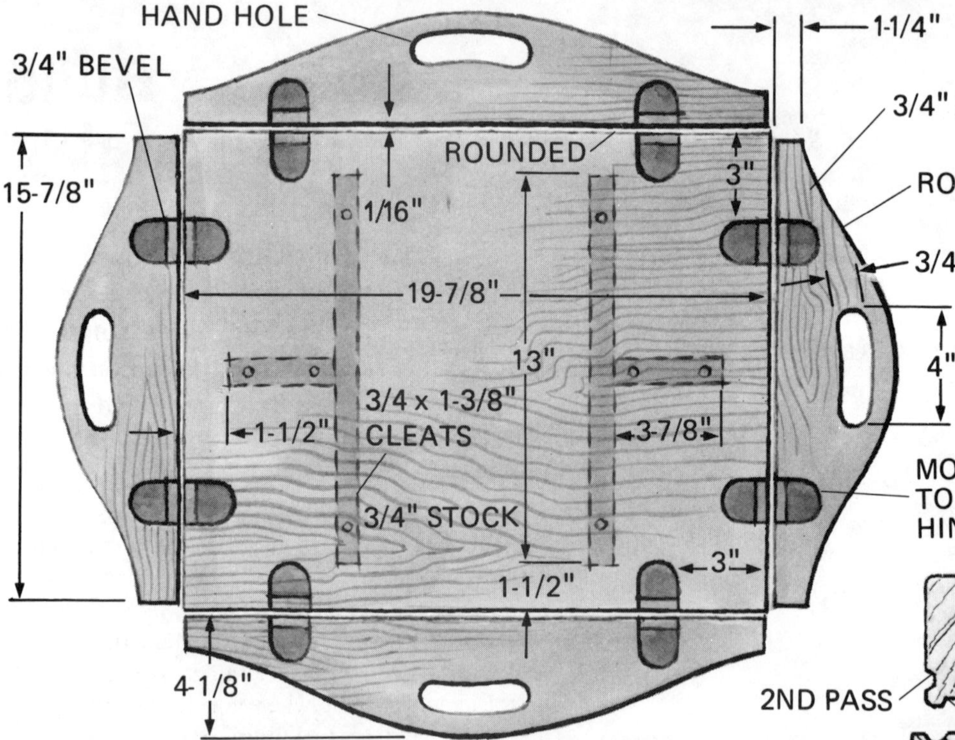

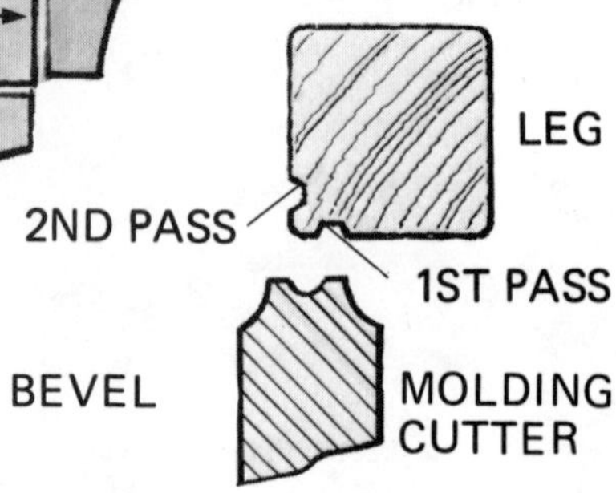

TRAY TOP

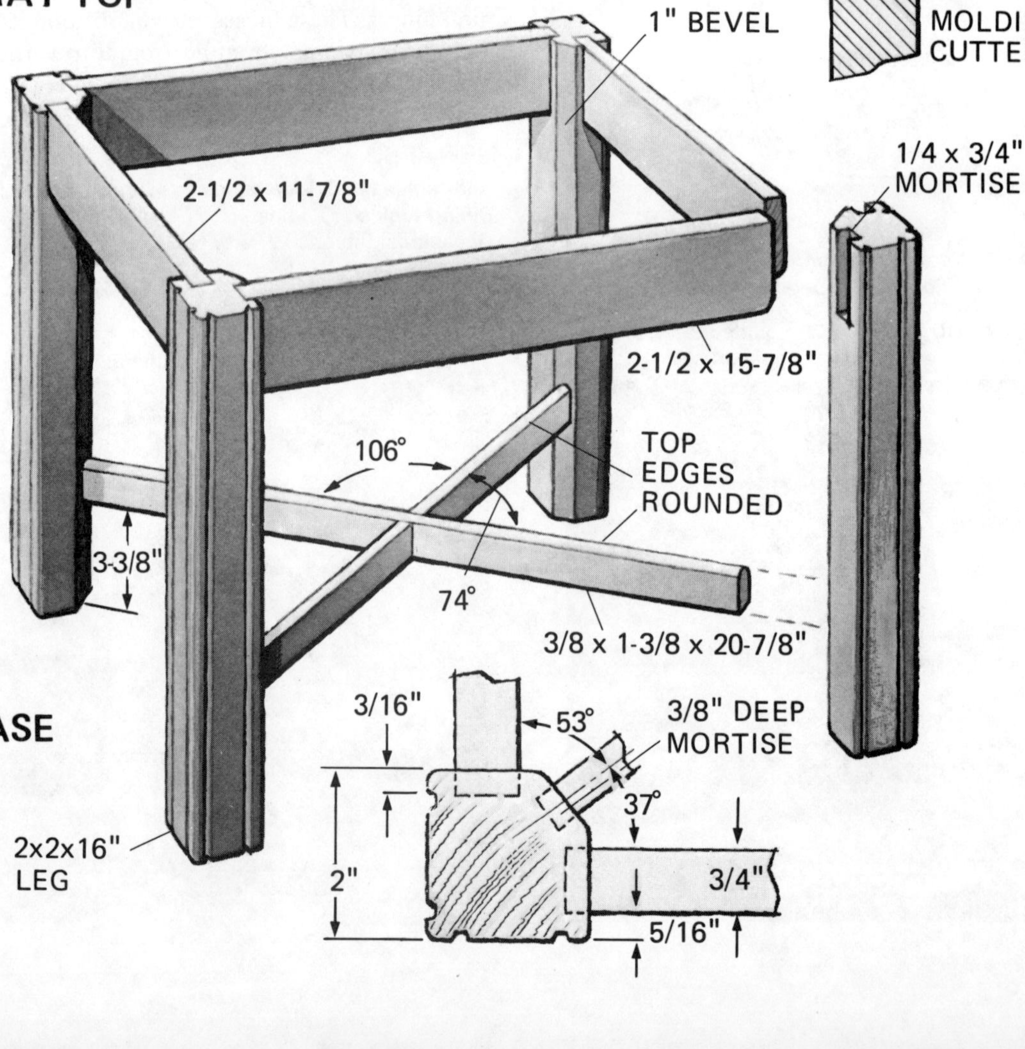

BASE

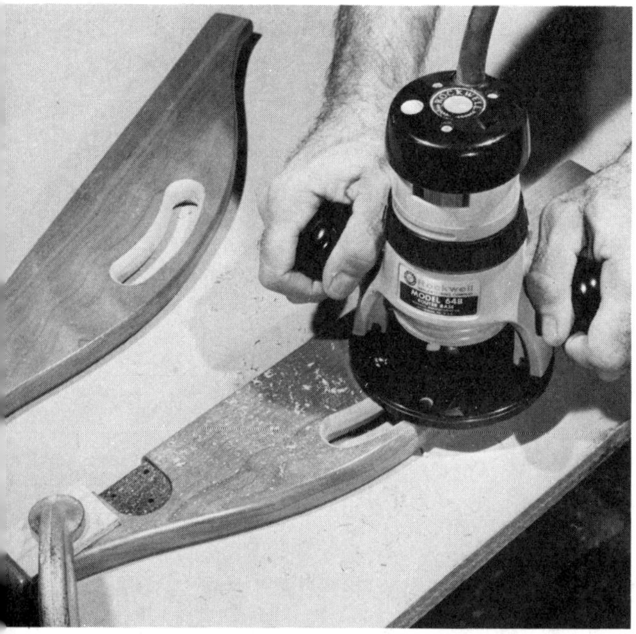

AFTER YOU FORM the curved openings of the built-in tray handles with a ¾-in. drill bit and sabre saw, use a router to carefully round the edges.

CLEATS FASTENED to the underside of the tabletop fit inside the aprons to register the top automatically with the base when placed in the correct position.

cleats on the underside cleverly position the tray/top on its four legs so it can't slide off.

You can convert these plans to just about any size table. If you buy one like it in the store it will usually be 33x44 in. I made mine smaller than this, for I found the bigger size and greater weight make it impractical for a woman to use the top as a tray.

Making this table and serving tray is not a difficult job, but neither is it a hammer-and-saw project. A router will form the semi-circular hinge mortises and round the edges. A table saw and molding cutter will form the decorative corner beading on the legs, a sabre saw will cut the tray leaves and hand grips and a drill press will form the stretcher mortises.

make all legs alike

In the drawing on the opposite page, note that all four legs are made alike; the inner corners are first beveled 45°, then mortised at the top for the aprons and 3 in. up from the bottom for the stretchers. I used my table saw to rip the leg squares from a glued-up slab consisting of three ¾ x 12 x 16-in. pieces, then dressed the four sides to 2 in. square.

Since the legs are not set in a square relationship but rather rectangular, the cross stretchers must enter the legs at a corresponding angle. To determine the correct angle for the stretcher mortises, number the legs and stand them upright on a flat surface the proper distance apart. Place a straightedge diagonally across the center of the bevels of two facing legs and draw a line across the tops. Do the same with the other two legs. Now tilt your drill-press table to correspond with the cross lines on the legs and drill a series of ⅜-in. holes ⅜ in. deep in one pair of legs. Finally, do this for the others, tilting the table the other way.

now build the top

To build the top, you'll have to edge-glue several boards and join them with dowels. Each butler-table hinge has a single-thickness leaf and a double-thickness one. It's standard to rout both mortises to suit the thicker leaf, then shim under the thin leaf. A bevel will have to be hand-chiseled at the outer edge of each mortise for hinge clearance.

If your router has a 5-in.-dia. base (most do), you can make your plywood hinge-mortising template the size given; if not, cut it to suit. Use the template's centerlines to position it over the hinge locations and place cardboard between the top and tray leaf for clearance. Then hold template, plus top and leaf, with C-clamps. The eight hinges can be purchased from Armor Co., Box 290, Deer Park, New York 11729, for about $16 postpaid.

Build a picturesque poolhouse

By SVEN CORSAK

Don't let its mini-size fool you. This little house not only is attractive, but also functions five ways to add fun to your pool

■ IT DIDN'T TAKE LONG after the christening of our new pool for us to realize that we needed a pool-side cabana to save wear and tear on the main house. Using simplified construction techniques, and inexpensive materials, when I built the poolhouse shown here the cost was about $250. With higher lumber prices today, the structure could cost much more than that. Prudent shopping, of course, keeps total cost down. Though small, the house performs five functions: In addition to housing the pool filter and accessories, it offers a screened-in area for bugfree barbecues, a lavatory and dressing room, a deck for sunbathing and an upstairs playhouse for youngsters.

Originally I had planned to continue the rear roof past the back wall right on down to the ground. My plan was to use this overhang as a "carport" for my garden tractor. But since my wife was pleased with the little house as is, the idea was shelved. Another optional (but practical) feature is to install a separate septic tank for the lavatory rather than tying the plumbing system into the existing waste system.

The building rests on a 4-in. concrete slab poured on a perimeter footing. For framing I used 2x3s for studs and 2x4s for joists. The cedar shingles on the A-roof and gable ends are No. 4 and the exterior siding is V-grooved ⅜-in. exterior plywood.

YOUNGSTERS CAN'T resist second-level play house, use it frequently for overnight sleep-outs. For contact with house, solid state intercom is used.

SEE ALSO

Carpeting, outdoor . . . Decks . . . Fences . . . Garden shelters . . . Gazebos . . . Patios . . . Poolhouses . . . Pools, swimming . . . Screened summer rooms . . . Swimming pools . . . Yard lighting

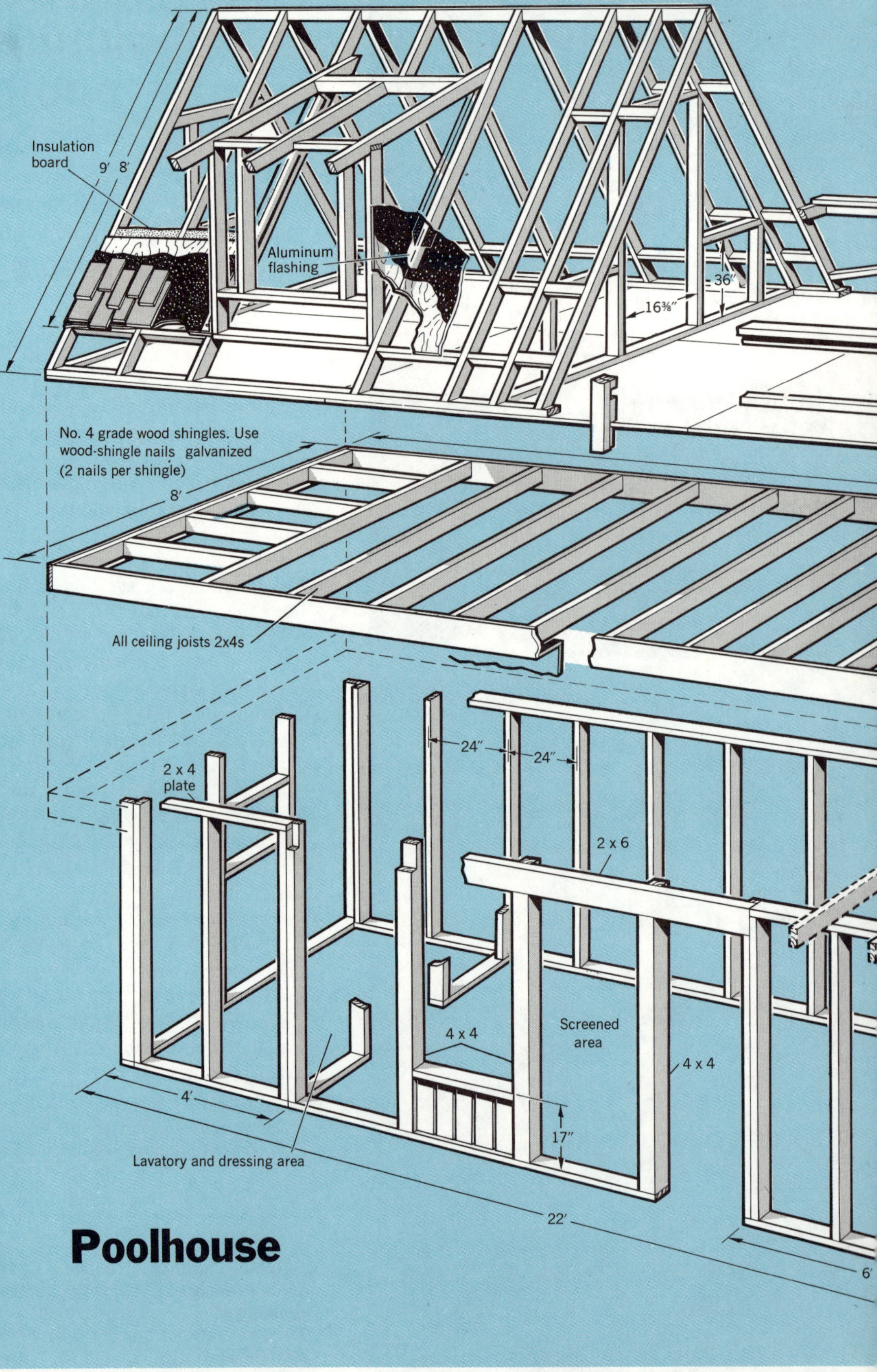
Insulation board
9′
8′
Aluminum flashing
36″
16⅜″
No. 4 grade wood shingles. Use wood-shingle nails galvanized (2 nails per shingle)
8′
All ceiling joists 2x4s
24″
24″
2 x 4 plate
2 x 6
Screened area
4 x 4
4 x 4
4′
17″
Lavatory and dressing area
22′
6′

Poolhouse

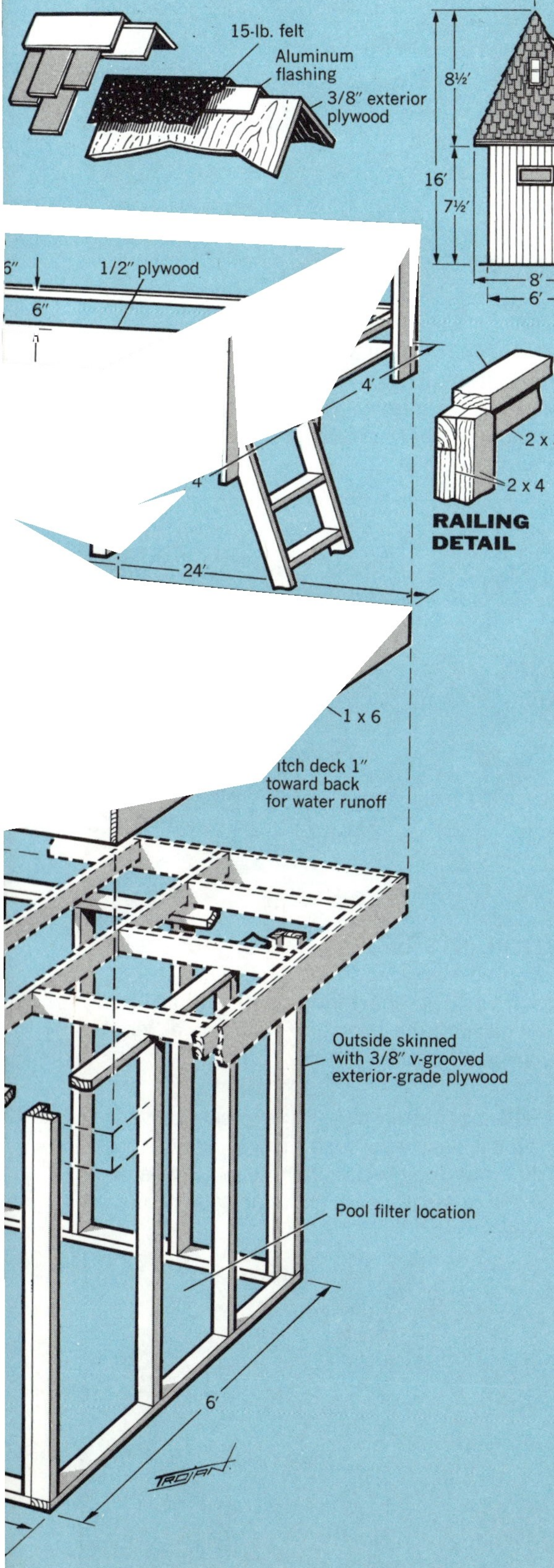

RAILING DETAIL

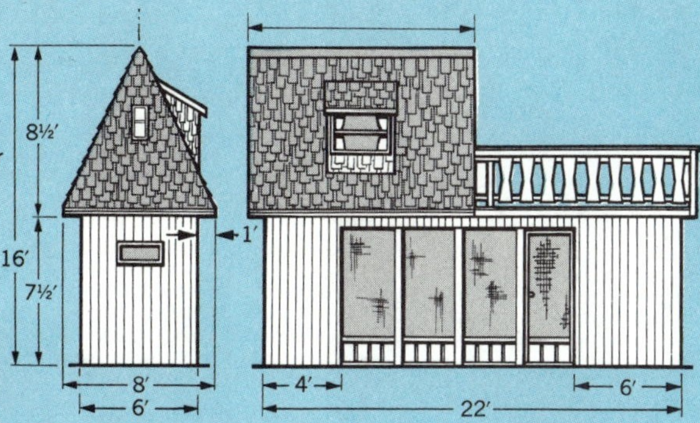

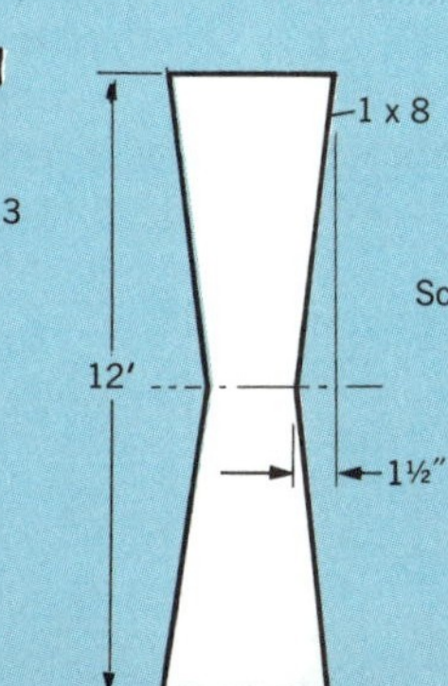

BALUSTER DETAIL

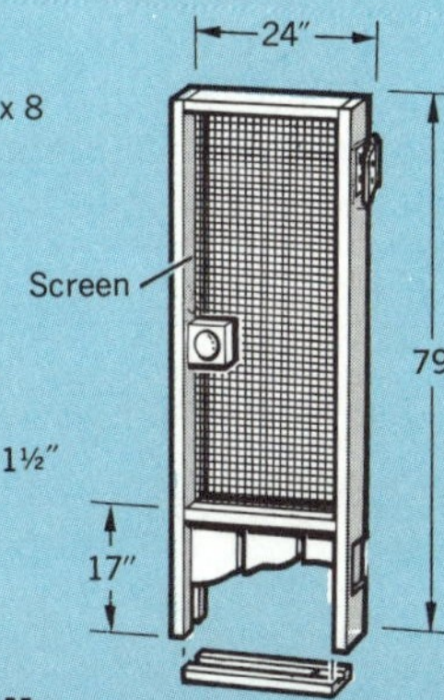

DOOR FRAME

I chose to use fin-type windows. They are extremely easy to install and, once in place, are practically maintenance-free. In my case they were also a good buy; I got them at a local lumberyard during a sale for about $7 each.

Since indoor-outdoor carpeting is used on the sundeck, absolute waterproofing is a must. To do it, cover the ½-in.-plywood sheathing with two layers of overlapped 15-pound felt. Next, to protect the carpet from stains, put down a cover of 6-mil. polypropylene plastic. Notice that the deck is slightly pitched to provide positive drainage. Rainwater passing through the carpeting is carried over the plastic to the edge of the building for runoff.

To finish the structure, I chose a cocoa shade of Cabot's creosote shingle stain.

NOTE: While the author used 2x3s for studs, conventional 2x4 construction is indicated in the drawing.

A SCREW driven into the end grain of one member of a joint will hold far better if a dowel is installed—perpendicular to the screw—for the latter to bite into. Then it won't be able to work loose.

YOU CAN PROTECT wood surfaces from wreckingbar mars by covering the rocker end with a short length of garden hose. When not needed, simply slide the rubber hose up the shank and out of the way.

SANDING A CONTOURED surface is easier if the sanding block is resilient enough to conform to the irregular surface. Several layers of glued-up corrugated cardboard is one way to solve this problem.

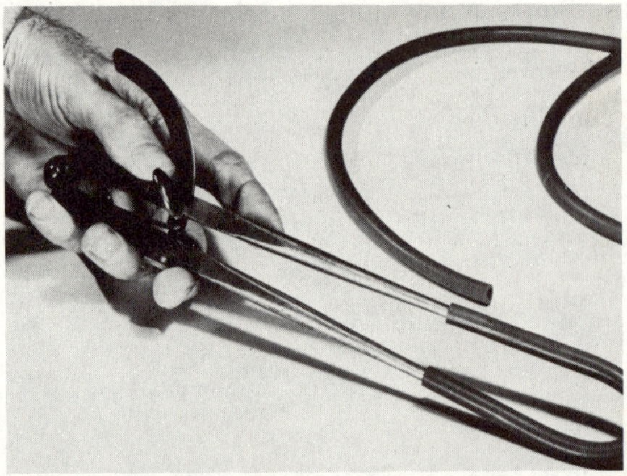

DIVIDER POINTS (on compasses and the like) can be prevented from becoming blunted in the toolbox if you slip short lengths of rubber tubing over the ends. Such tubing is available at most hobby stores.

SLIP A PAPER CUP over your drill bit (below) the next time you have overhead drilling to do, and shavings and plaster dust will fall into it, rather than on your face or down your sleeves. Hold the cup in place with tape.

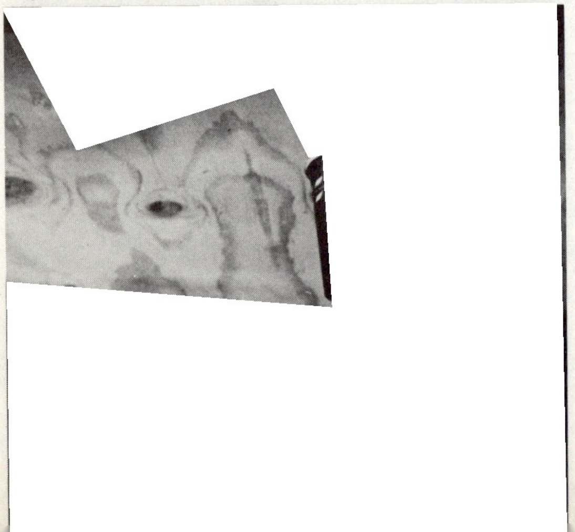

DRILLING a centered hole transversely through a rod or pipe is easy if you use a metal sleeve of the same diameter (below). Make hole in guide-sleeve the same size as bit used, and clamp both pieces in the vise.

METRIC CONVERSION

Conversion factors can be carried so far they become impractical. In cases below where an entry is exact it is followed by an asterisk (*). Where considerable rounding off has taken place, the entry is followed by a + or a - sign.

CUSTOMARY TO METRIC

Linear Measure

inches	millimeters
1/16	1.5875*
1/8	3.2
3/16	4.8
1/4	6.35*
5/16	7.9
3/8	9.5
7/16	11.1
1/2	12.7*
9/16	14.3
5/8	15.9
11/16	17.5
3/4	19.05*
13/16	20.6
7/8	22.2
15/16	23.8
1	25.4*

inches	centimeters
1	2.54*
2	5.1
3	7.6
4	10.2
5	12.7*
6	15.2
7	17.8
8	20.3
9	22.9
10	25.4*
11	27.9
12	30.5

feet	centimeters	meters
1	30.48*	.3048*
2	61	.61
3	91	.91
4	122	1.22
5	152	1.52
6	183	1.83
7	213	2.13
8	244	2.44
9	274	2.74
10	305	3.05
50	1524*	15.24*
100	3048*	30.48*

1 yard =
.9144* meters
1 rod =
5.0292* meters
1 mile =
1.6 kilometers
1 nautical mile =
1.852* kilometers

Fluid Measure

(Milliliters [ml] and cubic centimeters [cc or cu cm] are equivalent, but it is customary to use milliliters for liquids.)

1 cu in = 16.39 ml
1 fl oz = 29.6 ml
1 cup = 237 ml
1 pint = 473 ml
1 quart = 946 ml
= .946 liters
1 gallon = 3785 ml
= 3.785 liters
Formula (exact):
fluid ounces × 29.573 529 562 5*
= milliliters

Weights

ounces	grams
1	28.3
2	56.7
3	85
4	113
5	142
6	170
7	198
8	227
9	255
10	283
11	312
12	340
13	369
14	397
15	425
16	454

Formula (exact):
ounces × 28.349 523 125* =
grams

pounds	kilograms
1	.45
2	.9
3	1.4
4	1.8
5	2.3
6	2.7
7	3.2
8	3.6
9	4.1
10	4.5

1 short ton (2000 lbs) =
907 kilograms (kg)
Formula (exact):
pounds × .453 592 37* =
kilograms

Volume

1 cu in = 16.39 cubic centimeters (cc)
1 cu ft = 28 316.7 cc
1 bushel = 35 239.1 cc
1 peck = 8 809.8 cc

Area

1 sq in = 6.45 sq cm
1 sq ft = 929 sq cm
= .093 sq meters
1 sq yd = .84 sq meters
1 acre = 4 046.9 sq meters
= .404 7 hectares
1 sq mile = 2 589 988 sq meters
= 259 hectares
= 2.589 9 sq kilometers

Kitchen Measure

1 teaspoon = 4.93 milliliters (ml)
1 Tablespoon = 14.79 milliliters (ml)

Miscellaneous

1 British thermal unit (Btu) (mean)
= 1 055.9 joules
1 calorie (mean) = 4.19 joules
1 horsepower = 745.7 watts
= .75 kilowatts
caliber (diameter of a firearm's bore in hundredths of an inch)
= .254 millimeters (mm)
1 atmosphere pressure = 101 325* pascals (newtons per sq meter)
1 pound per square inch (psi) = 6 895 pascals
1 pound per square foot = 47.9 pascals
1 knot = 1.85 kilometers per hour
25 miles per hour = 40.2 kilometers per hour
50 miles per hour = 80.5 kilometers per hour
75 miles per hour = 120.7 kilometers per hour